Blood Sport

The Program for Cultural Cooperation Between Spain's Ministry of Culture and United States's Universities generously provided financial support toward the publication of this volume

Blood Sport

A Social History of Spanish Bullfighting

Timothy Mitchell

With an Essay and Bibliography by
Rosario Cambria

upp

University of Pennsylvania Press
Philadelphia

Cover photo. Paco Camino and the masterful *temple* of his *derechazo* (Madrid, 1967). Photo by Rosario Cambria.

Photos page 112–119 taken by Rosario Cambria.

U. S. Library of Congress Cataloging-in-Publication Data

Mitchell, Timothy (Timothy J.)
    Blood sport : a social history of Spanish bullfighting / Timothy Mitchell ; with an essay and bibliography by Rosario Cambria.
        p.   cm.
    Includes bibliographical references and index.
    ISBN 0-8122-3129-5. — ISBN 0-8122-1346-7 (pbk.)
    1. Bullfights—Spain—History. 2. Bullfights—Social aspects—Spain—History.   I. Title.
GV1108.5.M58   1991
791.8′2′0946—dc20   91-7231
                                                                                      CIP

Contents

vi   Contents

Preface

I ARRIVED IN SPAIN toward the end of the summer of 1984 with a Fulbright grant in one hand and a map of the gigantic Biblioteca Nacional in the other. My intention was to spend a year searching for traces of ritual violence in old manuscripts. But then fate intervened: On September 28th, Spain's most famous bullfighter was gored to death in a third-rate bullring in the province of Córdoba. Although at the time I knew little of bullfighting, I had heard of Francisco Rivera (alias Paquirri); my wife, a native of Madrid, had even met him years before when he was an up-and-coming *novillero*. And although she took it well, the nation was quite unprepared for Paquirri's tragic death. Spain went into shock, it seemed; people spoke of nothing else—not just aficionados, but people in all walks of life. Newspapers, magazines, and the state-run television devoted vast amounts of space to the bullfighter's rise and fall. Some aficionado had been present with his home video camera when Paquirri's luck had run out; as an act of patriotism (he later said) the aficionado turned down astronomical foreign offers and sold his videotape to Spanish television for a paltry two million pesetas. As a result, the whole country was able to witness the awful moment, again and again in slow motion. At the traditional cocktail party for new Fulbrighters, it was the same story. I remember the night well. While everyone was distracted with the subject of Paquirri and the sport of bullfighting, the American Embassy's cultural attaché quickly wolfed down most of the caviar.

Suddenly, my original research topic seemed too humdrum. How could I devote so many months to searching for traces of ritual violence in medieval ballads when all around me a modern, industrialized society could be turned upside-down by the death of a matador? Was this not the real opportunity to observe the role of violence in shaping culture? Had I not lucked into a chance to observe a myth in the process of being made? What I really needed, I soon convinced myself, was to put the ballads on the back burner and immerse myself in bullfighting lore.

Had I known at the time just how much bullfighting lore there was to get immersed in, I might have thought twice. But my ignorance shielded me even as my curiosity pushed me forward. And when I finally realized what I had gotten myself into, there was no turning back. Time sped by, and just when I was getting a handle on the bibliography, my Fulbright stipends ran out. Fortunately I found a new backer (the Newcombe Foundation), and I was able to stay in Spain for one more fertile year. My game plan for the second year was to attend as many bullfights as possible—not in the great plaza of Madrid, mind you, but in the humble plazas of the towns and villages. This is where Eugenio Noel had said that the *real* Spanish barbarism was to be located. It seemed to me that the patronal festival was the genuine context for bullfighting and the most promising key to its interpretation (in small towns bullfights are always held on the patron saint's feast day). The bullfight in Madrid had become too secularized: you could see one every weekend if you had the money. I didn't have it, and that was what really clinched it. Goodbye Madrid, hello Cercedilla.

Eugenio Noel was an early twentieth-century Spanish journalist and social reformer. He is remembered today as the greatest enemy bullfighting ever had. With his sharp wit and poisoned pen, he marshaled every argument imaginable in a quixotic attempt to close down his country's bullrings. Although I appreciated his anti-taurine tirades, I was glad he had failed. If Spain had renounced "barbarism," my research would have been archival drudgery instead of fiesta after fiesta. Besides, bullfighting was no longer the vicious spectacle it had been years before. I would no longer see the phenomena Hemingway had celebrated: horses tripping on their entrails, or nighttime encounters featuring bears versus bulls, lions versus bulls, elephants versus bulls, . . . etc. I will say, however, that I did see one or two things during the course of my fieldwork that sorely tested my status as a card-carrying cultural relativist. Here I am not thinking of the brave and photogenic thirteen-year-olds risking their lives for a few moments of applause. Nor am I thinking of these same youngsters getting tossed around like straw dummies by eight-hundred-pound dogies (usually without consequence). Nor am I thinking of the many bulls who refused to die on cue, preferring instead to spoil their killers' victory with a prolonged, anti-climactic, anti-aesthetic agony. I am not even thinking of the slightly drunken picador who was vilified by a thoroughly drunken crowd when he clumsily picced the bull's ribs instead of his withers. I am thinking, instead, of the first and last "comic bullfight" that I attended.

The place: it doesn't matter. Comic bullfights are put on by troupes of performers who go all over Spain keeping up with the summertime schedule of patronal festivals. The date: that doesn't matter either, since they've been doing it since around the turn of the century. Suffice it to say that it was the feast of Santiago in a small town in Old Castile. I had the good fortune to be accompanied by Paco, a middle-aged *madrileño* with a lower-class background and a first-class mind. Paco had the kind of reflexivity that anthropologists only dream about. He was my Virgil, my sounding board, and my pal. I had great regard for his opinions and his thoroughly Spanish sense of humor. He had never attended a comic bullfight either, as it happened; so we set out for the makeshift *plaza de toros* with open minds and a sense of discovery, glorying in the Velázquez-blue sky and brilliant sun of Spain's northern *meseta* (plateau).

The crowd we were to share the experience with was, at first glance, the same sort of crowd we had seen at normal small-town bullfights. The organizational nucleus of every traditional fiesta was there in force, that is, the *peñas*, or social clubs, that raise money to buy the bulls, contract for the taurine performers, decorate the streets, furnish the music, participate in the saint's procession, and so forth. The town in question had two such peñas, each with its own band, colors, and other identity signs; now they occupied their respective territories in the stands of the jerry-built bullring, vying with each other to see who could make the most racket and quaff the most wine from pigskin *botas*. The other spectators, locals or visitors from neighboring towns, observed this pre-game warm-up with good humor. What made this crowd different from that of a regular bullfight was the large number of women and children present. And of course the mind-frame was not the same: people had gathered not for thrills and chills but to have some laughs.

And laugh we all did when the stars of the show marched out into the sunny arena: five dwarfs dressed in the regalia of full matadors and a normal-sized youth dressed as a rodeo clown. After a routine series of pratfalls and other antics, a gate was opened and a skittish *torito bravo* appeared, a little bull of brave blood who immediately followed the dictates of his genetic makeup and chased everyone behind the barriers. The bulls used in comic bullfights are usually one-year-olds, about three feet tall at the shoulder and weighing some 250 pounds. Small as it was, the torito looked big next to the gang of midgets.

Appearances can be deceiving, of course. Taurine insiders know that it is not so much the size of a bull but his age that matters: the older the bull, the smarter and more dangerous he is; the younger the bull, the easier he is to fool. The diminutive bullfighters began to make cape passes with the torito that would have been suicidal under normal circumstances. The

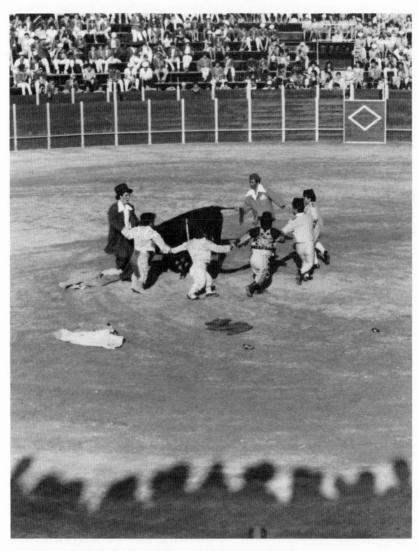

A troupe of *toreros cómicos* plays "ring-around-the-bull" in a small-town arena. Photo by Timothy Mitchell.

With this provocative gesture the "matador" proves that the bull is dominated and ready to be killed. Photo by Timothy Mitchell.

diminutive bull followed his noble instincts and played into their hands again and again. The dwarf with the fewest deformities played the role of matador; the others formed part of his *cuadrilla*, or crew. Some of them were so misshapen that it was hard to see how they could remain upright, let alone stick banderillas into the bullock's back. But they did. And when they had used up their repertory of tricks and stunts, the miniature matador took up his sword, marched out to the middle of the arena, and looked his fourfooted foe right in the eye (he had to look up). To the surprise of Paco, myself, and a lot of other people, the dwarf was going to attempt to kill the bull in the normal, orthodox way; the little man's bravura was immediately rewarded with a round of frenzied applause. As the "moment of truth" approached, the crowd fell silent. One or two people got up and moved toward the exits, unable to stomach what was coming. The dwarf had a little red cape in his left hand and brandished a sharp *estoque* in his right. As he raised the sword, the torito charged and trampled him underfoot. He got up, dusted himself off, squared up, raised his sword, and got trampled again. No one was laughing. His honor on the line, the dwarf squared off a third time. He got the jump on the bull, drove the sword a few inches into his withers, and was repaid with a sharp butt in the stomach. The torito shook the sword loose and began running around. An uncomfortable feeling of anti-climax was in the offing, quickly defused when the clown stepped forth to finish the unlucky midget's work. And what a finish! The clown played the agony of his bovine patsy for all it was worth. He began with a series of fake swordthrusts and finally mounted him backwards. As the little bull trotted along, the clown stuck a dagger into his neck again and again. They finally fell together and rolled around in the sand, with the clown still stabbing. When the torito stretched out his skinny legs and expired, the clown doffed his ragged top hat and bathed in the acclamations.

The show was over. But the fiesta was in full swing in the streets outside the bullring. As we made our way through the crowds, Paco and I compared our reactions to what we had just seen. He was bemused and philosophical. I was simply dumbfounded. Not shocked or angry or disgusted, just bewildered. My schemas had been thoroughly dislocated. Never had such demands been placed on my sense of humor.

In any given year, between seven and eight thousand bullfights are held in Spain, with approximately twenty-five thousand bulls killed altogether (the numbers steadily increased through the 1980s). In the interest of a broad perspective, therefore, it must be pointed out that midget bullfights represent only a tiny fraction of the total number of taurine spectacles offered every year. They do represent, for me, the most enigmatic aspect of Spanish bullfighting. Perhaps they owe their existence to the traditional Spanish fondness for the grotesque. From a formal point of view, of course, comic bullfights get by with an age-old repertory of clowning, farce, and slapstick. Perhaps people enjoy them for this alone. Or perhaps, at a more symbolic level, comic bullfights subliminally communicate the message that even the small and the weak can triumph in this harsh world. (This is the wisdom that the late Bruno Bettelheim retrieved from the most violent and gruesome fairytales.) Or, as another possibility, perhaps comic bullfights function as a culturally sanctioned escape valve for relieving feelings of inadequacy or inferiority, feelings that "serious" bullfighting might foment with its implicit demand that men be supermen. In this sense, a midget bullfighter may be the perfect embodiment of the "failed" bullfighter—a man unable to be a superman, hence condemned to be less than a man, for reasons that have more to do with fate (genes) than with personal shortcomings. But this is enough speculation for now. I deal with the whole issue of youth, bullfighting, and personal failure in Chapter 3.

Meanwhile back in 1985, the long summer finally came to an end and I returned to my station at the Biblioteca Nacional for a longer winter of note-taking and meditation. As I delved into two centuries of taurine writing, I discovered that most interpretations of the bullfight had come from historians or anthropologists of religion. For them the central question had been whether or not the bullfight was in some sense a sacrifice and the bullfighter a priest. Scholarly theories of the bullfight's alleged religious significance had greatly influenced the pseudo-philosophical or belletristic interpretations that came into style in the 1920s and 1930s and have not gone out of style since.

To make a long story short, most writers had begged the question as to what a sacrifice is, even as they took for granted that it was the Ur-ritual. But if one adopted the perspective that sacrifice was just another ritual interpretation of an older and less accessible phenomenon, then the whole question of whether the bullfight was a sacrifice became secondary, even moot. The theories of René Girard played an important role in helping me see through the misunderstandings that had plagued previous interpretations of the bullfight. Girard never mentioned the word "bullfight" himself (in contrast to other French anthropologists of desire like Michel Leiris or Georges Bataille), but his research into the victimage mechanism was utterly àpropos. Equally vital to me was the work of Spain's premier anthropologist, Julio Caro Baroja, who had spent years investigating the sociocentrism and violence of Spanish rural life.

In the light of such scholarship, it was easy to see what the bullfight wasn't. It wasn't a sacrifice in the conventional meaning of sacrifice; it wasn't a crypto-religion; it wasn't about man's sexual domination of woman; it wasn't about woman's sexual domination of man; it wasn't a daring violation of the menstrual taboo. (Each of these views has been advanced in perfect seriousness by one anthropologist or another.) In *Violence and Piety in Spanish Folklore* (University of Pennsylvania Press, 1988), I placed the bullfight alongside all the other Spanish rituals, games, fiestas, and folk dramas that mythify a victim. Generally speaking, folk communities mythify victims in two ways. (1) Persecutory mythopoesis seeks to hide the fact that a victim is a scapegoat by imputing him or her with a variety of malevolent traits. (2) By contrast, martyrological mythopoesis makes a hero of the victim and fetishizes his or her sufferings and death. It is easy to see how bullfighting provides abundant opportunities for both kinds of mythopoesis to take place: on the one hand, a bull's blind aggressivity prevents his being perceived as innocent; and on the other, the tree of bullfighting has never ceased to be nurtured by the blood of gored, and subsequently glorified, matadors.

This is by no means the end of the story, but only the sketchiest outline of an archetypal, ahistorical plot. There is much more to be told, for unlike the other rural rituals to which it is kin, bull-baiting underwent a dynamic phase of historical development and urbanization. It came to occupy a central place in Spanish life. The first bullrings were built in the eighteenth century, and ever since then people have flocked there to vent their passions and affirm their values.

For the past several summers I have returned to Spain in search of new information and insights. *Blood Sport* represents my culminating outlook on bullfighting. I hold that it is no trivial pastime, but the very mirror of Spain's social and historical traumas in the modern period. How this came to be so, and why, and the psychological consequences, are the subjects that my study treats in depth.

Although a thorough exploration of bullfighting is desirable in itself, for me it is more of a means than an end. The end I have always in view is a better understanding of the people of Spain, and therefore of humanity in general. I cannot emphasize enough that I do not see Spaniards as "the Other." Smug ethnocentrism, or its evil twin, chic adulation of différance, are equally alien to me. Tolerance of cultural diversity is a very good thing, as long as it does not entail a perverse unwillingness to criticize. After all, nothing created by human beings is sacrosanct or beyond reproach, and every cultural tradition develops facets of human nature that we all share. In other words, the reflection of Spain in the mirror of bullfighting is our own, warts and all.

Acknowledgments

THE STUDY I UNDERTAKE is complemented by that of Rosario Cambria. In 1974, Professor Cambria published a book that was destined to become a standard work of reference on the cultural implications of bullfighting. In *Los toros: tema polémico en el ensayo español del siglo XX* (Gredos), he systematically reviewed the wide variety of perspectives that Spanish intellectuals had adopted vis-à-vis their country's most famous institution. Every serious treatment of the subject since 1974 has relied on this work to one degree or another. For *Blood Sport*, Professor Cambria has prepared a new survey that includes both Spanish and English language intellectuals, along with an up-to-date selected bibliography of taurine sources. As it happens, Professor Cambria is as gifted a photographer as he is a scholar; most of the splendid illustrations that appear in this book were taken on one or another of his sojourns in Spain. With the addition of this material, I believe *Blood Sport* to be the most complete introduction to taurine culture ever published in English.

I would like to express my appreciation to the College of Liberal Arts of Texas A&M University for a generous Summer Research Award that enabled me to complete this project.

Once again, the encouragement of Patricia Smith and her colleagues at the University of Pennsylvania Press was invaluable to me.

For their kind help and suggestions at different stages of the project, I am much indebted to Angela Fernández, Francisco Fernández, Diane Christian, David Gilmore, and Wulf Koepke.

Introduction

THE INITIAL PREMISE of this book is very simply stated: bullfighting can best be understood when we see it in the context of Spanish society and history. Surely there is nothing in this affirmation that could cause anyone to raise an eyebrow; one would think that *any* human custom or institution is best understood in the context of the society in which it has evolved. Nevertheless, almost everything that has been written about bullfighting has taken it out of its sociohistorical context in one way or another. This is an altogether amazing circumstance. It implies that the Spanish *corrida de toros* has been widely misunderstood—by Spaniards and non-Spaniards alike. In fact, if we examine the major ways in which bullfighting has been taken out of context, we will quickly realize just how shaky and unreliable our knowledge of the entire affair is.

One of the twentieth century's prime interpretations of bullfighting has managed to take it not only out of Spanish historical context but out of history altogether. I am referring, of course, to the notion that the bullfight is a sacred or quasi-sacred ritual. Agog with the archaeological discoveries of Sir Arthur Evans and others, intellectuals and artists of the 1920s and 1930s were convinced that the matador could only be portrayed against a backdrop of minotaurs, bull worship, Cretan-style blood sacrifice, and so forth. (Ironically, this counter-historical perspective flowered in the very epoch when bullfighting itself had reached a high degree of rationalization and was quickly being converted into an industry.) I will take up this issue in greater detail in "The Magical Bull," part of Chapter 1. For now, suffice it to say that there is indeed a religious element in bullfighting, but one that has little to do with the high-flown fantasies of a Lorca, a Picasso, or a Montherlant.[1]

Another view of bullfighting, one that stands in sharp contrast to the mythico-religious, is that of moral condemnation. Now, it is entirely possible that bullfighting is immoral or unethical in some way or in every way. Extreme caution must be exercised, however, when applying personal or abstract moral standards to specific aspects of cultural performances. What at first sight appears to be evil may be mere brutishness; the genuine evil can be camouflaged or hidden in a dozen ways. If bullfighting is seen in terms of the ethical standards of the taurine subculture itself—the mores of the so-called "planet of the bulls"—then condemnation will naturally be impossible. The corrida de toros has been a perfectly normal and legal pastime in Spain and has been enjoyed without guilt by people of the highest moral caliber for centuries. It can be shown without difficulty, moreover, that for many people the bullfighter exemplifies important values like honor, integrity, rectitude, and so forth.

This does not place bullfighting beyond reproach. It simply means that, to be legitimate and credible, any condemnation of bullfighting would have to proceed from an evaluation of the cultural complex of beliefs and behaviors that sustains it. For this reason we can salute Eugenio Noel (1885–1936), a man who ardently attacked bullfighting but who knew everything there was to know about it, as well as how it related to Spain's social and political plight. In other words, it is the context itself that has to be put on trial, and not a few acts extracted from it. It is all too easy, and certainly far more common, to condemn without due process of law, as it were; instead of weighing dispassionately the pros and cons and complexities of the bullfight phenomenon, many people become fixated on the bloodletting and indulge in an unreflecting reaction of disgust. Paradoxically, such an emotional reaction is the counterpart of the unthinking enthusiasm of bullfight fans, those who cheer or insult the matadors, those who enter spontaneously into the passion of the spectacle—never bothering to inquire into its nature, never feeling the need to question its ethicality. In either case, knee-jerk condemnation or exaltation, people follow the typical human tendency to take the line of least resistance and react in accordance with received habits of mind. But to understand the *why* of Spanish animal-baiting in general, bull-baiting in particular, and finally the urban corrida de toros, is a more complicated and demanding task. It would seem to require a sense of perspective and an intellectual curiosity that the merely disgusted or the merely enthusiastic cannot attain.

In listing the ways in which bullfighting can be taken out of context, a place of honor must be reserved for the aficionados. Along with the bullfighters and cattle breeders themselves, the aficionados are the ones who best appreciate the complex technical aspects of the bullfighting craft. Specialized knowledge, an unimaginably rich and esoteric vocabulary, long years of experience, a discriminating eye—these are the characteristics of the true aficionado. But it is precisely this obsession with technical expertise that prevents aficionados from seeing—or caring about—bullfighting in societal or political or some other kind of broad perspective. We might say that aficionados cannot see the forest for the trees, as long as we remember that they were never looking for the forest in the first place. In many ways, the attitude that an aficionado adopts with regard to bullfighting is that of a fetishist. As Spanish philosopher José Ortega y Gasset put it:

> The aficionado, as such, indulges himself by keeping the object to which he is devoted present, uncovering every minute detail of its past and present forms. Thus, he always begins with the reality that stimulates his devotion and proceeds to, let us say, caress it lingeringly with his attention. Now then: to speak seriously of something is not that; it is a much graver, more dramatic task, an almost cruel one.[2]

Ortega complained that many of the people who seemed to know the most about bullfighting knew the least. In Ortega's opinion, even José María de Cossío, the creator of a massive and much respected taurine encyclopedia, had approached his subject with the curiosity of an aficionado instead of the scientific rigor of . . . an Ortega.[3]

Obviously it is a bold step to claim that bullfighting aficionados do not truly understand bullfighting. It would be even bolder to make such an assertion about the high priests of the planet of the bulls—the critics. Nevertheless, I am prepared to do just that. Even this elite group, with a tradition going back 150 years, composed of people with the most acute aesthetic sensibilities, does not or cannot or will not approach bullfighting with the requisite rigor. In view of the seriousness of this charge, I shall proceed at once to substantiate it, and in so doing I hope to convey the nature and advantages of my own approach.

In order to make a case against the critical elite, I must first present their case in as fair and honest a way as possible. At its higher levels, taurine criticism is built on two propositions: that bullfighting is a fine art, and that as such it can only be understood and appreciated from an aesthetic point of view. The first of these assertions is not particularly difficult to establish. In fact, bullfighting can even be considered sublime if we adopt Edmund Burke's perspective. As explained by a noted authority on aesthetics:

> The feeling of the sublime, to begin with, involves a degree of horror—controlled horror—the mind being held and filled by what it contemplates. Thus,

> any object that can excite the ideas of pain and danger, or is associated with such
> objects, or has qualities that can operate in a similar way, can be sublime.[4]

A moment's reflection will confirm that the bullfight fulfills this definition better than most arts. In the manner of, say, Sophocles' *Oedipus Rex*, the horror-arousing and sublime bullfight can be appreciated or even admired by anyone with a truly aesthetic attitude. But here is the rub: as John Hospers reminds us, the aesthetic attitude must not be confused with a practical, moralistic, or personalized attitude. Any work of art, in other words, must be experienced and enjoyed on its own terms, without reference to its possible utility, rightness or wrongness, or relation to our own lives.[5] Now, if we rigorously apply these criteria, most of the people who watch bullfights will have to be relegated to non-aesthetic categories.

Easiest of all to eliminate, perhaps, are those animal-rights activists who would vehemently deny that public animal slaughter could be classified as art. As Hospers would point out, however, the aesthetic attitude is independent of the moral attitude; an object that is objectionable on moral grounds can still be admired for its form, elegance, grace, economy of means, and so on.

In the case of the average spectator, any number of factors can intervene to short-circuit or impede the formation of a genuinely aesthetic attitude. For one thing, the planet of the bulls has traditionally been divided and subdivided into associations known as *peñas, tertulias,* clubs, or *círculos,* organized to foster a passion for corridas in general, for a particular style of bullfighting, or, most often, for a particular bullfighter. All major matadors, and numerous minor ones, have enjoyed the loyal support of these fan clubs. Like the toreros themselves, the fans tend to rival each other both outside and inside the bullrings. Like Spain itself, bullfighting has been factionalized almost from the start. In the late eighteenth and early nineteenth centuries, taurine enthusiasts divided themselves into partisans of the Ronda school of bullfighting (supposedly more sober and technically precise) and the Seville school (supposedly more lighthearted and graceful). This issue had barely been settled when Spain began to be rocked by countless verbal and physical clashes among the partisans of rival matadors—*lagartijistas, frascuelistas, esparteristas, guerristas, gallistas, belmontistas,* and so on, and so forth. The point is this: if you attend a corrida de toros to cheer on "your" bullfighter and vituperate the other, then you will not be in a position to evaluate the artistic merit of either. A fan's self-affirming identification with his or her hero is a type of personalized attitude and is, as such, inimical to the aesthetic attitude.

Not that one must belong to a peña to have a personalized attitude. As Fernando Claramunt points out, one never knows what kind of private psychological problems a bullfight spectator might be projecting onto the spectacle:

> There are afternoons in which the number of "pure" aficionados is at a minimum and the bullring overflows with fanatics, believers, and overexcited people, affectively involved with the incidents of the corrida in a substantially irrational way. Aesthetic values attract a certain number of spectators, but the majority are not motivated by meta-necessities of artistic creation and sublimation; above all those who show up at the ring with whistles, bells, and projectiles well-adapted to the need to express excremental impulses, known in psychoanalysis as forms of anal-sadistic aggression.[6]

Such information sheds new light on a confession made by Ernest Hemingway in *Death in the Afternoon*:

> I believe firmly in the throwing of cushions of all weights, pieces of bread, oranges, vegetables, small dead animals of all sorts, including fish, and, if necessary, bottles provided they are not thrown at the bullfighters' heads, and the occasional setting fire to a bull ring if a properly decorous protest has had no effect.[7]

In a conference held in Spain on the twenty-fifth anniversary of Hemingway's suicide, a number of scholars psychoanalyzed his love of bullfighting to find castration anxiety, latent homosexuality, hatred of women, and similar elements.[8] Interesting as these observations may be, they ought to be taken with a grain of salt. In the first place, may he who is not a latent homosexual cast the first stone. In the second place, and more to the point, we must not be misled into reducing spectator behavior to individual traumas of one kind or another. People are what their societies have made them, after all; so to trace the social traumas underlying spectator behavior stands to be a more fertile pursuit in the long run. As I will discuss in Chapter 4, the word "machismo" cannot even begin to describe Spanish criteria of dominance and submission, nor ideas of what men should be like in general and matadors in particular, nor the legacy of arbitrary authoritarianism that underlies such ideas. If Hemingway fit in so well at bullrings it was precisely because he had assimilated the Spanish worldview so completely.[9]

The values that Hemingway adopted and adapted to were, and remain, personalistic in the extreme. Whether they are members of the El Cordobés Club or free-lance sociopaths, bullfight spectators tend to take every part of the performance personally. Perhaps this is why there is no public in the world that is as experienced and as ingenious at hurling insults. In the view of sociologist Tierno Galván:

> It is a profoundly personal kind of insulting in which the abuse, far from being just a shout or indignant exclamation, conserves every shade of the ad hominem offense. This specific intentionality, plus the irony that is almost always present, give the taurine insult a special vigor and a characteristically sarcastic tone. Ordinarily the insult bursts forth with extraordinary violence when the matador shows some sign of fear. The public scolds him passionately, alluding to the qualities that define manliness, and even inclines toward personal aggression.[10]

One man I sat next to at a bullfight in Salamanca province kept jumping to his feet to shout such insults; many of them were extremely funny and all of them alluded in some way to the allegedly inadequate virility of the matador, Palomo Linares. Similarly, Hemingway filled his *Death in the Afternoon* with numerous catty, sarcastic, and utterly ad hominem descriptions of bullfighters. What all insulters have in common, of course, is their thoroughly personalistic approach to bullfighting, a perspective that is devoid of the detachment and distance required of the aesthetic point of view.[11]

The *taurinos*, or fans, are not to be confused with the aficionados. Surely the members of this numerically smaller group, it might be thought at first, know how to derive authentic artistic pleasure from bullfighting. Nevertheless, even aficionados are prone to a kind of personalism, one that paradoxically uses aesthetic criteria to defeat the aesthetic vision. In one of the better taurine essays of the 1980s, Spanish philosopher Fernando Savater distinguishes between the physical or mental inebriation of the public at large and the special moods of frustration and melancholy that characterize the genuine devotee. Savater traces such moods to a metaphysical dilemma: the aficionado has already seen the perfect taurine performance in the mind's eye, and having already seen it, cannot see it again. It all begins one day when an ordinary spectator or tourist is watching a given matador's performance and is suddenly struck with an intuition of the "Eternal Performance":

> He is from then on a true taurine aficionado, with his own pet peeves and idiosyncrasies that perhaps arise in part from the circumstances that surrounded

the revelation of the Eternal Performance on that particular afternoon. . . . He can go on to see in his lifetime a hundred better performances than that which served to awaken him to the Eternal Performance, but such an awakening takes place only once. From that moment on, the intuited archetype presides from its radical and arbitrary isolation over everything that is to be seen in a bullring. The aficionado now knows what he wants out of bullfighting; and he also knows, obscurely and unconsciously, that he will never have it.[12]

Savater offers a sophisticated way of accounting for the existence of a familiar denizen of the planet of the bulls, the *laudator temporis acti*, or praiser of times past, for whom bullfighting's golden epoch usually coincides with that of his youth. The tendency of such individuals to nostalgically glorify long-gone bullfighters and dogmatically heap abuse on those of today is notorious. Related to this species of aficionado are the taurine writers who give us ecstatic descriptions of performances that took place long before they were born.[13] The point is this: people under the influence of a metaphysical Eternal Performance are not in a position to judge or appreciate what they see in a fair-minded way. Like the hero-worshiping fan or the moralistic animaliarian, the melancholy aficionado replaces the aesthetic attitude with a private myth.

It should be clear by now that genuine aesthetic appreciation of the bullfight is not easy to attain. The three major types of non-aesthetic attitudes described above are like hurdles that must be overcome, or temptations that must be avoided, on the way to developing the proper sensibility. The entire process is best exemplified by a twentieth-century poet and essayist named José Bergamín (1897–1984). In dozens of essays published over a period of five decades, Bergamín established himself as one of Spain's most articulate legislators of taurine aesthetics. In so doing, he explicitly distances himself from the moralists, the *taurinos*, and the nostalgic aficionados. For Bergamín, the purveyors of sentimental bourgeois morality are unable to grasp the sublime beauty of the cruelly intelligent corrida. "Cruelty is an unavoidable condition of beauty because it forms part of an uncluttered sensibility. . . . A corrida de toros is an immoral spectacle, and therefore educational."[14] With regard to the masses of hero-worshiping spectators, or those obsessed with questions of virility, Bergamín asserts that the aesthetic emotion is only possible when such personalistic perspectives are overcome. The multitudes never accept the truth of art, says Bergamín, because it seems a lie to them, preferring any lie that seems true: "They reject the miracle and create the myth."[15] Ironically, Bergamín's defense of the aesthetic emotion—immoral by definition—acquires puritanical overtones when he condemns any excitement arising from danger:

> Since the true emotion of bullfighting is the emotion of art, the spectator who gets emotional for another reason destroys it by replacing it with a kind of mortal pornography that converts him into a suicidal masochist and a sadistic assassin all at once: both things are only imagined, of course, and unknown to himself, as he feels pleasure and pain in the frustrated manner of an unconscious phantasmagorial onanism.[16]

In keeping with his stringent philosophy, Bergamín affirms that a bullfighter's death in the line of duty is not tragic, nor honorable, nor glorious, but quite irrelevant to the only thing that matters—art.[17] Finally, Bergamín takes aim at those aficionados who have eyes but do not see, prejudiced as they are with dogmatic canons or mythicizing memories.[18] For Bergamín, the magical, miraculous beauty of bullfighting is available at any time, at any given corrida, for the right sensibility. Bullfighting is the art of *birlibirloque*, of *visto y no visto*, of "now you see it, now you don't." As a performance impossible to rehearse, the bullfight conveys "the eternally fugitive mystery of art" with special purity and luminosity.[19]

This completes my presentation of the case for an aesthetic approach to bullfighting. Now, more briefly, I will show why bullfighting cannot be understood or explained by such an approach.

As the critical elite has itself acknowledged, and indeed prided itself upon, most spectators are not capable of truly aesthetic emotions. As it happens, however, the personalistic criteria that keep the masses from having an aesthetic attitude are nothing less than the social and economic basis of the bullfighting phenomenon. In other words, if it were not for the ignorant, passionate, hero-worshiping multitudes who pay to have their non-aesthetic emotions stimulated, there would be no art for the aesthetes to savor.

Moreover, and in contrast to other spectacles, there is no such thing as an unknown but critically acclaimed bullfighter. On the planet of the bulls, mass popularity always precedes, and outweighs, critical scrutiny. Let us take two examples. The twentieth-century matador that most influenced the aesthetic canons of bullfighting was unquestionably Juan Belmonte. But the vast majority of spectators flocked to see him not for his art but because they were sure he was going to be gored with every cape pass. They were drawn, in other words, by the sort of morbid curiosity that Bergamín termed pornographic, quite indifferent to the critical ballyhoo.[20] Similarly, in the 1960s, the poisoned pens of the entire critical establishment were unable to keep the suicidally valiant El Cordobés from winning over the crowds and amassing an immense fortune. Never was the social irrelevance of the *arbitri elegantiarum* more in evidence.

So even as we admit that there is such a thing as an aesthetic perspective on bullfights, we must admit that it has precious little to tell us about why people go to them. In the process of showing that the majority of bullfight spectators answer to motivations that are non-aesthetic in nature, we demonstrate that bullfighting exists because of non-aesthetic reasons. There is a crucial point to be deduced from this: the aesthetic approach, to be such, must necessarily take bullfighting out of its context, that is, the circumstances under which it exists. Consequently, the aesthetic approach is just as narrow and misleading as the moralistic approach, or the mythico-religious approach, or the technical approach. What they all have in common is a tendency to focus in on the bullfight performance, select and isolate certain elements, and omit everything else from consideration. In my view, any approach to bullfighting that proceeds by taking it out of context cannot be a legitimate way to understand bullfighting.

All of us, surely, would like to think that we are capable of feeling refined aesthetic emotions. I myself fancy that I have felt them at one point or another. It is an attractive and satisfying approach to bullfights—and that is precisely why it must be defined, rebutted, and dismissed. Of all the ways to close one's eyes to the raison d'être of bullfighting, the aesthetic view is at once the most seductive and the most possessive. In fact, if anyone realized just how much the aesthetic approach is incompatible with any other, it was Bergamín. "There is no 'sociological point of view' from which to observe bullfighting," he asserted, "because in that way it is simply *not seen*."[21] This statement is clearly consistent with his entire philosophy, in which epistemology is one with aesthetics and what you see is what you know. But to fall under the spell of taurine art is to abandon all hope of accounting for it. This was well understood by Eugenio Noel, a man with a superb aesthetic sense who was nevertheless unwilling to turn his back on the social reality of bullfighting.

> This barbarity has undoubtedly inspired works of art. No one denies that. The artist elevates and dignifies what he sees and even what he doesn't see. His genius works miracles. And it is no small one to convert a work of popular force, of inconsistency, of catharsis, into a work of art. . . . But now the time has come for the sociologist, not the artist, to intervene.[22]

When it comes to the art of bullfighting, the sociological or the sociohistorical perspective can encompass the aesthetic one, but the aesthetic perspective must, by its very nature, flee from the other.

There is another important aspect to this issue. Unlike other fine arts, bullfighting cannot make a conscious, deliberate comment on the society at large in the manner of, for example, Picasso's *Guernica* or Dreiser's *Sister Carrie*. The canons of bullfighting are far more rigid and ritualistic than those of painting or literature; there is no way that a matador can modify his style of killing in order to express protest, satire, or any other idea whatsoever. Ideas can only appear when bullfighting becomes the subject matter of another artistic medium, such as a Blasco Ibáñez novel or a Solana painting. The "artistic" techniques of bullfighters themselves are unidirectional, non-referential, unreflexive, and inarticulate.

For many poetically and mythically minded writers, bullfighting's inability to make social comments of any kind constitutes a license to fantasize, to see it as a separate creation, its own closed universe, timeless, unchanging, and absolute. Indeed, it is almost as if bullfighting itself wished to throw up a smokescreen around its own reality, masking its historical and social determinants to cast a spell over spectators. More than an art, then, bullfighting could be seen as stylized shamanism; and there is nothing shamans like better than to hoodwink people about their human, all-too-human nature. Aestheticists willingly suspend disbelief and give themselves over to the illusion. For Bergamín, of course, illusion was the very basis of bullfighting's aesthetic thrill; the truth of art was to be located precisely in *birlibirloque*, hocus-pocus. There is something touchingly childlike in all this; one would no sooner interrupt the poet in his taurine reveries than tell a four-year-old that there is no Santa Claus. Sooner or later, however, the pleasure principle must yield to the reality principle. Our role model need not be the Grinch, but Toto, the little dog who pulls back a curtain to reveal that the awesome Wizard of Oz is just a wily charlatan at a control panel.

What I have tried to establish is this: if most of what we thought we knew about bullfighting comes from moralists, fans, aficionados, and critics who have taken bullfighting out of context in judgmental or passionate or fetishistic or aesthetic ways, then we have to start all over again, from a new perspective, one that is radically committed to understanding bullfighting in the only way it can be wholly understood—holistically. To the degree that we succeed in seeing the bullfight in the context of Spanish society and history and politics, all the other incomplete views should fall into their proper place as well. It would certainly be inadvisable to ignore the considerable contributions made from one or another of the "mainstream" approaches; they simply need to be harnessed in the service of a more global perspective. Both taurine and anti-taurine writings ought to be scrutinized and set over against one another, and then measured against the insights of social scientists and humanists. Above all, we ought to approach bullfighting in much the same way that a bullfighter approaches a bull: we should close in and confront our subject with nerve, tenacity, and finesse while remembering to keep a very prudent distance.

1. Fiesta de Toros

IT IS NOT UNCOMMON for books on Spanish bullfighting to begin not with its current reality or even its historical development but in the dark eons of prehistory. Authors delve into ancient myths of taurine deities, minotaurs, sacrificial rites, and so on, eagerly citing examples of cave paintings and bull worship in the Iberian peninsula. The implication, of course, is that somehow the modern bullfight has descended from or evolved out of these primordial precedents.

The only thing that can be affirmed with certainty, however, is that a predatory species of mammal known (wisely or not) as *homo sapiens* has taken advantage of a herbivorous mammal species known as *bos taurus* for at least fifty thousand years. Spanish bullfighting, like American bullriding, clearly demonstrates that human utilization of bulls is not merely utilitarian. It is not simply a quest for food but a question of recreation or fantasy or cultural drama. This much we can affirm through observation alone. But to proceed to affirm, as many authors do, that bullfighting is related in specific ways to primordial manhandling of bulls is to enter the terrain of hypothesis and conjecture. And although these things certainly have their place in the quest for knowledge, they do not strike me as the best way to *begin* the quest.

The present study, therefore, begins with facts in context, with the ethnographic present, with bulls as they are actually handled by ordinary Spaniards during their local fiestas. In any form it takes—rural or urban, spontaneous or legislated, "barbarous" or "civilized"—bullfighting is always known in Spanish as *la fiesta de toros*, the fiesta of bulls. And since this fiesta is at its most festive in rural Spain, it behooves us to begin our investigation there, bearing in mind that (1) the bull is not the only species to be pressed into service and made to honor the patron saint of a given locality; and (2) the animals thus victimized can be grouped with other categories of victims of a symbolic or inanimate nature. Indeed, only when we have grasped the entire context of animal-baiting, Judas-burning, and

Moor-killing in village festivals can we begin to understand the significance for ordinary Spaniards of the fiesta de toros.

One Year of Fiestas

To achieve this goal in as agreeable and profitable a time as possible, let us embark on a tour of festal Spain. Imagine that it is January and that you, the reader, have arrived in Spain with unlimited funds, an unquenchable if somewhat morbid curiosity, and an iron constitution. You find preparations underway all over the country for the Fiesta de los Reyes Magos, the Feast of the Three Kings, when good children receive presents and bad ones get coal stuffed into their shoes. You journey to Cañada, a little town of Alicante, and watch a two-day play put on by the people themselves that culminates in the Massacre of the Innocents. This is mild stuff indeed compared to what awaits you up north, in the patronal fiestas of Guarrate (Zamora), where fattened cocks have been hung by their talons from a rope running across the town plaza. Mounted on horseback in the middle of the plaza, young men about to enter the army (Spain still practices universal conscription) recite long autobiographical verses that draw peals of laughter from the assembled crowd. When they finish, they draw their sabers, gallop toward the squawking cock, and do their best to decapitate it. You then go south to Arquillos (Jaén) to watch a strangely costumed "*pelotero*" chase people all over the village, after which you go to Caniles (Granada) to watch a simulated "theft of the patron saint" and a simulated recovery of the icon that has turned into a bloody melee on more than one occasion. You round out your first month with a visit to San Pablo de los Montes (Toledo), where a transvestite known as the "Madre Cochina" or Piggish Mother runs wildly through the town, accompanied by two acolytes dressed as cows who clobber outsiders with staffs and lift women's skirts with impunity.

In February you part for Bocairente (Valencia) to attend the five-day *fiestas de moros y cristianos*. Neighborhood organizations dress their members like Christians or Moors, and after many a seesaw battle in the streets, the latter capitulate and accede to the torching of a giant effigy of the prophet Mohammad.

You immediately set out for Zamarramala (Segovia) for the famous *festividades de Santa Agueda*, yearly celebrations that would warm the hearts of feminists everywhere. All events are organized and protagonized by the women of the town. First they extort funds for the fiesta by brandishing huge, old-fashioned girdle pins known as *"mata-hombres"* or men-killers. Then they award a solid-gold *mata-hombres* to the woman who has done the most for her sex during the previous year. Then they carry the icon of their saint in solemn procession; Santa Agueda is seen holding the heaven-sent palm with which she healed herself after losing her breasts to Roman cruelty (this saint is now the patroness of nursing mothers all over Spain). And finally, a giant straw dummy representing man is hung by the neck in the Plaza Mayor and set on fire while eloquent local women assail the male condition in comic verse.

Carnival is fast approaching, so you hasten to Villanueva de la Vera (Cáceres) for the *fiesta del Pero-Palo*. A man draped in a sheet is riding around on the oldest and most wretched burro in town while people chant hoary verses that combine rambling invectives with legends of evil-minded Jews:

El año de ochenta y uno	Back in eighty-one
nos dieron la jugarreta	we were double-crossed
entre judíos e intrusos	by Jews and intruders
y gente de mala jeta. . . .	and ugly-looking people. . . .
Judíos ponéos al punto	Jews, watch out
que viene la Inquisición	the Inquisition is coming
que ha salido de Llerena	it has left Llerena
que nuestro Rey lo mandó.	as ordered by our King.
Si se acabara la casta	If the caste were finished off
mejor para el mundo fuera;	it would be better for all;
mejor fuera para Dios	it would be better for God
si de esa casta no hubiera. . . .	if there were no such caste. . . .
El Pero-Palo nosotros	We want the Pero-Palo
queremos para quemarle,	to burn him up,
que son Judas que hacemos	it is Judas that we make into
afrenta de su linaje.	the shame of his race.

The man on the burro is replaced by the effigy of Pero-Palo, which is then carried through the streets and spun around (or "jewed") on a pole by the young women; some pretend to weep upon hearing that Pero-Palo may be pardoned for his crimes. Public jests proliferate until the effigy is blown to bits by a firing squad.

You then make your way to Lloret de Mar (Gerona) to join in a *romería*, a fiesta-pilgrimage-procession that leads people to some isolated shrine and back again. This one was specifically created to give men and women an opportunity to beg heavenly forgiveness for all the sins they committed during their riotous Carnival celebrations.

By the middle of March you have arrived in Alcira, just one of dozens of Valencian towns that have spent vast amounts of time and money to create enormous satirical sculptures. Known as *ninots* or *fallas*, they are all put to the torch to honor San José.

As Holy Week approaches you are beset with indecision, for there are as many ways to celebrate this solemn fiesta as there are towns in Spain. Should you go to Ciudad Real province to attend one of its *procesiones de borrachos* and see how men with hoods and tunics sin and repent at the same time? Should you attend a rustic Passion Play put on by the entire population of Riogordo (Málaga)? Should you travel to Valverde de la Vera (Cáceres) to see men rope rough-hewn beams to their shoulders and trudge along in agony all night? Should you make your way to Baena (Córdoba) to see the mock mob violence of "White-tailed Jews" pitted against "Black-tailed Jews"? You finally decide on Doña Mencía, a little town in the same province where the most pathetic images of Christ and the Dolorosa are carried through the streets and folk *rezaores* chant long romances whose similarity to Scripture is purely coincidental. On Easter Sunday you are on hand in Alcaudete de la Jara (Toledo) to see dozens of Judas dummies getting lynched and shotgunned all over town.

A week later you are on hand for the Day of the Drink in La Alberca (Salamanca). In ostensible celebration of the occasion when the local mountain women whipped would-be invaders from Portugal, two colossal wine barrels are set up in front of City Hall. Unlimited quantities of red wine are consumed by all present while a number of young men rush off and return half an hour later with a rooster. The cackling bird is hung feet up; the men mount their swift steeds and gallop forth one by one. This time, the object is to snap the cock's head off with one's bare hands, a feat that challenges the coordination of the inebriated horsemen to the maximum.

It is now the third week of April and you hurry to Alcoy (Alicante) for the splendid spectacle of Christians quashing Moors in honor of San Jorge. You are tempted to proceed to Corcubión (La Coruña), where no feast of San Marcos has ever gone by without the death of a local father or mother, but decide instead for the festival in honor of Our Lady in Tauste (Zaragoza). The highlight of the five-day fiesta is to be the *toro de fuego*, a brave bull with torches attached to his horns that makes a striking picture as he flees headlong through the darkened streets. As all towns that have this custom know, the metal apparatus that fixes the flares to the bull's horns allows the fun to last a lot longer than when the horns themselves are set on fire. As the month ends you realize that you will have to miss the cock-fights of Vejer de la Frontera (Cádiz).

As May begins you are relieved to discover that not an animal but a vegetable focuses the sacrificial enthusiasms of towns all over Iberia: a *mayo*, also known as a *maya*, made out of a tree or trees and set up in the town plaza by the unmarried males of the town. Thinly disguised as a cross in some places, the obviously pagan fertility symbol brings about a verita-ble explosion of erotic folklore. You arrive in Santoña (Santander) to find hordes of young women dancing around a towering pine and singing verses like

Maya bendita,	Blessed *maya*,
palo larguero,	lengthening pole,
que nuestro Santo	that our Saint
ve placentero.	looks on with pleasure.
Todas las mozas	All the girls
a ti te alaban,	praise you,
por lo derecha,	for being so straight,
por lo pinada.	for being so erect.
Tu punta ostenta,	Your tip enjoys,
gallarda y maja,	gallant and handsome,
nuestro tributo y	our tribute and
nuestra alabanza.	our praise.
Todas presentes	All [the girls] present
damos las gracias	give thanks
a nuestros mozos	to our boys
por esta maya.	for this *maya*.
¡Vivan los mozos!	Long live the boys!
¡Viva la maya!	Long live the *maya*!

The feast of San Miguel finds you in Torres de Berrellen (Zaragoza), watching a parade of huge papier-maché figures known as *gigantes y cabe-zudos*—giants and big-heads. Then you are off to Oya (Pontevedra) for the *rapa das bestas*, Galician for the "shearing of the beasts." A multitude of diminutive wild horses are rounded up and barbered while people eat and drink to the bursting point. Then you travel to Villareal (Castellón) and spend ten days watching the delirious public emotions caused by the *bous embolats*, Valencian for *toros embolados*. These are bulls that run wild in the streets at night after large balls of coal tar are affixed to their horns and set on fire.

The great feast of Corpus Christi is fast approaching, so you hasten to the town of Benavente (Zamora). In the morning you see groups of laughing children pulling calves through the streets with ropes. At seven in the afternoon you realize that the children are only the appetizer for the adults, who attach a one-hundred meter, one-ton rope to the horns of a giant bull and begin a three-hour tug of war in which as many as two hundred people join in. An old man informs you that the real danger is not from the bull but from the rope, for it is heavy enough to crush a person or "cut him in two." You are also informed that the young men of the town have become such sissies that they no longer wade around in the bull's blood when he is finally slaughtered in the square.

A week after Corpus you are on hand in Castrillo de Murcia (Burgos) for one of the most peculiar fiestas in Spain. The main street has been lined with two dozen mattresses, and each mattress has a newborn baby lying on top. When a procession bearing the Holy Eucharist passes by, a bizzare clown known as the *colacho* appears out of nowhere, jumping over the babies like a kangaroo and striking onlookers with a horse's tail attached to a stick. When the ruckus has subsided, the mothers snatch up their crying babes, now believed to possess a special invulnerability to disease.

June leads you to Benabarre (Huesca) and its famous folk comedy, La Pastorada, wherein the locals mock each other and satirize the events of the preceding year in dialogue form. A week later you are in Malpica de Bergantiños (La Coruña) for its famous romería.

Finally the fiesta you have been waiting for arrives—*la noche de San Juan*. As you enter San Pedro de Manrique (Soria) at dusk, the sky glows eerily. The reason: tons of oakwood are being consumed by a bonfire in front of the church of the Virgen de la Peña. At the same time, liquid tons of a sugary sweet wine known as *zurracapote* are being consumed by the assembled crowd. As the blaze begins to die down, two old men start spreading the embers on the ground and a dozen young men with red cumberbunds take off their shoes. Their girlfriends climb up on their shoulders, and the young men tramp barefoot over the carpet of burning coals. No harm comes to them and the crowd shouts its congratulations. A first-aid station has been set up nearby to attend to the inebriated outsiders who attempt to duplicate the feat of the locals.

The ancient Celtic ritual marks the official beginning of summer. All over both Castiles, bull- and cow-baiting is already well underway. From

May through October, hundreds of towns will thrill to *toros de fuego, toros de soga* or *de cuerda, toros embolados, toros de andas y volandas, toros de aguardiente, fiestas de la vaca* or *de la vaquilla,* and so on. (Even in towns that go in for exactly the same kind of bullplay, the fiestas will go by different names.) There will be *encierros,* wherein people run along with the bulls through the streets. There will be *capeas,* where everyone has a chance to show off his bravery in improvised bullrings. There will be *becerradas* in which brave-blooded yearling calves are fought and killed. There will be *novilladas,* showcases for the aspiring young toreros of a given region. There will be any combination of the above.

On the 24th of June you opt for the "*Sanjuanes*" of Coria (Cáceres). Young people have come from all over Extremadura to attend these fiestas. Morning and afternoon, a brave bull is set loose in the main plaza, conveniently ringed by boarded scaffolding. Impoverished would-be bullfighters known as *maletillas* show off their skill and daring for coins and applause; at the same time, scores of less-daring young men behind the barricades are throwing firecrackers at the bull or using blowguns to stick darts in him. You are assured that the darts, hand-made out of cardboard and sewing needles in the true fashion of a folk art, never actually penetrate the bull's hide. The people strongly resent the bad press their fiesta has acquired, so anyone with a camera is asked to put it away or be thrown into the plaza to face the bull. It takes from two to three hours for the *toro de Coria* to grow weary. When he does, a hunter fires his shotgun right between the horns. As the bull plummets to the ground, a mad rush ensues. The men trample each other to be the first to grab onto a coveted trophy: the bull's testicles (which are subsequently chopped off by a butcher and handed over to the winner). The fiesta has remained more or less the same for centuries.

July has come and you have reached the halfway point of your educational journey through the world of Spanish fiestas. Your insatiable if rather morbid curiosity takes you next to Fuentesaúco (Zamora). In this locality, a prearranged but heated battle takes place between men on horseback trying to drive the brave bulls one way and crowds on foot with the opposite intention. A novillada is held in a makeshift bullring in the afternoon, a once-a-year opportunity for the neighborhood clubs to flaunt their colors, dance to their deafening brass bands, swig wine out of *botas,* and pay far more attention to their own hellraising than to the bovids being fought below.

The fiestas of San Fermín, or *Sanfermines,* are now upon you. You wisely reject Pamplona and head for Pasajes de San Pedro (Guipúzcoa), where bold Basque youths run the bulls for ten days without tripping over tourists and the nights are animated by *toros de fuego* and steaming cauldrons of bull stew. You are then tempted to go to Segovia to hear folksongs about mountain women breastfeeding bullocks, but opt instead for La Puebla de Montalbán (Toledo), where people are up at daybreak to scorch their throats with *aguardiente* (raw brandy), set a few bulls loose, and run for their lives. Then you hasten to Denia (Alicante) for the fiesta of *bous en la mar*, when enormous bulls are pushed off the docks into the sea and people swim for their lives.

The feast of Maria Magdalena finds you back in the north, in Anguiano (Rioja), watching in amazement as eight young men dance and gyrate down a steep cobblestone street on stilts. You are off at once for Lalin (Pontevedra), where dozens of men and women who believe themselves to be possessed by devils have come for help from the so-called Virgin of the Bodice. Some of these people are paralyzed and have to be pushed in wheelchairs; others are spasmodic and have to be restrained; all stare at you with haunted eyes.

Then the feast of Santiago arrives and Spain turns into one giant fiesta. You pause in El Carpio del Tajo (Toledo) to see horsemen tearing the heads off geese at full gallop and proceed on to Molvizar (Granada), where exciting skirmishes between Christians and infidels come to a climax with the burial of the "traitorous Moor."

As August begins you head for the ancient city of Sagunto (Valencia) to see the locals use their Roman amphitheatre, or what is left of it, for their fiestas of *toros embolados* (the ones with burning tar on their horns). The feast of the "proto-martyr" San Estéban finds you in Oyarzún (Guipúzcoa), where the fiestas are a veritable anthology of bull-baiting modalities. And then on the 15th you hasten to Vinuesa (Soria) for another violently feminist fiesta. *La Pinochada*, for so it is called, commemorates the great day a few centuries back when Vinuesa fought neighboring Covaleda over an icon of María discovered under a pine tree (hence *la Virgen del Pino*). Vinuesa won thanks to its women, apparently, and they have never let the men forget it. In the morning about four hundred women and girls appear in the streets, wearing their *piñorra* dresses and wielding pine branches they call *pinochos*. Meanwhile, the men divide themselves by marital status and play sword games in the town plaza. But the pine is mightier than the sword: the females invade the plaza and start thrashing the males with their branches. Every time one gets struck, he must say "thank you," to which the woman responds "until next year." People kiss and make up afterwards, then feast for three days straight.

Fiestas in honor of some version of the Virgen María break out all over on August 15th, and numerous bovids are manhandled and sacrificed, purportedly in the Virgin's honor, all week long. You travel to Sabiñan (Zaragoza), where people pray "Give us this day our daily bull of fire." Needless to say, their prayers are always answered.

A different kind of holocaust takes you next to the little seaside town of Llanes (Asturias). On the eve of San Bartolomé, people join together for the *quema de brujas*, wherein effigies of witches are sent up in smoke as a stern warning for the real ones to stay away. And it never fails.

The feast of San Agustín finds you in Toro (Zamora). It is fitting that a town with a name like this boasts one of Spain's more unusual taurine rituals. Tradition calls for a five-hundred-liter vat of lemonade-flavored wine known as "bull-broth" to be set up in the middle of the town bull-ring; everyone shows up with a jar or a pitcher to fill. At the very moment the spigot is opened, a huge *toro bravo* is set loose in the ring. Although the dangers of drink were never more apparent, the local lads and lasses glee-fully accept the challenge, working together to distract the bull with daring feints while filling their pitchers.

As August draws to a close you hurry off to Buñol (Valencia) for *La Tomatina*, quite possibly the world's largest food fight. In the space of one furious hour, some 12,000 people splatter each other with 62,000 kilograms of overripe tomatoes. Wading through the streets afterwards, you are struck by the incredible variety of red pigments caked into the hair and clothes of gleeful ex-combatants.

As September begins you are pleased to note that both your health and your single-minded enthusiasm for Spanish customs remain intact. The great summer cycle of fiestas has begun to slow down, but there are still dozens to choose from on a given date. You take off for Ibi (Alicante) to attend extravagant battles of *moros y cristianos* that culminate in the solemn execution of a dummy called "the double-crossing Moor." Then you proceed to Tordesillas (Valladolid), where Spaniards and Portuguese gathered centuries ago to partition the world and where people now flock to see the (in)famous *toro de la Vega*. Held in honor of the Virgin of the Rock, this hoary ritual is like no other encierro you have seen. Weeks of careful search-ing have gone into the selection of the bull, for much is to be demanded of him. First he is let out of a truck near the main plaza, where apprentice bullfighters are waiting to make a few showy passes and fix a pair of banderillas into his withers. He is then herded down narrow winding streets to the bridge over the Duero River. After crossing the bridge he finds himself in a wide open plain known as the Vega, where hundreds of men and boys are waiting with cudgels, swords, and spears three yards long. Out of a salutary sense of fair play, motor vehicles are prohibited from taking part in the "hunt." In reality, only a small number of *toroveguistas* have the courage to draw close to the bull with their lances, and most of them will be forced to drop everything and climb a tree. The trick is to get the bull to charge while holding the lance firmly enough to rip into his heart. The fellow who pulls off this feat is awarded the bull's testicles on the spot, which he mounts on his spear as a symbol of his superior sang-froid.

Following this fiesta you depart for La Puebla del Caramiñal (La Coruña), a little town on the Atlantic coast that puts on a *procesión de las mortajas* in which people carry their children around in open caskets as a kind of innoculation against real death. The feast of San Miguel Arcángel finds you in Mora de Rubielos (Teruel), where bulls with burning balls on their heads are yoked together in the interest of variety. And you finish up the month in Rus (Jaén) for three days of wild albeit unseasonable carnival with its origins in a bout of bubonic plague that almost wiped out the town four hundred years ago.

October arrives and you are amused to discover that a number of towns throughout the peninsula will hold encierros and other bull-baiting fiestas in honor, ironically, of San Francisco de Asís, the very saint who cherished all animals as his brothers and sisters. You pass them up in order to see Moors versus Christians at its most rustic: in Quentar (Granada), the hoary folk drama culminates in the "baptism" of all the neighbors who have played the role of infidel. You then make your way to Arenas de San Pedro (Avila) for the feast of its patron, San Pedro de Alcántara. Sorely aware that their saint is venerated almost nowhere else, the people have prepared a huge variety of festivities, including band concerts, romerías, processions, fireworks, and—naturally—bulls. Shortly after midnight the locals release four *toros de fuego* on the main street; but unlike other fiery bulls you have seen these have been outfitted as rocket launchers. But even stronger emotions are in store. People make their way to the bullring to drink and carouse while they wait for their unique "black-out capea." At about three in the morning, men young and old put down their wine, pick up their capes, and rush from the stands to meet the bull set loose on the sands of the ring. What makes this capea especially exciting is that from time to time the plaza lights are extinguished, leaving bull and players in total darkness. (And anyone in San Pedro will tell you that bulls have excellent night vision.)

The fiesta of an even more obscure saint takes you to the cliffs overlooking the Duratón River in Segovia. On October 25, great masses of *segovianos* gather to honor San Frutos, the provincial patron, in a shrine built into the very edge of the ravine. Ignoring the erudite wet blankets who question the saint's existence, the people bring his icon out of the shrine and dance themselves sick in his honor. Then, while the majority feast on succulent lamb ribs, a few enter the shrine to engage in a peculiar ritual. They approach the altar, get down on their hands and knees, and crawl into a narrow passageway beneath the altar where the miraculous rectangular rock of San Frutos is located. After going around the rock three times, they rest assured that they will never be bothered by another hernia.

Now it is November. The waning sun that casts long shadows over Iberia's villages is more than enough to warm the hearts of the children waiting in gleeful anticipation for the next great fiesta—*la matanza del cerdo*, or the slaughtering of the hog. This fiesta differs in certain ways from the others you have seen, for it is a community affair and a family affair all at once. In addition, the sacrificial destruction carried out possesses an unmistakable element of practicality: every family in a given town is actually supplying itself with numerous porcine products that will serve it well during the coming winter months. In sharp contrast with the pious and stuffy character of many an American Thanksgiving, the Spanish *matanza* gives people yet another excuse for carnivalesque merrymaking and excess. San Martín is one of this fiesta's tutelary saints. His feast finds you in Moreda (Asturias), caught up in a veritable orgy of folklore. All over town the high-pitched squealing of dying swine is accompanied by traditional riddles, jokes, and nonsense poetry. Families pool their resources and know-how in the non-industrial manufacture of hams, sausages, bacon, and many other items that give Spanish stews their unique taste. Several pigs are roasted in public bonfires and everyone overeats.

But you are off to Medinaceli (Soria) to see the famous *toro júbilo*, your last chance to see festal bull-baiting before your year runs out. Under the supernatural auspices of not one but five obscure saints—Arcadio, Probo, Pascasio, Paulino, and Eutiquiano—a giant bull is brought out at sundown and tied fast to a post. Mud is rubbed all over his body and his horns are augmented by iron horns with tips made of pitch and paraffin. Meanwhile, the main plaza has been barricaded and bonfires have been ignited in each of the four corners and the center. The bull is released and the fun begins.

Every time he charges a running figure, his metal horns burn brighter and even throw sparks. And since the mud protects his body from burns, the nightmarish scene lasts until dawn.

After the bull and the hog, of course, the rooster is Spain's third favorite totemic animal. So you are off to Salas de los Infantes (Burgos), where the finest cocks in town have been fattened for the role of piñata in unwilling homage to Santa Cecilia. While blindfolded young men try to club a rooster that is being swung back and forth by their pals, their grandmothers sing off-color songs about the lascivious behavior for which the cocks have been condemned. People laugh hysterically throughout.

You hurry off to Mollo (Gerona) for another hog-slaughtering fiesta. Here in Catalunya the fiesta is known as the *matança del porc* and in this particular town it is accompanied by *habaneras*, a style of singing roughly equivalent to the American barbershop quartet. The pre-winter cycle of fiestas comes to an end with the feast of Santa Catalina, whose gruesome martyrdom is recounted in children's games all over Spain. You are off to Barro in Asturias to see who can eat the most roasted chestnuts and drink the most cider while bands blare and fireworks roar.

December has arrived and your year of fiestas will soon be over. Preparations are underway all over Spain for the feast of the Immaculate Conception, which celebrates the idea that María, like Christ, was conceived free of original sin. Several centuries of Iberian stubbornness finally made the Church accept this dogma; so the accompanying fiesta has a special resonance in Spain. You travel to Torrejoncillo (Cáceres) to see hundreds of villagers cover themselves with immaculate white sheets, mount their horses, and fire their shotguns in unison.

The real star of the winter cycle of fiestas is not María, however, but the masked, costumed, trickster-like figure known as *botargas* (or a score of stranger names). A *botargas* can play many roles in a given fiesta: he can be a dancer, a minstrel, an actor, an impersonator of animals or devils, a pseudo-shaman like the *colacho* you saw in Castrillo de Murcia in May, or a generalized disturber of the peace. He specializes in outrageous behavior, violence, and chaos, and he is just as apt to get a beating as give one. Christmas in rural Spain would not be the same without him. You journey to the village of Sanzoles (Zamora), where the *botargas* is called a *zangarrón* and wears stockings of two different colors, a checkered suit, and a black leather mask with a red nose. He wields a stick festooned with swollen bladders as he dances down the street accompanied by musicians and transvestites. While his companions ask for donations, the *zangarrón* steals everything he can stuff into a large sack tied to his back. Children hurl rotten fruit to provoke him into frenetic pursuits. And then a most curious thing happens: an icon of San Estéban is brought out of the church and, while the eight-hundred-odd citizens of Sanzoles insult and pretend to attack the holy image, the *zangarrón* fends them off with his bladder-stick.

As the year draws to a close you realize that you will be unable to attend the *feira do capón* in Villalba (Lugo), with its ritual chicken slaughter. New Year's Eve finds you in Santurce (Vizcaya), where a gigantic effigy of the *olentzero*, a survival of the Basque country's pagan past, is paraded through the streets and joyfully put to the torch. As flames leap up into the chilly night air, you realize that you have attended your last Spanish fiesta.[1]

The Timeless World of Bull-Baiting

The fifty-nine fiestas the reader has had a glimpse of are only the tip of Spain's festal "iceberg." One could return a second, a third, or a tenth time and go to completely different places and experience new sensations. The fact that many of the feasts are moveable (Carnival, Lent, Holy Week, Corpus Christi) introduces a constant element of diversity. For further variety one could concentrate on the large urban festivals and discover how their neighborhood-by-neighborhood organization replicates key features of rural fiestas. One could concentrate exclusively on the processional pilgrimages known as romerías, or spend a year going from one culinary orgy to another. Although many fiestas have been lost forever due to industrial and demographic changes, an increasing consciousness of local identity in Spain's many regions has led to the revitalization of many fiestas that had lapsed. The main objective of our excursion into the world of Spanish fiestas, of course, was to place the fiesta de toros in its natural context. We have been able to discern the close connection between bull-baiting and popular religion. Indeed, it may seem to many a great paradox that the most violent acts toward animals are carried out under the auspices of a town's patron saint, with at least the tacit and oftentimes the wholehearted collaboration of the local religious authorities.

In the interest of a balanced perspective, it must be pointed out that there are many Spanish fiestas that do not revolve around violence and victimization. In addition, real Spaniards do not go from fiesta to fiesta at a breakneck pace as the reader has been asked to imagine doing. The whole point of a fiesta is the temporary replacement of humdrum reality with ludic emotion; even if it were possible to live a permanent fiesta, which I doubt, it would be not only unhealthy but ultimately meaningless without the context of a humdrum reality to refer back to. It is precisely the knowledge that the fiesta cannot last forever that spurs people to make the most of it. The ethnographic evidence would seem to indicate that whenever Spaniards want to get the maximum emotion from their festal periods, the forces of aggression and destruction are sure to be conjured up. In this sense the above itinerary is broadly representative of the different varieties of mock or real violence that natives of Iberia employ to enhance their fiestas. And although they do not always recur to such means, the sheer number of effigies burnt and animals slain boggles the mind.

Animal-baiting has been an important part of Spanish fiestas for many centuries. It can be affirmed in general that towns and villages originally imposed their own criteria and norms in this area without outside interference. This situation began to change in the early 1960s as Spain began to develop her modern tourist industry and government officials became wary of offending foreign visitors. In November 1962, a group of British reporters associated with the Royal Society for the Prevention of Cruelty to Animals saw Medinaceli's *toro júbilo*. (The reader will recall that this is the bull that wears an iron apparatus fitted with flares.) The reporters inflamed their readership and in due time Franco's government felt compelled to act (or appear to act). An edict promulgated in November 1963 officially prohibited all spectacles "involving cruelty or mistreatment of animals even though they may be traditional."[2] The mayors of Spain's towns and villages were urged to make the local populations understand that the prohibition was necessary for the good of the country. In reality, of course, no Spanish mayor was going to expose himself to the wrath of the people by telling them they could no longer celebrate the fiestas they associated with their childhood, their relatives living and deceased, and their very social identity, just because some foreigner found them offensive. So they either looked the other way or employed euphemisms in the official festival announcements. In Medinaceli, for example, people gathered for the fiesta-as-usual under the new name of "An Exhibition of Cattle and Parade of Torches."[3] Since part of the stability achieved by Franco rested on his non-interference in matters of popular culture, the highest authorities looked the other way as well.

Franco finally died, democracy came to Spain, and a new generation of progressive and European-minded men came to power. Whatever their private views might have been, they ended up following the same laissez-faire policy that Franco found so politically useful. A small number of urban Spaniards concerned about rural barbarism formed the Asociación para la Defensa de los Derechos del Animal and began to place advertisements in the national newspapers, targeting specific fiestas like the *Sanjuanes* of Coria or the *toro de la Vega* in Tordesillas. In addition, they attacked the many Socialist mayors who had never attended a fiesta in their lives but who now promoted encierros and novilladas as good public relations. As one of the ADDA's ads put it: "Why have they not been prohibited? Until when will our leaders remain impassive before the progressive brutalization of the masses? Is it that the only thing that counts are votes?"[4]

Spain's long-awaited entry into the European Community also galvanized animal rights activists in other countries, especially the United Kingdom. One of these activists, a member of the European Parliament named Andrew Pearce, went to Coria incognito to see its famous fiesta firsthand. As the reader will recall from our own armchair visit, the young men of this locality pursue the bovid with blowguns and rival each other for the possession of the bull's testicles after he is shotgunned. In defense of their fiesta, the young people of Coria affirm that the darts never penetrate the hide and that their combat with the bull is "clean" and "face to face," as evidenced by the many people wounded every summer by the bulls that participate in the fiesta. Unable to contain his indignation, Pearce called the fiesta "cruel and sadistic" on Radio Nacional, at which point the Socialist mayor, Eugenio Simón, dared the Englishman to attend an autopsy of the slain bull with two veterinarians and attempt to discover evidence of hematomas or puncture wounds. Pearce refused, stating that he had urgent business elsewhere. As menacing crowds gathered, the mayor assigned two municipal guards to cover Pearce's retreat.[5]

Yet another revealing anecdote can be cited. On September 12, 1989, the mayor of Cardona (Barcelona) defied a new directive imposed by the government of Catalunya and permitted his people to celebrate their traditional *corre de bou*. In gratitude, the bullfighters carried him around the ring on their shoulders while the whole town applauded wildly. His re-election is considered likely.[6]

Due notice taken of a few well-meaning but somewhat quixotic individuals, Spaniards and non-Spaniards, it must be pointed out that there has never been anything approaching a "public outcry" against bull-baiting in Spanish fiestas. For every visitor shocked or outraged by what he or she has seen in Spain, there are a hundred who have gone to Spain in pursuit of thrilling and atavistic experiences. And for every Spaniard who condemns the barbarous practices of her or his compatriots, there are a hundred who go on doing what they have always done without the slightest guilt. This does not mean that the minority is mistaken, but it does suggest what it is up against.

Now that we have a general idea of the festal context in which Spaniards have dealings with animals, let us narrow in on that segment of the local fiesta most closely connected, in both a structural and historical sense, to the modern urban bullfight. This "missing link," as it were, is the capea. Although capeas have been going on in Spain for longer than anyone can remember, it is not to the historians that we can look for information about them. Historians have traditionally been preoccupied with violence on a grand scale, with wars and revolutions and coups. For a picture of violence on a small scale, we must turn to Noel, Barea, Blasco Ibáñez, and other writers who have inserted fascinating and sometimes dreadful portraits of Spanish customs into their essays, travel accounts, and novels. The actual date of the account is immaterial, for capeas have remained basically the same for many centuries.

Unlike an encierro, which is a running of a bull or bulls through the town streets, a capea takes place in any enclosed space. The space can be a permanent or portable bullring, but is more often a plaza, square, or intersection that has been barricaded in some way. In the old days, horse- or mule-drawn carts served the double purpose of barricade and grandstands, as seen in Arturo Barea's 1907 description of a bull-baiting fiesta in Brunete:

> The village square was unpaved, full of ruts, with an iron lamppost on a stone base in the middle. Round this plaza people would draw up their carts on the eve of a bullfight; the shaft of each cart was riding on the bottom planks of the next and all of them were roped together so that they could not slide apart. This was a sort of barrier and a gangway with an uneven floor, where people could stand. The village lads and the children would squat between the wheels, in reach of the bull's head, and from there they would watch the fight or sally to take part in it. The bulls were kept penned up in a blind alley opening into the square, where the butcher had his corral. It was called Christ Alley.[7]

Thus, the stage setting of the capea will vary in accordance with the anatomy of any given town or village.

This is not the only element of variety. Unlike a formal bullfight with its strict time limits and numerous rules, the duration of a capea is only limited by the number or vigor of the bulls and the only rule applied is that of "anything goes." A capea need not be limited to cape-passing, therefore, but can include all the practices noted in our sojourn through festal Spain—dragging the bull by a rope, fixing rockets or flares to his horns, blowing home-made darts at him, and so on.

The third and most notable factor making for variety is the local population itself, which will differ not only in size from one place to another but also, more importantly, in its mixture of personalities. A capea can be seen as a kind of folk dramatic spectacle in which everyone in the village can be an extra, have a supporting part, or aspire to a leading role (the role of patsy is reserved for the bull, of course). In the words of Eugenio Noel, Spain's greatest describer of these festal dramas:

> Just as there is no bull quite like another bull, you can be sure that no two capeas are alike. . . . I don't know what sort of devilish creativity towns employ in conceiving and developing them, but with the forced participation of a little bull, or a cow, or an ox, they devise skits, epic theater, comedies, and farces that are admirable in their novelty.[8]

This theatrical element is an important one to bear in mind, particularly as it relates to the everyday role-playing of village social life. What gives a local capea its special flavor may often be the participation of a colorful local personality. And in keeping with one of the principal social functions of Spanish fiestas, colorful local personalities make use of capeas to confirm their identity or enhance status. A capea celebrated somewhere south of Toledo in 1838 may serve as an example:

> The young bull appeared at last, as I was saying, and after the brave fighters had caped him and amused themselves at his expense, several voices were heard shouting "Let Uncle Wild Boar come out! Let Uncle Wild Boar come out!" And immediately a gigantic figure appeared on the scene, porcine and swarthy, with an athletic build and terrifying countenance. . . . Making the sign of the cross like a good Catholic facing danger, he approached the young bull and began to incite him, calling him a coward, a tedious ox, a son of a bad father, and other even more insulting epithets with which he meant to offend the beast's sense of honor. As was to be expected, the latter finally grew inconvenienced, and scraping the ground and raising a cloud of dust with his snorts, he charged his opponent. Uncle Wild Boar gave him such a mighty punch on the snout that it sounded like the handclap of a giant, and this wasn't the worst thing for the bull, for then he stuck his fingers into the nostrils and grabbed onto the horns with such skill, that with little effort he twisted the head and thrust it to the ground, in the midst of thunderous "vivas" and acclamations. The poor animal got up sneezing and fled to a corner while his adversary

shouted to his admirers: "Why are you so amazed? Thus have I demolished the novillo! And am I not made of flesh and blood just as he?"[9]

The role of bull-baiter is by no means limited to hulking rural brutes, nor even to members of the male sex. In his description of a capea in Medina del Campo, an indignant Noel recounts how

> a certain very old woman, with heavy hips, places herself in a large opening [in front of the bull] and fearlessly calls him with a large green shawl. . . . Another woman, whose face is a large crust of grime and mange, says good-humoredly, "If you want really good bulls, take the ones that killed my husband." I shiver with rage, I tremble: that's how my race talks. My whole lineage speaks from the mouth of that wicked widow.[10]

Capeas are indeed the showcase for colorful personalities, which easily lend themselves to caricature and condemnation at the hands of Regenerationist writers like Noel. Still, as a form of participatory theater, the major role is played by the collectivity as such, by the people acting en masse. It is a given local population acting *as one* that presumably enables each individual to escape inhibitions and join in the "fun." Noel reserves his best lines for describing the crowd, and few can match his ability to make it seem like one massive living organism:

> The multitude flows, recedes, circulates, flees, gathers itself, pushes itself, crushes itself, spreads out, comes, goes, gesticulates, shouts, moos, calls, rages, laughs, and jokes all at once, all in a second. Immersed in an immense cloud of dust it moves convulsively. At times it opens in great extensions that tear its mass asunder and reveal the bull in an empty space; at other times it initiates a mass attack that looks like a plundering raid. If the beautiful young bull remains still, frightened, or surprised, the populace harrasses him, charges him, pricks him, and passes before him to hurl insults.[11]

The fiesta in Brunete described by Barea is a textbook case of *el toro del aguardiente*, or raw brandy bull, so named because it takes place at dawn and in the old days it was common for men to "breakfast" on raw brandy. Such a bull-baiting event is often the one that kicks off a three- or four-day festal period. What the people actually do with the bull differs from place to place and from crowd to crowd. Brunete's treatment of its early morning bull was apparently as harsh as the raw brandy it was named for:

> At first the little bull attacked and threw the lads. But he was so small and young that they managed to hold him by the horns, drag him to the ground, kick him

with their heavy boots, and beat him with their sticks. At eleven in the morning he reeled on his legs and gave no more fight, but fled from the gang of lads and boys who by then all dared to come out into the plaza. He backed against the wheels of the carts, but from there they pricked at him with knives and the old men held their burning cigar butts against his haunches to make the beast attack again in blind rage. And so it went on till noon.[12]

The calf-bull of Brunete would have been unsuitable as a *toro del aguardiente* in the town of Turégano, where the dawn's early light finds the entire populace hanging onto a rope tied to the horns of a full-grown animal. Noel's description of the affair dates from 1915, but in the timeless world of Spanish bull-baiting, it could have been written last week. The *toro de la cuerda* or *toro de la maroma*, as it is also called, remains a standard festal practice throughout rural Spain. Noel's account provides us with a valuable glimpse of the special code of honor that becomes operative in all thrilling but dangerous capeas:

> The first man on the rope was Pascualón; the last one—if that rope, like that of hanging victims, had an end—could not be seen. Half the province was pulling on it. Once someone had grabbed on, he did not let it go again for no reason, since letting go constituted an unspeakable shame. People fought each other for a place on the rope and some even offered money for one. When a sudden charge of the bull put them in the worst predicament, some fled, others fell, most held on tighter and all turned around with eyes wide open, since the slightest carelessness was all the bull needed to recoup with fatal results. But he who fell would get up again without looking at himself or dusting himself or thinking anything of his wounds. Nobody helped anybody, nor was it possible, and this was yet another charming aspect of the much-awaited barbarous fiesta. He who had been on the point of getting gored was congratulated as a hero. . . . He who had received a blow felt dignified and showed off the bruise to anyone who wanted to see it. One who had been knocked down and had his arms trampled by the bull showed them off everywhere, swollen, black and blue, and those arms were laughingly acclaimed by all.[13]

Thus far we have seen that a provincial fiesta de toros can be a theater of cruelty, a stage for social role confirmation, and a showcase for popular concepts of honor and valor. But that is not all. It is also the setting for serious injury and sudden death. This is perhaps the feature of rural bull-baiting that is hardest for us to understand; for although there are very few towns in Spain that cannot recount the tragic goring of a neighbor or a visitor during the town fiesta, the fiesta goes on. People will blame fate or the bull, never themselves or their time-honored festal practices, and there will be no popular outcry to stop the bloodshed. Indeed, it may well be that the certain shedding of animal blood and the possible shedding of human blood are the two main factors that make capeas so thrilling for participants. The testimony of Hemingway can be cited in support of this idea:

> One bull which was a great favorite in the capeas of the province of Valencia killed sixteen men and boys and badly wounded over sixty in a career of five years. The people who go into these capeas do so sometimes as aspirant professionals to get free experience with bulls but most often as amateurs, purely for sport, for the immediate excitement, and it is very great excitement; and for the retrospective pleasure of having shown their contempt for death on a hot day in their own town square.[14]

A few recent incidents can be cited to demonstrate that, in their festal bull-baiting, Spaniards stage not only comedies but also genuine tragedies. On August 13, 1989, a fifty-five-year-old man was fatally gored by a bull during the fiestas his home town of Pinto dedicates to Our Lady of the Assumption. According to newspaper accounts, Fulgencio Sanabria was very well known in Pinto for his extroverted character, his enthusiasm for bulls, and his noticeable limp. On the first day of the fiestas, Sanabria climbed one of the many posts that the town sets up for the protection of the participants. From there he called to one of the bulls, and the bull came straight toward him at high speed. According to eyewitnesses, Sanabria had not climbed high enough and in an instant the bull crushed him against the post and gored him twice. He was rushed to a hospital in nearby Madrid where he died on the operating table. The patronal festival of Pinto continued as scheduled.[15]

There was a worse accident, if these things can be called accidents, in Ciudad Rodrigo (Salamanca) in February of 1986. Ciudad Rodrigo is famous for its Carnaval del Toro, which combines everything associated with Spanish Carnival—wine, disguises, chaos, and bands of wandering minstrels known as *charangas*—with every variety of Spanish bull play—encierros, becerradas, novilladas, even a raw brandy bull. People come from all over the province to join in the fun; such was the case with Miguel Angel Garzón, a twenty-eight-year-old native of Matilla de los Canos. On Shrove Tuesday, Garzón was on hand for the *desencierro*, where bulls that have already been played with (and are therefore "smarter") are driven back from the ring to the corral by crowds of masked thrillseekers. As luck would have it, the one with the sharpest horns got separated from his fellow bulls, spotted Garzón, knocked him to the ground, and set to work. Somehow the bull was able to introduce his horn into the young man's mouth and with one violent thrust destroyed his brain stem. Death was instantaneous.[16]

If we are to believe writers like Domínguez Sánchez or Noel, the people involved in rural capeas remain indifferent to fatalities when they occur. The former describes a fiesta in an impoverished area of western Spain known as Las Hurdes, in which a bull trying to escape from his attackers tried to jump over a cart loaded with people. A child was crushed in the ensuing panic but the show went on. A few moments later, the bull caught hold of a young man and began to toss him from horn to horn like a dummy "offered up by the beast to a public gorged with blood."[17] For his part, Noel portrays the people of Medina del Campo at a great public dance following their capea, where women rival each other for the company of those who acted the bravest and gaily comment that this year's body count is nothing compared with last year's.[18]

Such portraits cannot be taken at face value. Noel and those who shared his outlook were not ethnographers but social activists. Valuable as their observations are for us today, we must recognize that they include devices that all reform-minded writers employ, such as caricature and hyperbole. It is certainly an exaggeration to imply that Spaniards remain unaffected by the violent deaths of their fellows. The fact that the fiesta goes on despite the death of a participant does not mean that the dead participant will not be mourned. The evidence: rural capeas and encierros have been a fertile source of "martyrological" folklore, brief stories or ballads that serve to pass on the news of a fatality and mourn the victim. A moment of carelessness or bad luck and the presence of some eyewitness with literary ambition can combine to produce a poem that enters local tradition and stays there for years. The ballad that recounts the death of one Mariano Mera during the patronal festival of Matapozuelos (Valladolid) may serve as an example. The mishap occurred in 1935; the verses floated along in oral tradition until a folklorist recorded them in 1981:

Tarde muy triste de toros.	A very sad afternoon of bulls.
Pueblo de Matapozuelos.	Town of Matapozuelos.
Muy tristes quedamos todos	We were all very sad
por la muerte de este obrero.	at the death of this worker.
De Valladolid llegaba	From Valladolid he arrived
el pobre Mariano Mera	poor Mariano Mera
sin pensar que le acechaba	without thinking that

esa muerta traicionera.	traitorous death lay in wait.
Apenas llegó a la plaza	Barely had he got to the plaza
el toro le atravesó	when the bull pierced him
y la cornada le alcanza	and the horn thrust penetrated
hasta el mismo corazón.	to the very heart of him.
Ninguno culpa ha tenido.	No one can be blamed.
Sólo la fatalidad.	Just fate.
Pero Mariano ha venido,	But Mariano has come,
y ya no vuelve a su hogar.	and now he'll never go home.
¿Cómo creerá su esposa	How will his wife believe
ni su niñito tampoco	or his little boy either
que sin vida ya reposa	that lifeless he now reposes
el que contento hace poco	the erstwhile happy man whom
llevó la muerte alevosa?	perfidious death has taken?[19]

We have seen how capeas can go from farce to tragedy in a split second. But we have yet to discuss the final and most important of its dramatis personae, the one who is exposed not only to the horns of the bull but to the wrath of the crowd as well. I am referring to the teenage aspirant known as the maletilla. Pronounced ma-le-*tee*-ya, the word means literally "little suitcase" and refers to the young man's meager belongings. The Spanish capea, historically, has been the proving grounds for the Spanish bullfight, serving to weed out thousands of boys over the years—the incompetent, the unlucky, or those unable to replace wholesome fear with crowd-pleasing temerity. Although some have managed to avoid capeas by getting born into established bullfighting families with important connections, the majority have had to undergo this harsh apprenticeship. Until quite recently, most famous bullfighters started out as maletillas, proving themselves with the sort of bull that their fame and clout eventually enabled them to avoid. But for every bullfighter who survives and prospers, there are many more who never make it past the capea stage. This selection process is the final "functional" element of rural bull-baiting, a ruthless application of the principle of survival of the fittest.

In *Blood and Sand*, an early twentieth-century version of what we today would call a docudrama, Blasco Ibáñez presents a true-to-life portrait of a band of pathetic maletillas trudging from village to village with their homemade capes, sleeping out in the open, and scavenging food from nearby fields.

When they reached their destination, tired and footsore from their long tramp and with mouths and eyes full of dust, they went straight to the mayor, and the leader of the group made a speech in praise of the talents of his party. They thought themselves lucky if municipal generosity provided them with a lodging in the inn stables, and a dish of stew which was cleaned up in a few seconds.[20]

Municipal generosity varies greatly from town to town. In the best of cases, there will be some sort of official or semi-official body set up to recruit novice toreros, organize becerradas or novilladas with reasonably small bulls, and distribute reasonable rewards afterwards. This is how things work in Ciudad Rodrigo, the town in Salamanca province that sponsors the Carnaval del Toro mentioned above. In such places, the care and feeding of penniless maletillas is motivated by a commendable spirit of charity, or perhaps by guilt feelings over the risks that young aspirants must run for their rewards. But in other places, the very fact that the aspirant is an outsider can serve to reduce concern for his fate. Terrible as this may sound, in many cases Spanish mayors have deemed their own popularity to be more important than the welfare of a wandering maletilla. Aware that their power is partly based on their ability to satisfy the local appetite for strong emotion, they have frequently hired the oldest and biggest bulls they can for the climax of the capea, bulls that Blasco Ibáñez described as "mountains of flesh covered with scars and scabs, with huge sharp horns; beasts that had seen fighting in provincial fiestas for many years; veterans whose cunning and knowledge of the game was such that they were said to 'understand Latin'."[21] If the fiesta budget permits, the mayor will actually buy a bull instead of renting one, a "bull of death" such as the one Barea saw in Brunete:

> He had to be killed by a team of four maletillas, torero-apprentices who went round the villages fighting bulls and starving. As they did not come from this village, the mayor had bought a huge old bull with enormous horns, taller than any of the little bullfighters. The poor lads cowered when he came into the square and they saw his bulk, but the village people began to shout and some of the young men jumped into the ring, brandishing their sticks. It was a pitiful thing to see those lads in their shabby, patched-up bullfighter's costume, its gold spangles tarnished or missing, running around the bull's head in little spurts and flicking their capes under his nose, only to flee, and then to clamber up the lamppost when they were driven away with sticks from the cart barrier.[22]

Both taurine and anti-taurine writings abound with these descriptions of desperate youngsters trapped between some mayor's mammoth bull and a menacing public. It must be emphasized that such episodes do not belong to the realm of fiction. According to statistics compiled by Ramón

Carande, the category of "young aspirant" accounts for more taurine fatalities than any other category. From 1786 through 1962, at least 153 young aspirants died of wounds inflicted by bulls.[23] For each death Carande supplies the date, the name, the rank, the ring, and the cattle brand of the death-dealing bull.

It might be instructive to look into an eyewitness account of one of these statistics, the one that took place on September 15, 1948, narrated by Santiago Araúz de Robles in one of the few sociological treatments of bullfighting that we possess. The author recalls how his father, a rancher and amateur cattle breeder, sold a gigantic nine-year-old seed-bull to the town of Cariñena (Aragón). The bull was only meant to be harrassed in the streets as the yearly *toro de ronda*, but then "someone" in a position of influence had the bright idea of taking it to the bullring and using it for the novillada as well.

> They had contracted a poor apprentice matador, a barber in Zaragoza. The bull occupied the entire plaza with his terrible demeanor. The public had overflowed the boarded scaffolding and occupied the *burladeros* [camouflaged wooden fences bullfighters hide behind]. That public, possibly somewhat inebriated and depersonalized by the fiesta and its own numbers, berated the maletilla, Luis Miguel Sanz by name, hounding him to confront a bull that had already been fought during his selection as a stud. The boy came out into the ring. He essayed a few cape passes, but the bull gained ground on him with each one. He dropped the cape and fled toward the *burladero*: it was so jammed with people that he couldn't get in. The bull caught up with him at the entrance: with the left horn he punctured his thorax, going in at the nipple and ripping him to the shoulder. He died instantly. Afterwards the people dedicated tributes and ballads to Luis Miguel Sanz. The glory of toreros is just this terrible.[24]

The statistics cited above do not cover the past quarter-century, they do not cover non-fatal injuries or mutilations, and they do not even include capeas. At this point in time we have no figures for the number of boys who have been slain or maimed in improvised provincial bullrings. We have, instead, dozens of written descriptions of such casualties, folk ballads of tragic mishaps, and numerous biographies of successful bullfighters who remember their days as maletillas with horror and recall their friends whose careers ended in one God-forsaken village or another. As we will see in a later chapter, capeas can leave psychological as well as physical scars on the young men who subject themselves to the brutality, triumph over their bovine adversaries, and survive to fight another day.

One could be tempted to say that, after all, the maletillas go to capeas of their own free will and are therefore responsible for the consequences. Perhaps the same thing could be said about Fulgencio Sanabria, Miguel Angel Garzón, or any of the other men who were too clumsy or too slow on their feet to avoid a deadly bull being toyed with in a fiesta. From another perspective, it would be easy to place the blame on passive or cynical local officials. And what are we to say of those who breed brave bulls, sell them, and ship them all over Spain for profit? There is, in truth, no telling where we will end up if we begin to trace the complex web of complicities that maintain bull-baiting in small-town fiestas. In another chapter I will attempt to outline the connection between bullfighting and political corruption. But we must first attempt to account for popular demand, for the popular concepts of "fun" that put the whole machine in motion in the first place.

Therefore, having now reviewed the where and the how of the fiesta de toros at its most festive, we can turn our attention to the intriguing question of *why*. We will need to leave the sure ground of ethnographic fact and enter—at least temporarily—the uncertain but fascinating terrain of speculation. We must seek to account for three principal dimensions of community bull-baiting in festal context: (1) the dimension of belief; (2) the dimension of ritual actions; and (3) the dimension of the emotions that accompany the beliefs and actions. By focusing our attention in this way, we may begin to understand how the benighted capeas and encierros of village Spain were able to engender the great spectacle of the urban bullfight.

The Magical Bull

In all probability, the original human relationship with the bull was that of pure and simple predation. We were, and are, carnivorous creatures, and hunting has unquestionably been the master behavior pattern of our species. Everything about us, from our physiques to our technology to our aggressive impulses, may well reflect our predatory past.[25]

Like the other ferocious mammals that walked the earth in those days, the bull was hunted down and dispatched not by individuals but by groups. People made up for their relatively puny size by using slings, arrows, lances, and—above all—strategy. Exciting scenes of group hunting can be found in hundreds of cave paintings in Iberia and other parts of western Europe. The paintings may even have served a hunting function themselves (as magical preparation or propitiation). It therefore becomes possible to conjecture that Spanish capeas are somehow a survival of early hunting techniques. This was actually suggested in 1980 by a trio of Spanish scholars:

> If we look closely, the capea . . . , preceded by the scene of the encierro and brought to a close by the community feast, reveals in the order of its episodes and the goals of the same a structure analogous to that shown by the successive scenes of a primitive hunt. . . . The nutritive and tumultuous hunt of the wild bull is the archetype of the capea.[26]

What makes this interpretation attractive and plausible are the many rural fiestas in Spain that involve a frenzied group killing of the animal, in Tordesillas, Coria, and other places discussed earlier. It is hard not to think of a paleolithic hunting band when watching young men attack bulls with spears or blowguns, or when reading Hemingway's description of a bull being brought down by a crowd of villagers:

> every one swarming on him at once with knives, daggers, butcher knives and rocks; a man perhaps between his horns, being swung up and down, another flying through the air, surely several holding his tail, a swarm of choppers, thrusters and stabbers pushing into him, laying on him or cutting up at him until he sways and goes down.[27]

Suggestive as it is, however, the primitive hunt hypothesis of the capea is based on analogies that can be neither disproven nor substantiated. Too vast a stretch of time divides the cave paintings of Altamira from the patronal fiestas of modern-day Spain. The intervening stages are too many and too momentous to brush aside or skip over—the Neolithic revolution, the growth of organized religion and cults, the rise of the great civilizations of the Middle East, and so forth. Over time, killing for food in the manner of a primitive hunting group turns into ritual killing, a dozen different varieties of sacrifice, and scores of different rituals, each with its own rationale. Killing for sacred purposes even comes to be "sexualized" in the form of virgin sacrifice and phallus cults. In sum: whatever its original value for survival, human predation—like all other human behaviors—is eventually transformed to fulfill symbolic functions in widely differing cultural contexts.[28]

Our images and fantasies of the bull reflect the general development of culture over several millennia. At the danger of oversimplifying a very complex evolution, it can be said that the bull came to be conceived of in four successive ways: (1) as a totem; (2) as the embodiment of divine genesis or creation; (3) as a perfect partner for the Neolithic Mother-Goddess; and (4) as a magic agent of sexual potence and fertility.[29] Each one of these representations implies a different concept of the sacred. It has been surmised that more primitive groups locate the sacred in the mythical animal ancestor of the group, the totem who established the taboos people live by. In "higher" religions, the bull-god in the sky enlists the help of a heavenly cow-god in his creative efforts. Patriarchal nomadic herdsmen, for their part, are prone to a primordial "male mystique" and find the sacred at work in every ejaculation of their potent seed-bulls.[30] A new view of the sacred will be formulated when these nomads mingle with the sedentary agricultural peoples of the Neolithic who worship the fertile feminine earth: henceforth their Great Mother will be provided with tauromorphic mates whose regular sacrifice maintains crop production at optimum levels. As a final stage in this process, rural cults spring up all over the Mediterranean basin to harness the generative power of the bull for community or individual purposes.

All of this leads us to a new group of theories, those that derive Spanish bullfighting from ancient religious practices of one kind or another. This mode of interpretation was greatly stimulated by a major exposition of ancient bovine artifacts organized in 1918 by a Spanish aristocrat and several archaeologists. Almost overnight the fiesta de toros was linked to the sacrifices that ancient peoples had made to their divinities. Only a few years later, Sir Arthur Evans undertook excavations on the isle of Crete and soon discovered striking statues and mosaics of young people performing acrobatic stunts on the backs of giant bulls. Such rituals were common, apparently, and took place somewhere deep inside the labyrinthine palace of Minos. After the bull had been played with for a lengthy time, the priest would thrust his fingers into the bull's nostrils, grab a horn, and violently snap his neck.[31] (The reader may recall that this same technique was employed in a capea by Uncle Wild Boar, the hulking rustic brute described earlier.) Evans' use of bullfighting terms to interpret the taurine images he had unearthed at Cnossos served to fan the fires of the revolutionary "Neolithic" thesis. Scholars of several different nationalities subsequently elaborated the Cretan-origins hypothesis of the Iberian fiesta de toros. One even argued that Theseus was the first bullfighter and the Labyrinth was in reality the sacrificial dance of the Minotaur.[32]

Was the bull a performer in ceremonies and sacrifices in ancient Iberia? We know, to begin with, that the *bos taurus* species had gone forth and multiplied with particular success in the Iberian peninsula. When Hercules had to steal bulls, mythology tells us, off he went to what is now the province of Cádiz. Apart from his utilization for food, the bull was quite possibly a totemic figure and/or sacrificial victim for some or most of the races that populated Iberia during the Bronze Age. These local cults were eventually blended with beliefs and practices common to the entire Mediterranean area, disseminated by the same currents of war and trade that disseminated the Phoenician alphabet or the art of shipbuilding. As a result, we have pottery fragments from Catalunya and the Balearic islands that depict young men dancing around horns; we have a bull-shaped sacrificial altar from Galicia; and we have bronze bull heads, statues of bulls with human heads, and carvings of winged bovids from numerous Iberian sites. All of these items were in use thousands of years before Christ.[33] One of the more spectacular discoveries was made in the ruins of Termes, an ancient city in what is now Soria province: archaeologists unearthed a primitive amphitheatre and discovered numerous knives, axes, and bull horns. Spectators were gathering to see public bull sacrifices, apparently, at least a hundred years before the arrival of the Romans.[34]

Roman armies did not have an easy time subjugating the fierce peoples of Iberia, but eventually their tactical superiority enabled them to extend their rule over most areas of the peninsula. The new colonies of Hispania were to be among the richest of the Empire, a reward for military service and a future home to Caesars. With Roman law came Roman language, religion, and a number of bull cults that had originated in one part of the Empire and spread throughout. Chief among these was the cult of tauromorphic Bacchus or Dionysus, which became firmly entrenched in the Hispania of Roman days.

The parallels between the fiesta de toros and Dionysian rituals were first pointed out by the fathers of the Church (who portrayed the devil himself in taurine/Dionysian terms) and continue to interest scholars. Gómez-Tabanera has associated a totemistic Dionysus with certain capeas that, according to Eugenio Noel, ended with the bull being cut to pieces.[35] Caro Baroja, for his part, has examined a now-defunct nineteenth-century fiesta of Extremadura known as the "Bull of Saint Mark" and found it to hark back to the cult of Bacchus/Dionysus, buttressing his argument with both erudition and solid data.[36] Other folklorists have identified Dionysian or totemistic aspects in fiestas that commemorate a given saint's power to make wild bulls mild.[37]

Bulls were by no means confined to the sphere of cult in Hispania. They were also used for public spectacle. In nearly every land they ruled the Romans constructed oval circuses for horse-racing and grand amphitheaters for gladitorial combats, executions, and exhibitions of hunting prowess. Spectators were treated to the slaughter of countless lions, panthers, leopards, stags, boars, bears, bulls, and even hippopotami. Animals were often made to fight each other; they were frequently turned loose on criminals or Christian martyrs.[38] In Hispania, the amphitheater of Itálica (near modern Seville) held twenty thousand spectators; those of Mérida and Tarragona fifteen thousand each.[39] Surely here, it might be thought at first, we have a clear chronological antecedent of the fiesta de toros. Spanish theologians of the sixteenth and seventeenth centuries were convinced that the Spanish love affair with the bull was directly descended from pagan Rome. But there is no evidence for such an historical link. To the contrary: the Visigothic barbarians who invaded Hispania at the fall of the Roman Empire had no interest in animal-baiting; the grand amphitheaters were abandoned and never used again; and as will be seen, the bullfighting on horseback that Spanish aristocrats preferred was itself an offshoot or derivation of the capeas. Even if we granted for the sake of argument that the cruel spectacles of Rome constituted an antecedent, we would have to explain why they did not bear similar fruit in any other former imperial colony. (I will take up this issue from a different perspective in the last chapter.)

To keep our search going for the roots of the capea, we must return to the realm of ritual. As the reader will recall, the bull as a symbol of the sacred underwent a slow but steady transformation over millennia. The great cosmogonies of celestial bull-gods and earth mothers, and the mystery religions of Dionysus or Mithras, eventually dissolved into cult techniques that sought to harness the bull's sexual potency for human purposes of fertility or procreation. It is interesting to note that paleolithic cave paintings never show bulls with exaggerated sexual attributes or potency; this notion of the bull is the humble magical end-product of the evolution of taurine symbolism. It was present in numerous rural regions of the Mediterranean before Christ, it survived the collapse of the great official cults, and it remained in the countryside after the fall of the Roman Empire. It was a pagan belief in the truest sense, for it survived among the *pagani*, or serfs.

The idea that bulls were fundamental to rural fertility rites during the Dark Ages in Spain was first advanced in 1950 by Casas Gaspar, found its most succinct formulation in 1962 at the hands of Alvarez de Miranda, and was carried to its ultimate consequences in 1986 by Delgado Ruiz.[40]

Alvarez de Miranda began by studying a number of old Spanish legends and folktales that associated the bull with miraculous transformations of women into men, or homosexuals into heterosexuals, and with magical cures for female infertility. He found that such stories could be paired with archaic folk rituals that actively sought to exploit the sexual magic of the bull that the old legends told of. The most important of these had been a wedding custom that called for the bride and groom to stick darts into a bull that their friends had tied to a rope. The object was not to fight the beast, still less to kill him, but to evoke his fecundating power by "arousing" him and ritually spilling his blood. Tradition called for the couple to stain their clothes, and sometimes their bedsheets, with the bull's blood they had drawn. We cannot say if the supposedly Christian peoples of medieval Spain engaged in this ritual of the "nuptial bull" in full consciousness of its pre-Christian magical character. But we do know that in certain areas it was an established practice at both upper and lower class weddings well before AD 1300.[41]

Alvarez de Miranda argued forcibly that the capeas of rural Spain have their origins in this antique custom of the nuptial bull. This is an exciting and plausible hypothesis. As we saw earlier, there are many village fiestas that feature a *toro de la cuerda* or a *toro de la maroma*—that is, a bull that is pulled around the plaza and through the streets by a heavy rope. The darts wielded by the bride and groom could have become banderillas, and their clothing and sheets might have turned into the capes that are fundamental to capeas. But that is not all: the Spanish scholar goes on to assert that the bull-baiting fiesta that accompanied the wedding celebrations of feudal nobles was soon transformed into a gallant knightly tournament. In the sixteenth and seventeenth centuries, this bullfighting on horseback came to be a great spectacle, with aristocrats eager to flaunt their power while the commoners looked on from the sidelines. The rural wedding superstition had come a long way:

> It is necessary to understand that the rite of the nuptial bull, as soon as it leaves the sphere of popular religiosity in which it was born, tends to lose its old meaning, its character, and sometimes even its essential forms. On the other hand, deep inside the popular environment that constitutes its cradle, the fiesta del toro continually finds a climate favorable to its lasting for centuries.[42]

A certain play element was already present in the original custom of the nuptial bull. Alvarez de Miranda reasons that since the custom did not invoke or depend upon any sort of divinity, the play element came to be the dominant one over time and people simply lost consciousness of the original purpose of sexual magic.

> It is a slow and murky process whose intermediate stages are always difficult to identify. It is never accomplished entirely [in other Mediterranean countries]. Its complete cycle is wholly developed only in especially adequate times and places and in exceptional environments that boast a great conservative tenaciousness of the archaic element.[43]

In other words, we are not likely to find many examples of the slow transformation of an ancient fertility rite involving bovids into a popular spectacle. The presence of numerous brave bulls in rural Spain can be seen, therefore, as a necessary condition, but insufficient in itself. The crucial ingredient was a conservative and anachronistic populace that steadfastly clung to festive rituals even as it forgot the primordial beliefs that had originally engendered them.

The ground-breaking discoveries and interpretations made by Alvarez de Miranda have recently been elaborated and transformed into a bold theory that seeks to account for the psychological significance of every fiesta de toros, not only rural capeas but the urban bullfight itself. According to Manuel Delgado Ruiz, weddings are indeed at the heart of things, or, more exactly, the wedding night. What happens to a groom on a wedding night in Spain, says Delgado, is essentially the same thing that happens to a bull or to a rooster in a popular Spanish fiesta. In other words, he becomes a victim; led on by his irrepressibly virile libido, he walks straight into the trap that has been set for him; and as he consummates his marriage, he is actually being castrated (symbolically) and domesticated and absorbed into the matriarchal community that set the trap in the first place. The bull and the cock are to be taken as symbols of masculinity, the same masculinity that must be neutralized if small-town society is to exist.

What keeps Delgado's theory from being dismissed (at least initially) as nonsense is his painstaking effort to document his claims. He accumulates an impressive number of references to many of the fiestas we observed earlier—the rooster-beheadings, the chasing and killing of bulls by gangs of young men, the occasional extirpation of the genitals, the small-town feasts that feature bull stew, the transvestite cow-boys of San Pedro, the defunct Bull of Saint Mark ceremony, and, above all, the tradition of the nuptial bull. Delgado appropriates all of this folklore and recasts it in the light of his scholarly obsession—matriarchy. Then and now, he asserts, the sexual magic of the bull is a transparent metaphor of the domination of men by women (not women by men, which is what everyone else thought was going on). A wild bull is toyed with and slain for the same reason that a vigorous bridegroom becomes a henpecked husband; each is "seduced" into a tragic ritual—bullfight or wedding night:

> The fiesta de toros, and in general every public sacrifice in which death is administered to an animal representative of extreme virility, illustrates . . . all the actions that a society adopts to prevent and control the danger to its stability that masculine instinct in a free state implies. But, at the same time, the rite recognizes the high value attributed to the impetuous sexuality of young men, making it clear that it is a socially irreplaceable raw material, from which the community expects to profit by strengthening parental institutions and guaranteeing reproduction. . . . On a symbolic level, the nuptial rite implies the turbulent lynching of the groom by the collectivity, which tears him apart and devours him, assimilating his sexual vigor and dissolving it. . . . The trap has been revealed, the machination perfectly contrived against him from the very beginning by the great mother culture, by society, which is no other than the society of mothers, their realm.[44]

If Delgado were to stop here, we might be able to applaud his intuitions and originality. But this is only the beginning. Delgado goes on to see the fiesta de toros as part of the cult of the Virgin Mary, which is to be understood in turn as a "cult of tragic virility" in which Christ offered himself up as a sacrificial animal to the greater glory of matriarchy.[45] Popular Christianity itself, Delgado claims, is really the disguised ideology of the dominant force in traditional society—mothers. The Christ archetype is drilled into young men to socialize them in accordance with a tame, self-castrating, tragic, fatalistic, and utterly manipulable concept of their manhood, and that is not all. Delgado proceeds to associate Christ, the Antichrist, the bull, and the matador—all four—with the archetypal bull-deities sacrificed to a lunar-solar mother-goddess (whose Spanish representative is María).[46] All these vigorous young bridegrooms, Delgado asserts, are so many hermaphrodites who symbolically protagonize tragic carnal acts to the greater glory of matriarchy. Christ is just like a matador, says Delgado, and "hardly distinguishable" from the other juvenile bull-gods who animated tragic virility cults in other epochs—Attis, Dionysus, Mithras, and so on. Such is "the religion of Mary and the bull," where "life and death are venerated for themselves."[47]

We have now come full circle. As the reader will recall, we began with totemism and traced the evolution of bull symbolism through the Bronze Age and the rise of the great religions, seeing how complicated concepts of taurine theology finally dissolved into pagan fertility rites. Alvarez de Miranda believed that rural capeas came about when people forgot about the magical meaning of the nuptial bull ritual and elaborated on the ludic or play elements that did not depend on any religious concept. Delgado's reasoning goes in exactly the opposite direction: he starts with the secular fiesta de toros and shows (or attempts to show) that in reality it belongs not only to popular religiosity but to Christianity itself, and even harks back to the great mythological systems of antiquity—precisely those that give off the strongest aroma of totemism.

Elsewhere I have shown how Delgado's theory can be punctured, torn apart, and boiled down to almost nothing.[48] Something does remain, however: the idea that the fiesta de toros functions as a sort of rite of passage, serving to inculcate community norms into adolescent males and channel their potentially antisocial sexuality into the socially desirable institution of matrimony. As it happens, this is the one part of Delgado's case that might be supported by statistical evidence. According to figures compiled by Pérez Díaz for the first decade of the twentieth century, the number of illegitimate births in regions with traditional fiestas de toros (the Basque country, Catalunya, and both Castiles) was much lower than in regions with no such fiestas (Galicia and the Canary Islands).[49] Let us leave Delgado, then, on a positive note, and enjoy the irony: that somehow despite its barbarous and chaotic appearance a capea can be a mechanism of social control.

The interpretations of the fiesta de toros that we have discussed so far share an assumption common to many folkloristic or anthropological theories; that is, they take for granted that the people involved do not really know why they do what they do. Spanish capeas, with their fiery bulls and raw brandy bulls and bulls on a rope, along with other animal-baiting fiestas, might be considered as "nothing more than the expression of something that is done automatically."[50] From here it is only a short step to the idea that the people of small-town Spain cannot help themselves, that they could not stop baiting bulls and beheading roosters even if they wanted to. Although there is something to be said for this line of thought, it tends to lose sight of something basic: the festive feeling itself. The emotions of excitement and glee that people experience in a fiesta are rewarding enough, in themselves, to make it likely that the fiesta will go on. To characterize a fiesta only in terms of the beliefs it could have descended from or the ritual motions it entails, is to miss the crucial element of emotion. If we put aside the theorists and return to the many writers who have actually witnessed popular capeas and encierros, we realize that the instantaneous gratification of impulse is everything to the people involved. No one can remain impassive when a fiery bull is charging at you in the dark. And few can refrain from giving vent to aggressive impulses when the whole community is lending its loud approval.

Strong emotion is the most immediately apparent motivation for rural fiestas de toros and it is the motivation that we can most readily understand. This does not mean, by any means, that therefore emotion is too superficial a phenomenon to consider seriously. To the contrary: emotion can be seen as the nucleus or the root or the motor of Spanish fiestas in general and the fiestas de toros in particular. In the emotional dynamics of the fiesta we can distinguish several major dimensions. We have, for example, the dimension of the sacred. The search for *ekstasis*, the desire to be transported out of one's body and into a state of overpowering emotion, forms part of almost every known religious tradition. What some might describe as an attempt to escape reality can be seen as the wish to accede to a different sort of reality, one in which the contours of space and time themselves are determined by emotion. People have always felt that at certain rythmically recurring moments they can have immediate access to the *really real*; logic and history alike can be put aside, indeed must be put aside, in order to comprehend existence with the superior vehicle of feeling. According to Gómez-Tabanera, the space-time warp produced by the ecstatic approach to reality is

> a most important principle if we wish to grasp the significance of the popular fiestas of the Iberian Peninsula. For we must not forget that people of archaic mentalities, or folk communities, do not perceive time in quantitative terms, constantly oriented in one direction, but as a continuous substance full of affective and dynamic qualities.[51]

Not that one must belong to a folk community to affectively transcend the limitations of the past and the future: festive emotionality is available to us all to one degree or another. For example, no one can celebrate Christmas without remembering other Christmases of long ago spent in the company of loved ones, family members who have died but who seem to live again in our minds as we enter a peculiar emotional state known as "the Christmas spirit." Everyday egocentric reality loosens its cold grip on our hearts and our wallets. Traditional substances are consumed to facilitate the festive emotionality. Laughing and/or weeping become likely.

Even in this mild form, festive emotionality implies a certain degree of rupture, not only with quantitative time and logical thought processes, but also with one's own carefully guarded sense of self. Individuality must be transcended if proper communication with the beyond or the "other" is to be reached. The greater the rupture, the more one gets "carried away" (i.e., achieves ecstasy). The fiesta can be defined as a community-sanctioned apparatus for facilitating communal ecstasy through some kind of rupture—an excessive consumption of food, wine, or other substances; an unlimited exchange of gifts and offerings; an explosion of energy in the form of dancing, shouting, fireworks; incessant competitions; and mock or real violence directed at a third party. In cultures that have not been overly contaminated by "modern" concepts of time, rationality, and decorum, the festal apparati will tend to be less inhibited, that is, capable of channeling a large amount of violent rupture. The greater the violence, the more intense the ecstasy. With more ecstasy, everyday concepts of individual self-preservation tend to be eroded. Enter Spain.

As the twentieth century draws to a close, the people of Spain remain committed to their ecstatic and dangerous fiestas. To take two recent examples: On the night of August 13, 1990, the traditional fireworks battle of Elche (Alicante) left 277 people with burn wounds serious enough to require medical attention, with five people in critical condition.[52] And on the final day of Pamplona's *sanfermines* (July 14, 1990), six gigantic bulls installed a reign of terror in the streets that sent 42 to the hospital; the most serious injuries were sustained by a twenty-one-year-old American girl named Stephanie Kern.[53] Natives and foreigners alike can be sucked into the Spanish festal vortex.

Considerable amounts of space and time have now been expended in our attempt to clarify Spain's small-town fiestas de toros. Fascinating as they are in themselves, local bull-baiting fiestas are important because they have been the spiritual reservoir for the urban corrida de toros. Capeas are not a minor, unpleasant "aspect" of Spanish bullfighting, as some taurine apologists would like us to believe. To the contrary: they are bullfighting's "collective unconscious," the source of many of its techniques, the proving-ground for its young aspirants, and the wellspring of its mass psychology.

2. The Rise of Modern Bullfighting

TO THE EXTENT that any human behavior is capable of it, the capea has existed largely outside of history. It reflects ancient, half-forgotten fixations and ritual practices. It operates on a huge underground supply of emotional vitalism. Now the task will be to see what happens when the capea, timeless and counter-historical by definition, enters history. As we shall see, village Spain's fiesta de toros will be transformed into the *fiesta nacional*, and will go on to touch nearly every aspect of Spanish society. According to a major twentieth-century philosopher, in fact, what is at stake in the history of modern bullfighting is nothing less than the modern history of Spain itself:

> I affirm, in the strictest way possible, that no one can properly comprehend the history of Spain from 1650 to the present day without having rigorously elaborated the history of bullfights in the strict sense of the word; not the fiesta de toros that has existed in the peninsula more or less vaguely for three millennia, but what we currently call by that name. The history of bullfighting reveals some of the best-kept secrets of Spanish national life during almost three centuries.[1]

Unfortunately, José Ortega y Gasset died before he could properly reveal the secrets he refers to. Perhaps we can ferret a few of them out in the pages to come.

Lords and Lackeys

For a long time it was assumed that modern bullfighting had evolved out of the *toreo de rejones*, or bullfighting with lances, that was practiced in gaily decorated urban plazas by dashing aristocrats mounted on gallant steeds. This half-military, half-equestrian sport became popular among Iberian bluebloods during the Middle Ages and reached its zenith during the seventeenth century. It was, more than anything else, a showcase for the status of the seignorial class as a whole.

In grandiose spectacles organized to celebrate a royal wedding, birthday, or anniversary, a military victory, the visit of a foreign monarch, or virtually anything else, the common people were permitted to crowd into the plaza and hang from the balconies to watch their lords rival each other in magnificence and valor. When the nobles finally lost interest in the affair—so goes the theory—commoners too poor to own horses took their place and invented the revolutionary art of bullfighting on foot. We now know, however, thanks to the work of Alvarez de Miranda and other scholars, that what happened in the eighteenth century was a kind of "reconquest," wherein the common people recovered what had been theirs in the first place, long before it had been appropriated and monopolized by their *señores*. Innovations did occur, to be sure, but in most cases they can be seen as developments of capea-style bullfighting.

Historians tell us that the same aristocrats who flaunted their power and wealth at public spectacles were roundly incompetent in the sphere of public service. Hapsburg Spain was already bankrupt, economically and morally. The spectacular Baroque rituals of the seignorial class took place against a backdrop of injustice, corruption, racial and religious intolerance, anachronistic concepts of honor, mendicity, commercial restrictions, and the resultant multiplication of socioeconomic crises of all kinds. The sixteenth-century Spanish monarchs were even worse than the nobles—the weak Felipe III, the lazy Felipe IV, and the imbecile Carlos II, alias Carlos the Bewitched. In truth, the entire country seemed to be laboring under a curse. Spain, affirms J. H. Elliott, was the victim of its own greatness; its governing class lacked the strength of character to shake off the inertia of defeat and abandon its fantasies of imperial glory.[2] With Carlos the Bewitched unable to sire an heir, the Hapsburg dynasty died with him at the end of the seventeenth century.

The devastating War of the Spanish Succession brought a new dynasty into power, the Bourbons, and a new idea of ruling-class decorum. French-born King Felipe V did not care for bulls; members of the Spanish nobility who closely identified with the court developed a similar dislike almost overnight (to do otherwise would have been lese majesty). Aristocrats hastened to adopt the prestigious new behaviors of France, if only out of courtesy toward the new monarch. Much to the disgust of the common people of Madrid, no bullfights were to be held in its plazas for a space of two decades. And when the king finally gave in to popular demand, the aristocratic sport of *toreo de rejones* was already in its death throes. In the last days of July 1726, Madrid's Plaza Mayor bore witness to the fading taurine skills of three aristocrats and the increasingly popular skills of their assistants, men known only by utterly plebeian nicknames like Little Angel, John the Lefty, the Sheep, Baldy, the Andalusian, the One-Eyed Man, Francisco the Jumper, Lord Cesar's Berber, and so forth.[3] By the end of the century, the aristocrats had been banished altogether and their former lackeys reigned supreme over the so-called planet of the bulls.

To better envision how this fascinating development took place, it might be useful to employ a "country mouse" and "city mouse" analogy. The reader is already well acquainted with the popular pastimes of rural Spain; we were able to confirm in Chapter 1 that the fiesta de toros has its roots in archaic superstitions and maintains itself with savage but reward-ing thrills of every description. The "country mouse," then, would be all the serfs, peasants, churls, and rustics who have baited bulls in diverse ways for untold centuries. With the growth in power of the Spanish monarchy and the development of a courtly/bureaucratic imperialism, many of the feudal lords left the country to live a more refined urban life; most of the serfs were left behind to keep on producing wealth from the land, but oth-ers were transformed into servants. The "city mouse," therefore, would be this new subordinate class, all of the lackeys, footmen, valets, cupbearers, cooks, maids-in-waiting, and coachmen, as well as African slaves, who formed the retinue of some important lord at court or in the provincial capitals.

In the meantime, the nobles continued to perfect the skill of lancing bulls that they had inherited from the wedding customs of their ancestors, refining the protocol and surrounding the act of animal slaughter with nu-merous chivalresque ceremonies. As numerous eyewitness accounts of the seventeenth century attest, the gentlemen who were to lance the bulls typ-ically presented themselves in the plaza with large numbers of elegant liv-eried servants, sometimes as many as a hundred, the better to flaunt their wealth and power. Afterwards, a small number of lackeys would remain with their *señor* to assist him in his battle with the bull. Both the lord and his footmen had their respective audiences: the former was out to impress the king, his fellow bluebloods, sometimes a paramour; the latter were cheered on by their own kind, the teeming ranks of plebeians who filled the plaza—some sixty thousand in the case of the Plaza Mayor of Madrid (there were no bullrings at this time). Only a fine line divided the actions of the footmen that were necessary to aid their master and the "knavery" that was not really needed and served mainly to show off the skill or the valor of a given knave. Already in 1620 a nobleman of Seville, Don

Francisco Morovelli, complained of what he considered to be the servants' excessive desire to be protagonists of the spectacle.[4] As the seventeenth century wore on, the daring lackeys began to assume an ever greater role in the course of the corrida, adorning their feats with haughty, crowd-pleasing gestures. On innumerable occasions, their lords were unable to kill the bull with a lance thrust, and the underlings were only too glad to take over. According to a foreigner on hand for a Madrid bullfight at the very end of the seventeenth century:

> There are people of the lower class that are quite daring and quite skillful at sticking a dagger or a javelin between the bull's horns as they run past, and when the beast charges them and puts them in a tight spot, they throw their capes over its head or throw themselves to the ground face down, thereby escaping the fury of the bull.[5]

The eighteenth century will witness the rapid decline and retreat of the aristocratic *toreo de rejones* and its eventual replacement by bullfighting on foot. The evolution will not be smooth by any means, but accompanied by a good deal of anarchy and experiment. There will even be a curious transitional phase known as the age of the *varilargueros*, when men of humble origin sought to occupy the saddles vacated by the nobles. It is certainly a truism that the whole process was made possible by the changing tastes or the general lack of credibility of the Spanish aristocracy; but this necessary condition is insufficient in itself to explain the taurine enthusiasm, the bravery, and especially the technical know-how of the common people. These things can only be accounted for by the existence of an autonomous, non-institutionalized tradition of bull-baiting that had remained intact in the isolated villages of provincial Spain. Consider, for example, the banderillas and the cape that play such crucial roles in modern corridas (the cape is used in either the large-sized version known as the *capote* or the smaller *muleta*, or flannel). These implements did not exist in the aristocratic mode of bullfighting from horses. As Alvarez de Miranda demonstrated, both the banderillas and the cape originated in the nuptial bull fertility rite and were commonly used in the modest fiestas de toros that villagers conserved during the whole time nobles were showing off with their lances in the cities.

> The historians of bullfighting speak of the replacement of the nobility by the common people in the bullfights of the eighteenth century; they present it as a revolution in the art of bullfighting. It was precisely the opposite: it was a

restoration—taking advantage of the decadence of the usurping knightly to-reo—of the old popular custom of approaching the bull with cape in hand.[6]

If this "return of the repressed" hypothesis is correct, we should be able to find not only the cape but other important features of the capea coming to the fore in the course of the urban bullfight's evolution. And we do. Chief among them, perhaps, is the element of crowd psychology. It turns out that the urban proletariat, the "city mouse" of our analogy, tended to behave exactly like its country cousin on fiesta days. Historical records indicate that the lower class individuals that crowded into the plazas to watch bullfighting on horseback were always eager to make the affair as much like a capea as they could. The proletariat kept up a running battle with the authorities over who could enter the plaza and who couldn't; troops were routinely deployed to keep the crowd in line. A Jesuit priest writing in 1655 complains of the heat and confusion of bullfight days, and refers to people being beaten into conformity by the plaza guards.[7] Submissiveness has never been a feature of the Spanish underclass, however, and already in the seventeenth century there are numerous signs that the repressed are itching to return and make the fiesta de toros a real fiesta once again. Even from behind the barricades people struggled for an active part in the spectacle. Scenes like the following could be routinely observed in the Plaza Mayor of Madrid:

> If by chance the poor animal passes close to the bleachers, the rabble lashes out with a thousand swordblows, and when the bull falls they rush to see who can strike it the most with his saber and make off with the tail, or its shameful parts, that they carry in their handkerchiefs, showing them off like a trophy and an emblem of some great victory.[8]

It is hard to believe when reading this that we are not back in Coria or Brunete or one of the other isolated villages whose fiestas have included such sanguinary acts for centuries.

Another capea-type practice that was already gaining in popularity in seventeenth-century urban plazas was the *lanzada a pie*, wherein a brave commoner wedged a heavy lance into the ground and waited for the bull to charge in the hopes of being able to skewer him.[9] As the reader will recall from our festal sojourn of Chapter 1, this is precisely the maneuver most prized by the young men of Tordesillas in their annual "hunt" of the *toro de la vega*.

Still another fertile link between the festal reservoir of capeas and the urban corrida was the so-called *toreo pirenaico*, or Pyrenean bullfighting. This was a style of challenging the bull that emphasized both strength and agility, and its most able practitioners were young men from Rioja, Navarra, Aragón, and the Basque provinces (all close to the Pyrenees that separate Spain from France). However they developed this style, it certainly was not in the context of the aristocratic corrida (rarely seen in their hometowns anyway). That leaves only one possibility—their very own rural fiestas de toros. Cossío and a number of other taurine historians cite the names of sought-after toreros of the north to dispute the south's claims for priority in the development of the modern bullfight. There is evidence that the all-important art of delivering a sword thrust to a charging bull (known as the *suerte de recibir*)—something most people associate with the Romero family of Andalusia—was actually taught to the Romeros by bullfighters from Navarre.[10]

As luck would have it, one of the great artists of Europe left us visual testimony of the plebeian "invasion" of bullfighting that takes place in the epoch under discussion. In the series of engravings known as *Tauromaquia*, Goya portrayed not only the many *suertes*, or maneuvers, inherited from capeas but also the savage enthusiasm of the crowd that constituted the most important legacy of all. According to one critic, "Goya's vision of taurine combat was in reality a terrible one, and undoubtedly gloomy, because he knew or mysteriously intuited something of the deep primitivism of bullfighting."[11] The excited and altogether ferocious crowds that Goya sketched represent the most important historical connection between the rural capea and the modern corrida. For in the last analysis, it was the emotionality of the plebeian masses that served both to preserve some of the old festive techniques and reinforce the new *suertes* coming into use. (Eventually, as bullfighting becomes not only big business but the undisputed mainstay of Spanish popular culture, its mass psychology will change in subtle ways. I will discuss the whole issue in the fourth chapter.)

As García-Baquero and his fellow authors point out, the communal disorder and even anarchy that characterized capeas stood in sharp contrast to the status-display rituals and hierarchical impositions of knightly bullfighting.[12] By the middle of the eighteenth century, the waning influence of the nobility and the waxing pugnacity of the plebeians combined to bring about an entirely new idea of decorum. But here we must mention the men who ushered in a brief but important halfway stage between the aristocratic corridas and bullfighting on foot as we know it today. As the reader will recall, the fundamental weapon of bullfighting on horseback had been a short lance called the *rejón*. The gentleman on horseback dashed by, planted the lance between the bull's shoulderblades, and skillfully maneuvered his horse out of harm's way afterwards. As the nobles lost their prestige and began to withdraw from the urban corrida, their places were taken by commoners from the country, either modest ranchers or hirelings who tended bulls on the great landed estates. These new recruits arrived on horseback, but instead of *rejones* they wielded a much longer spear known as a *garrocha* or *vara larga*—a tool much like the one they employed in herding bulls in the fields. Obviously these men had been around for a long time, but only in the eighteenth century did they have the opportunity to show off their skills in public plazas. Instead of galloping past the bull like the aristocrats, the so-called *varilargueros* reined in their mounts, held their ground, and drove the tips of their spears into the bull's withers as he charged. The most famous varilarguero of them all, José Daza, even penned a detailed treatise of this fierce art. Unpublished until 1959, it contains numerous mocking references to the pomp and circumstances left over from the Baroque Age of bullfighting. A no-nonsense man of the country, Daza had no sympathy for the trappings of a failed aristocracy. At the same time, however, he lashed out against the scum and the dregs of society who behaved like animals in the plaza, thumbed their noses at the authorities, and threatened to turn every corrida into anarchy.[13] Daza exemplified the ideological "twilight zone" that the varilargueros occupied, halfway between the old and the new. Some scholars contend that despite their humble extraction the varilargueros were still too attached to the obsolete mentality of the aristocrats to comprehend the plebeian revolution that was transforming the urban corrida de toros; they unconsciously wished to bask in the reflected glory of the elite, even though they could never hope to bridge the great social gulf that separated them from that elite.[14] Whatever the case, the varilarguero was eventually subordinated to the matador on foot and in time became known as the picador. From a technical point of view, the picador's function is absolutely necessary: the proper piccing of a brave bull in the first suerte, or act, of the bullfight is what makes the second suerte of the banderillas and the third suerte of the flannel-work and killing possible. Nevertheless, the picador is nothing more nor less than the popular "villain" of the bullfight, the man most often accused of being a butcher, an executioner, or something even more insulting. It serves him right, as García-Baquero and his fellow authors seem to say:

Death of the Picador (1794), one of several bullfighting scenes painted by Goya two decades before the *Tauromaquia* series.

The Famous American, Mariano Ceballos (Goya, 1825). This South American Indian, the only bullriding bullfighter known to history, provoked mass frenzy in Spain's plazas.

Yesterday and today, picadors remain expelled from the essential drama of the fiesta, and in their eternal damnation they pass through the spectacle, mounted with unbearable sloppiness on squalid nags, haunting the ring as if they were debased and macabre replicas of their gallant old masters. The picadors, now and then, are prisoners of the curse of their social treason, and continue to suffer the rage of the public, for people see in them the abominable image of their lords.[15]

By way of summary, it might be said that the rise of bullfighting on foot represented the happy reconciliation of the country mouse with his es-tranged cousin in the city. The serfs and peasants of Spain's isolated prov-inces had evolved little over the centuries, and they had never abandoned their beloved bull-baiting festivals. When changing historical circum-stances and fashions led the aristocrats to abandon their own version of bull-baiting, the teeming underclass of the cities was able to draw on the great reservoir of the capea for both techniques and inspiration. In many cases, the first bullfighters on foot hailed directly from the archaic northern regions close to the Pyrenees. And after a short-lived equilibrium represented by the varilargueros, the balance was tipped permanently in favor of a new, thoroughly plebeian spectacle that has remained basically the same since the end of the eighteenth century.

Enough has been said, perhaps, to demonstrate that the rise of bullfighting on foot was a kind of "reconquest" of the festal territory of urban plazas or a restoration of popular techniques of manhandling bulls. But this is not the whole story. As we will see, the rise of the modern corrida possesses many characteristics of a *reaction* as well.

✳ Majismo

Bullfighting is an activity in which style counts almost as much as substance: the object is not simply to deceive and kill a bull, but to look good while doing it. Bullfighting as practiced by aristocratic horsemen placed great emphasis on the proper dress, behavior, and gesture. When bullfighting on foot replaces the knightly variety, it will retain "style" as an all-important category, but the dress and manners that it prizes will be radically different. In my view, it is not possible to understand the psychology of Spanish bullfighting, even today, without some exploration of the source of its body language—*majismo*.

As a phenomenon unique to Spanish culture, majismo has no direct equivalent in English. It can be defined initially as the personal presentation of style for both men and women of the lower classes of the eighteenth and nineteenth centuries; it was characterized by a bold, sexy, self-assured, and flippant manner of dressing, walking, and talking. The female equivalent of the swaggering, cocky *majo* was the proud and saucy *maja*. Although the words have now shed some of their original meaning, they are still employed with great frequency in Castilian Spanish. This definition will serve us for now; in a moment we will see that, despite the erotic component of the style, it was nevertheless held to be a reaffirmation of traditional virtues and old-fashioned concepts of honor and morality.

As with any other reactionary movement, it is important to understand what the majos and the majas were reacting against. As is well known, the Age of Enlightenment spoke with a French accent all over Europe. With

The Rise of Modern Bullfighting   57

the coming of the Bourbon dynasty to Spain at the beginning of the eighteenth century, the penetration of French culture into Iberia was unstop-
pable. Spain, the so-called "sick man of Europe," was not in a position to
compete with the advances in science and learning that were taking place
north of the Pyrenees; suddenly aware that they hailed from a "backward"
country, many of the Spanish elite rushed to embrace the prestigious new
styles. As we saw earlier, this wave of imitation had a major impact on the
corrida; numerous nobles began to abhor the *toreo de rejones* that their fathers and grandfathers had proudly practiced in the plazas of Spain. Now,
this might have been all to the good if the Spanish upper classes had entered fully into the spirit of the Enlightenment and had set out to renovate
and rationalize every aspect of their benighted land. But the number of
Spaniards who actually rose to the occasion was very small. Spanish philosophers and essayists like Jovellanos, Feijoo, or Iriarte were probably the
intellectual equals of Enlightenment figures elsewhere but quite without
their influence. Eventually there would be some important reforms and
administrative innovations carried out during the reign of Carlos III, if
only to further the cause of enlightened despotism. But even the much
publicized expulsion of the Jesuits in 1767 represented no threat to the
power and influence of the Spanish Church.[16] And the majority of Spaniards remained traditional in their customs and attitudes. Thus, to make a
long story short, where French culture had its biggest influence, its most
visible, day-to-day impact, was in the lifestyles of Spain's rich and famous.

By the middle of the century, the sons of aristocrats or the untitled well-
to-do had already begun to *correr cortes*—to spend time in the courts, cities,
and fashionable salons of France and other enlightened countries. A liberal
education was the theoretical justification for such trips; but instead of renovating their minds, most of the young travelers only managed to renovate
their wardrobes. They returned from Paris with a superficial polish of sa-
voir-faire; a lifetime supply of perfumes, creams, buckles, clocks, and handkerchiefs; a passing familiarity with minuets and other recherché dances;
an exorbitant love for everything foreign and a sneering contempt for anything Spanish, especially the traditional Spanish prejudice against bathing.
Their speech was so full of pedantic Gallicisms that they came to be known
as *petimetres* (from the French *petit maître*, or little master). As the eighteenth century wore on, an increasing number of non-aristocratic but
wealthy and status-conscious families sent their youths to acquire this Gallicized polish in speech, dress, mannerisms, and attitudes; the number of
petimetres increased accordingly. There was nothing in the prestigious

new lifestyle that was not designed for social display; other trademarks included cool composure, exhibitionistic courtesy, a fashionable scepticism in matters of religion, a dislike of violence, an abhorrence of facial hair, and a fawning and servile coquettishness with women. In other words, the petimetres rejected almost everything that traditional Spaniards cherished in order to embrace what had always been anathema. Let us yield the floor to an expert in this field, Carmen Martín Gaite:

> The masculine attitudes that the new mentality held to be excellent were those that contradicted the image of the brave and daring swordsman, forever ready to fight and kill for faith or honor, an image that for centuries bespoke the essences so automatically attributed to the Spanish race; now it seemed so totally revolutionary to oppose these essences, just like that, and unmask their barbarism. I think that unless we realize how a novelty like this must have been a provocation and an offense for traditional opinion . . . we will never understand the birth of a phenomenon that various authors refer to and that incubated in the lower strata of society as a reaction to the feminization of the nobles and their middle-class imitators: I am referring to majismo. The common people had retreated into an attitude that was completely hostile to foreign influences, and the men of low neighborhoods, as a revenge for their misery, entrenched themselves in this xenophobia and accentuated their contempt for rich petimetres. They considered themselves superior, and came to believe themselves to be the safekeepers and genuine representatives of the purest essences of the Castilian spirit. . . . And, in the process of consolidating that supposed authenticity and purity [*casticismo*], they created a highly distinct style, a mixture of aggressiveness, vulgarity, and insolence, that naturally enough came to be the reverse of the image they rejected, but just as much a caricature.[17]

Majismo, then, had an ideological component as well as a stylistic one. Or to put it another way, majismo was the stylistic component of Spanish casticismo, the broad traditionalist, conservative, and patently reactionary ideology that opposed the Enlightenment and all its works. Majismo was to caticismo what the petimetres were to the Enlightenment: each served, consciously or not, as the cutting edge for larger, more abstract movements. More is involved, therefore, than a mere question of dress or body language. Both majos and petimetres were cultural shock troops whose every pose and gesture came to symbolize one of the ideological systems that competed (perhaps still compete) for the Spanish soul. And the battle was first joined in the unlikely terrain of popular culture, in the heat and commotion produced by the irruption of plebeian art forms like bullfighting on foot. In the eighteenth century, writes Ortega y Gasset, all of Spain found itself divided into two great parties: on one side the immense majority of the nation, submerged in casticismo, impregnated with it and enthusiastic about it; on the other, a few groups whose contingency was numerically small but made up of men of greater quality—some nobles, men of science, governors, and administrators—educated in the French ideas and tastes that dominated the whole of Europe and for whom the popular customs of Spain represented ignominy. The clash between these two parties was harsh and grave.[18]

Perhaps it would have been better for Spain if Ortega's "men of greater quality" had won the battle to Gallicize their own country and do away with the supposedly disgraceful and atavistic attitudes and activities of their compatriots. As is well known, Jovellanos and nearly every other man of quality labored in vain to ban public bullfights. But such was not to be. The first great battle for the hearts and minds of Spaniards was won by the anti-French traditionalists. On the social front, the majos were able to quash the petimetres (and not simply because the former were good with daggers and the latter favored handkerchiefs and minuets). Let us briefly explore some of the key aspects of this triumph, for even if it condemned the country to decades of political stagnation and obscurantism, it helped to make Spain safe for modern bullfighting.

One of the chief reasons for the victory of casticismo was its moral message. Despite the best intentions of the truly Enlightened Ones of Spain, the men Ortega refers to, French styles and behavior patterns seemed ungodly and immoral. One example was the custom of the *cortejo*, whereby the wife of some aristocrat or rich bourgeois allowed herself to be "courted" by one or more petimetres without incurring an old-fashioned attack of marital rage. The custom of the cortejo was reinforced in turn by the dances newly imported from abroad, which all featured an intricate series of postures, steps, and pauses that facilitated flirtation and coquetry. According to Martín Gaite, the majority of extramarital affairs of this period were incubated in the elegant salons where such dances were held. She refers to a particularly popular dance (the so-called *contradanza de los maridos*) that featured a covert allusion to the infidelity it covertly fomented: while the women formed a circle with their hands behind their backs, simulating a bullring, the men held their fingers to their temples, simulating horns, and "charged" into the ring all at once.[19] In other words, the men playing the *maridos*, or husbands, were at the same time *cornudos* (horned ones), that is, cuckolds. The Spanish upper crust had obviously come a long way from the dark days of Calderonian honor, when the merest suspicion of adultery provoked murderous impulses in husbands. And that is not all: the new dances and the new freedom to flirt were accompanied by a flashy and expensive new lifestyle. Status-striving women were anxious to avoid the least stigma of traditional frugality and the lack of worldly sophistication that this implied. And affluent men, fearful of seeming hidebound and old-fashioned, found themselves at the mercy of their wives' competitive acquisitiveness and newfound taste for elaborate dresses, rococo furniture, shoes, fans, and all of the other paraphernalia essential to the good life of the eighteenth century. This new ethos of conspicuous consumption, which had first been introduced by the aristocrats, ironically contributed to the further erosion of the aristocracy. For now wealth mattered even more than lineage. Young single women began to subordinate considerations of rank to seek out a husband who could support them in the style to which they desired to accustom themselves. And lastly, the new styles and attitudes that had become the rage in Madrid began to spread to provincial capitals and "infect" good families living there.[20]

What the above paragraph describes is the decay and eventual loss of the moral authority that had once been a major hallmark of the Spanish upper classes. Preachers, moralists, and even a few of the more puritan intellectuals thundered against the perversion of traditional Spanish customs. The slavish bourgeois imitation of the Gallicized aristocracy proved that the latter was still exemplary—but now of immorality instead of morality. The petimetre quickly became the easiest mark: everywhere his effeminate mannerisms and showy indifference to religious matters made him the villain of numerous sermons or satirical tracts. The petimetre was unfavorably compared to the manly *homo hispanicus* of yesteryear who supposedly wielded a sword in one hand and a cross in the other. The female counterparts of the petimetres, for their part, were reviled as spendthrift, frivolous, and indecent. Where, then, were the real men and women of Spain to be located? The answer was already in place: exemplary virtue had passed from the Gallicized bourgeoisie to the chauvinistic majos of the lower classes, men who demanded utter fidelity of their majas and got it, men who put their honor ahead of their lives à la Calderón, men who despised anything foreign, men who could now pride themselves on being the authentic inheritors of the violent values of old.

The way in which moral exemplarity had shifted from the upper to the lower classes by the end of the eighteenth century is splendidly illustrated by an incident that took place in Madrid on Good Friday of 1798. On this holiest day of the church year, a number of trend-setting ladies of high rank dared to replace their traditional black *basquiñas* (short capes for outdoor use) with brightly colored ones. For the ordinary classes of Madrid, this brazen action was nothing short of sacrilege. As the ladies strolled proudly through the streets accompanied by their footservants, a group of majos began to insult them. The ladies insulted back. Things went from bad to worse, as they often do in Spanish arguments, and it was not long before the majos actually attacked the women in an attempt to strip off their *basquiñas*. The pages who escorted them drew their swords and fought off the majos. Result? A royal order issued the following year made black the only acceptable color for *basquiñas*, thereby confirming that the plebeians were the surer guide to proper public morals.[21]

History itself seemed determined to reinforce the traditional moral and political attitudes represented by the Spanish proletariat. The bloody anarchy of the French Revolution served to galvanize royalist and rightist forces all over Europe, and after Louis XVI was guillotined in 1793, an outraged Spain "threw herself enthusiastically into the war against the French Republic—with a patriotic fervor that can be compared only with the Spanish uprising against Napoleon fifteen years later."[22] In essence, the folly and bloodshed taking place north of the Pyrenees confirmed traditionalist Spain in its worst suspicions; henceforth the Spanish clergy missed no opportunity to denounce a new variety of "French disease" in the most graphic terms. The xenophobic lower classes needed little urging. Unlike the plebeians of Paris, the plebeians of Madrid were pious, conservative, and monarchist. The surly French troops that came to be stationed in that city under the transient rule of Joseph Bonaparte were hardly likely to win converts to *liberté, égalité, fraternité*. Neither Napoleon nor his brother had taken the measure of the people they presumed to dominate. Appropriately, the great War of Spanish Independence was set off by none other than the proud majos of Madrid in May 1808 (possibly to avenge the honor of some insulted majas) and enthusiastically seconded by their ferocious cousins of the countryside. As Ropp remarks:

> Those who like their history in neat packets find the Spanish resistance to Napoleon almost as hard to understand as did Napoleon himself. It was national, but not liberal, a super Vendée, peasant, Catholic, and royalist. . . . This was the war of Goya's famous *The Disasters of War*. Probably more people lost their lives in it than in any other war of the Napoleonic era. As many French officers were killed there as in Russia or Germany.[23]

A people given to careful calculation of the odds would never have risen up against the greatest army in Europe. But a people fond of blood sports and festive risk-taking would have, and did. Even clergymen and women got into the picture: monks grabbed their carbines and strapped cartridge belts to their chests while wildly valiant women with scissors struck terror into the hearts of the regicidal French Republic's soldiers.[24] As a number of Spanish historians have recognized, the Spanish aristocracy played a ridiculously small role in the resistance to Napoleon—yet another sign of their lack of exemplarity. Hence, the war reflected and gave new impetus to casticismo—not only to old-fashioned notions of honor and bravery but also to the entire constellation of Spanish popular values, including traditional religious beliefs and practices, and, above all, the attitudes and styles of majismo. Throughout the nineteenth and twentieth centuries, the charismatic heroes of the people will be those capable of masterful public demonstrations of risk-taking, such as bullfighters or caudillos.

In the meantime, many of Spain's Enlightened Ones had been forced to choose between two unpleasant alternatives: a progressive but ruthless France and their own valiant but reactionary native land. Many opted for the latter, thinking that their liberal ideas would prosper in the post-Napoleonic era; they even drew up a progressive new constitution in Cádiz. But they had not taken the measure of the man that thousands of blindly royalist Spanish peasants were dying for, Fernando VII, described accurately by Lovett as "cowardly, ignorant, and lazy, but cunning and vindictive as few men in high position have ever been."[25] Brought to power on a wave of xenophobic and almost messianic mass fervor, the reactionary Fernando and his cohorts restored Absolutism, re-established the Inquisition, and managed to keep the liberals in exile or in prison for years.

We have seen how casticismo triumphed over the eighteenth-century petimetres and even the Enlightenment itself because it breathed new life into traditional concepts of honor, valor, and morality—qualities that were never so much in evidence as in the successful fight to expel French armies from the peninsula in the first part of the nineteenth century. A series of fortuitous historical circumstances had actually demonstrated the vigor and ongoing relevance of a thoroughly ancien régime worldview and its curious combination of obscurantist Catholicism, monarchical fetishism, and xenophobia. Majismo, the cutting edge of casticismo, its stylistic and behavioral dimension, was all of this.

In the nineteenth and twentieth centuries, the Spanish bourgeoisie will succumb again and again to the cultural prestige of neighboring France, consuming French fashions and aping French customs. But France will never recover the hegemony it had at the beginning of the eighteenth century; and the popular classes will always be there to keep bourgeois snobs in check, not only through the devices of satire and ridicule but also through the nativist or nationalistic prestige of their own "genuinely Spanish" lifestyles. In strongholds of casticismo like Madrid, a whole category of Gallicisms will be assimilated to speech, but only under the condition that their accepted pronunciation should be as little like French as possible.[26] And even today when Spaniards want to pay something or someone the highest compliment, the word employed will be "majo."

The time has come to discuss the other major factor in the triumph of majismo, the one most closely connected with the triumph of bullfighting on foot, and the one that would almost seem to contradict everything that has been said about its moral exemplarity. For in what has to be considered the greatest irony of Spanish social history, the majos beat the petimetres at their own game and developed styles of dress and gesture that were the very epitome of eroticism.

In broad perspective, it is possible to see majismo as one more symptom of Spanish decadence; the whole wave of Spanish plebeianism, according to Ortega y Gasset, comes about because of the social vacuum left by a weak and fractious aristocracy. The people turned their back on their social betters and modelled themselves—on themselves.

> Beginning around 1670 the Spanish plebeian class turns in on itself. Instead of looking to the outside for its forms, little by little it nurtures and stylizes its own traditional ones. Out of this spontaneous, diffuse, and everyday labor will come the repertory of postures and gestures of the Spanish people of the last two centuries. This repertory has a characteristic that, I believe, makes it unique, to whit: that consisting of poses and movements that are as spontaneous as all things popular, those poses and those movements are already stylized. To execute them is not simply to live but to live *en forma*, to exist with style. Our common people created for themselves a sort of second nature that was already informed by esthetic qualities.[27]

In the previous section we followed the development of the Gallicized lifestyle originally introduced by aristocrats and subsequently copied by members of the numerically small Spanish bourgeoisie. The petimetres had their heydey in the first half of the eighteenth century. We saw how majismo represented a kind of class consciousness; it was inseparable from a conscious popular rejection of the alien and overrefined fashions and behaviors of the upper echelons of society. If this reaction had been limited to the lower classes, it might not have played the major formative role that it did in Spanish history. As it happened, however, majismo was so overwhelmingly successful that, in the second half of the same century, numerous members of the upper classes were doing their best to imitate the clothes and mannerisms of the plebeians.

The artificial and effeminate styles of the petimetres did not stand a chance against the frank and daring styles of majismo. As with any change of fashion, the "snob" element played a major role. But if this had been the only factor behind the aristocratic imitation of plebeian styles, it would have been a short-lived affair, as short-lived as any other caprice of the well-to-do. But majismo prospered, endured, broadened its base, and spread to every corner of Spanish society (as Ortega and other Spanish intellectuals have lamented). There must have been, therefore, something innately appealing about it, some unique quality or qualities that won people over and retained their loyalty. Majismo, in the words of Martín Gaite, "was the opposite of submission and obedience to rules; it was the defiance of one's own walk, one's own body, of *majeza*, of majesty."[28] In short: body language. Everything about majismo was designed to create an aura of insolence and sex appeal. And these characteristics were accentuated, and often taken to extremes, wherever and whenever majismo came into contact with the other current of imitation that had been set in motion in Gallicized aristocrats. The final irony is reached when the aristocrats forget about Paris and begin to take their cue from the proletarian neighborhoods of Madrid.

When we look more closely into this ironic turn of events, we discover a still greater irony: it was precisely the elegant and affluent natives of Paris and other prestigious European capitals who "discovered" majismo on their journeys to Spain and subsequently reoriented the tastes of the Spanish upper classes. The supreme irony, of course, is that foreigners should be so taken with a lifestyle in which hatred of foreigners played no small part. As Martín Gaite relates, many of these travellers were diplomats and intellectuals who were thoroughly familiar with the latest refinements; for this very reason they were ready to ignore imported styles and focus on the native, on the "genuine" Spanish styles, thus bringing them to the attention of "Spaniards of the elite who were prepared—then and always—to enthusiastically applaud anything that authoritative foreigners could point to as novel."[29]

This is not the only "snob" factor involved, however. Quite apart from the influence of prestigous foreigners, Spanish aristocrats were eager to put some distance between themselves and their pesky middle-class emulators. Majismo lent itself admirably to this strategy:

The courtly fashions born to satisfy the nobles' need to stand out had been used up, vulgarized because of their excessive appropriation by the middle class. And a group of ladies of the high aristocracy, nauseated by them, turned their gaze to the models of majismo that they spied upon and tried out with secret fascination. . . . Women of high rank continued to feel the need to elevate themselves over those of the middle class, distinguish themselves from them at whatever the cost.[30]

Apparently it was the Duchess of Alba, drawn or painted on innumerable occasions by Goya, who became the most audacious implanter of majismo at the top of the social pyramid.

Spanish women of the elite had another reason for throwing off courtly fashions, even more powerful than the two that have been mentioned so far. As it happens, their husbands had become bored with the opera and were flocking to the music halls to listen to and lust after the majas who sang there. The triumph of majismo in eighteenth-century Spain, in fact, was closely related to the triumph of popular musical theatre over the operatic theatre imported by Felipe V and his entourage. Like other refined activities promoted by petimetres, opera could not hold a candle to the wave of plebeianism sweeping over Spain; its place was quickly taken by the *sainete*, a versatile and dynamic one-act musical comedy featuring men and women of the proletariat, that is, majos and majas. Don Ramón de la Cruz (1731–1794) was the most famous of a series of playwrights and composers who were busily giving the people what they wanted to see and hear. Crowds of commoners were joined by foreigners and aristocrats anxious to see *The Faithful Maja, The Maja and the Sergeant, The Happy Maja, The Torero, the Maja, and the Petimetre, The Maja Without a Country, The Jealous Maja, I Am a Maja,* and so on. These titles alone indicate the enormous popularity of the maja character, as Caro Baroja points out.[31] The plot lines of the plays were simple: one or more desirable but class-conscious majas, normally employed selling fruits and vegetables, engage in amorous skirmishes with pugnacious majos, handsome sergeants, rich old men, petimetres, or lascivious priests. Provocative songs alternate with knife fights and neighborhood fiestas. In one anonymous sainete, Don Juan himself tires of the artificial coquettishness of his aristocratic paramour and throws her off in favor of a maja from the slums. Some sort of revolution was clearly under way.

Since literary histories reflect the class prejudices and ideologies of their writers, they rarely mention these plays and when they do it is with condescension. The secret of the sainete's success was not so much in the text as in the performance, however. The key was the singer-actress who interpreted the role of maja. A good number of beautiful proletarian women became rich and famous by playing themselves, as it were, by bringing to the stage all of the sauciness, insolence, bold stares, and frank talk that were the hallmarks of majismo. The most famous of all was María Ladvenant. Born in the slums of Madrid, she carried majismo to new heights of sex appeal and awoke vehement passions in men like the Marquis of Mora and the Count of Fuentes. Her death in 1767 at the age of twenty-five provoked a massive outpouring of grief in Madrid and her funeral was attended by the cream of Spanish society.[32] More than any one person, of course, it was majismo itself that electrified Spanish society; the sugary rituals of the court were no match for the salty spontaneity of the proletariat.

It will come as no surprise to the reader to learn that the greatest vehicle for the propagation of majismo was the bullfight. In its newly plebeianized format, the bullfight gave majos the same opportunities to rise in society as the popular theatre gave to their women.

The essential identity of the majo and the bullfighter cannot be emphasized too much, for in this identity lie the seeds of the bullfighter's ability to mesmerize the masses and fascinate the aristocracy. As is well known, Goya's etchings of majos are well-nigh indistinguishable from his portraits of toreros. The seductive body language of majos/toreros, what Caro refers to as their "exemplary narcissism," is well illustrated by a popular song making the rounds of Madrid in 1779:

Quien quiera ver torero	Whoever wants to see a torero
de fantasía,	from out of a dream,
aquí está este real mozo	here is this splendid lad
de Andalucía	from Andalusia
sin deshecho ninguno	without a single flaw
de abajo arriba.	from head to toe.
¡Esta sí que es pierna!	Now this is a leg!
¡Este sí que es cuerpo!	Now this is a body!
¡Este sí es columpio	Now this is swing
y este sí es manejo!	and this is flair!
¡Vea usted qué fachenda	See for yourself what style
y qué meneo!	and what swagger![33]

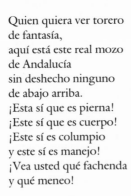

In the same way that noblemen lusted after the majas of the stage, more than a few noblewomen sought out lovers among the dashing young majos of the bullring. Gossip held that the Duchess of Alba herself—one of the first aristocrats to embrace the styles of majismo—had taken not one but several bullfighters to her bedchambers.[34] This gossip formed the basis of a steamy bestseller penned by the Duchess of Abrantes a few years later, one that set the tone for scores of similar works published in succeeding decades. According to one literary historian, the Duchess of Abrantes was among the first to capitalize on bullfighting's ability to mix the lowborn with the highborn; she showed how a plot derived from social reality itself could be thickened by adding more savagery and passion to the plebeian bullfighter and more lust or despotic capriciousness to the noblewoman.[35]

More will be said later about the erotic fantasies that bullfighters inspire. Let us remain for now in the sphere of social history, where truth often bests fiction anyway. There was a crucial difference between the sexy majas of popular theatre and the sexy majos of the bullring. Singing and dancing, after all, were relatively safe activities, and the plays majas appeared in were "make believe." But the bullfight was utterly real. To see a man act with nonchalant insolence in the face of a murderous bull was bound to be more exciting, and more addictive, than seeing the same gestures played out against the backdrop of a vegetable market. The real danger present in the bullring constituted the perfect validation of _vergüenza torera_, the pugnacious code of masculine honor that predated majismo and has outlived it as well. It may not have been a particularly edifying concept of honor, but it was more than enough to justify the flashy display and posturing of its adepts. And it can be unerringly traced back to the bad old days, when certain unsavory Spaniards used their blades not on bulls but on each other.

The Ethos of the Outlaw

It is well to remember that majismo represents the specific contribution of the urban proletariat to modern bullfighting. Most of the actual techniques, as we discussed earlier, had been developed over the centuries in rural fiestas de toros. But if the "country mouse" contributed the basic techniques of tauromachy, the "city mouse" contributed style, flair, and gesture. If we look into the social origins and personalities of the first professional bullfighters, men whose names still resonate in the minds of taurine aficionados today, we find that they were majos almost to a man, completely immersed in the ethos of the eighteenth-century urban slum. Some were even Gypsies, a group much despised—even today—by

Spanish peasants, but tolerated and even sought after by majos and aristocrats alike. And, as a final rural/urban disjuncture, the fact that most apprentice bullfighters were outsiders from the city often brought out the worst in the in-crowd at village capeas.

So whatever the rural roots of the taurine "performance" that emerges in the eighteenth century, the "performers" will be men of the urban proletariat. This much is undeniable. But García-Baquero and his fellow authors have argued that even the modern manner of killing the bull, with a single efficient swordthrust within a strictly measured period of time, was an urban creation as well. Their argument runs as follows. The majority of Seville's early bullfighters were one-time employees of the slaughterhouse who discovered they could earn more money by doing their job in public. In a rural capea, no one is in a hurry to see the bull dead, and when the time comes to kill him, any method will do, from a shotgun to a mass assault with knives. In the modern bullfight, however, it becomes crucial to show efficiency and know-how; the bull is to be dispatched cleanly (at least in theory) and quickly in a (relatively) methodical manner. It was the daily experience of killing bovids in the slaughterhouse that gave certain plebeians the necessary knowledge and skill. In time, the guild system then dominant in the workaday world served as the model for turning bullfighting into a true profession with rules, regulations, hierarchism, apprenticeship, seniority, and so on. And the emblem for all this modern timesaving expertise is a famous engraving of Pepe-Illo, a great early bullfighter from Seville, who posed with a sword in one hand, a timepiece in the other, and a dead bull at his feet.[36]

For the sake of argument, let us grant what the above argument takes for granted but what is by no means certain—that the modern bullfight was invented in Seville. Let us also grant that the slaughterhouse has been a vital source of experience and information for some, though by no means all, would-be bullfighters. But if know-how and efficiency were all there is to bullfighting, any slaughterhouse worker could become a bullfighter and make big money. And instead of building bullrings, why not just sell tickets at the door to the slaughterhouse so that people can see real expertise in action, cheering wildly all the while? Obviously something is missing here. And that something is the desire on the part of some to flaunt their virile valor and the desire on the part of many to watch them do it. The whole point of a bullfight, after all, is to give the bull a fighting chance. It takes a very special sort of person to face a large brave bull. One can have all the knowledge or expertise of a veterinarian and it will serve for nothing without a sufficient degree of temerity. And this holds equally for the eighteenth century and the twentieth. As bullfighters are fond of saying, "*los de valor a mandar, los del arte a acompañar*" (roughly, the courageous are to lead, the skillful/artistic to follow along). If slaughterhouses were set up to operate in the same way, we would have severe shortages of meat.

The argument presented by García-Baquero and his colleagues is invalid for another reason: the killing that goes on in a bullring is not utilitarian in nature. While it is true that the meat of dead bulls is sold to butchers or in the past was donated to hospitals and orphanages, the bulls are killed not in the interest of food distribution but for spectacle, sport, and entertainment. As it is, the slaughterhouse is almost the bullfight's antithesis— a purely utilitarian and functional processing of the bovid as object. Nothing could be further from the spirit of the bullfight, where people have anthropomorphized the bull and imagined him to possess many admirable qualities. The bull must be a serious adversary, the better to test the presumption of the majo/torero. If the latter takes unfair advantage of his opponent, he might receive the supreme insult—¡*carnicero*! (butcher). Ironically, when they cite Pepe-Illo holding his watch over a dead bull as the emblem of their argument, García-Baquero and his co-authors unwittingly compound their error. Taurine historians tell us that in order to demonstrate his valor at killing-time, Pepe-Illo liked to throw away the flannel and substitute a watch, a hat, or even a *peineta* (an ornamental comb used by women).[37] Pepe-Illo's gesture is not, therefore, a statement of efficiency but of exhibitionistic *vergüenza torera*.

Finally, while it is good Marxist form to derive cultural spectacles from labor relations and the circumstances of production, it would be grossly misleading to associate early bullfighters with any kind of a work ethic— Protestant, Catholic, or otherwise. In the beginning, bullfighting was only a little more respectable than smuggling tobacco; it was bound to appeal to violent men with nothing to lose and something to prove. (The big issue, of course, is why public animal killing became not only respectable but highly prestigious in Spain; I hope to have clarified this by the end of the book.) Men like Pepe-Illo were not the product of industrial modernization but the living proof of its failure; Spain was to remain, deep down, a very anti-modern country; and the rise of bullfighting on foot simply gave a new lease on life to a thoroughly primitive cosmovision.

In order to fathom the innate appeal of majismo, we need to look more closely into its nature and origins. For just as bullfighting on foot did not appear overnight but reflected an ancestral heritage of rural bull-baiting, the behaviors associated with majismo did not appear out of thin air but from the barracks, the prisons, the mountain camps of horsethieves and brigands, and the violent and vice-ridden urban slums far removed from the sleepy stability of peasant life. Majismo's origins in the basest spheres of Spanish society make its later success all the more ironic.

The time frame for this evolution is much the same one that we have employed thus far. By the beginning of the seventeenth century, an empire that had been founded on military conquest was already paying the social cost of its violent heritage. In the age of expansion, Spain's best men had put the honor of their lineage ahead of all other considerations. There was no better way to prove the nobility of one's blood than by spilling the enemy's; honor was something to be gotten or defended through one-on-one combat on the field of battle. In the age of collapse, this bellicose notion of honor underwent a process of, for want of a better word, plebeianization. It came to be identified not so much with military glory or conquest but with aggressive virility and a pugnacious sort of one-upmanship that was as much for show as for real and that included a distinct element of sexual prowess. The decline and fall of the Spanish Empire engenders a dangerous fruit, a young man

> who in order to demonstrate his superiority in everything connected with disorderly and juvenile living must not only be the one who risks his life more, kills more, gambles more, brags more, but also the one who conquers more women and employs greater ingenuity in seducing them. . . . In other words: the principle of honor through individual violence is always the ethics of the soldier that, as long as the risk and the venture last, are acceptable and even desirable, but which are unacceptable in civilian life.[38]

The reader will be quick to associate the figure of Don Juan with this spirit of braggart amorality described by Caro Baroja. But we are certainly not in the realm of fiction. For one thing, there were plenty of flesh-and-blood aristocrats who lived lives of murder, seduction, and blaspheming defiance—for example, Don Tiburcio de Redin, Don Miguel de Castro, Don Juan Diego, the Duke of Estrada.[39] More importantly, the donjuanesque ethos achieved its most complete expression in men who did not have the rank of "don." Among the rank and file or the down and outs, violence became the best and sometimes the only route to prestige. But the readiness to kill or die for the sake of reputation was not sufficient in itself to make a man a "legend in his own time." He also had to display this readiness with a maximum of nonchalance. Destruction had to be courted with style; enemies, death, and even divine wrath had to be countenanced with flippant indifference.

The innumerable military campaigns of imperial Spain provided the initial matrix for braggadocio and licentious behavior of all sorts; but the antisocial customs reinforced by war eventually spread to any situation in which vehement young men had something to prove, from the jail of Seville to the University of Salamanca. From the seventeenth century onwards, notes Bennassar, masculine honor was slowly assimilated to the willingness to risk death; a true "contagion of honor" infected Spanish society and the authorities were largely powerless before it.[40] The new ethos, now far removed from any military or social utility, took hold among all social classes. Where it held absolute sway, however, was in the criminal underworld. The double disposition toward homicide and narcissism that we have outlined became the trademark of an entire class of men living on the fringes of the law and known variously as *valientes*, *bravos*, *guapos*, *jaques*, and *majos*.

Although such men existed in cities all over Spain, they were plentiful in Madrid and legion in Seville. As the chief port and distribution center for goods arriving from or on their way to the New World, as well as the headquarters of Spanish colonial administration, Seville was a booming and contradictory city. It was characterized by extremes of wealth and poverty, piety and vice, licit and illicit affairs of all kinds. In *Rinconete y Cortadillo*, Cervantes provides us with a splendid portrait of Seville's criminal underworld, with power in the hands of a ruthless but clever barbarian and his two "enforcers"—all three of them bravos. They hold the highest positions in a confraternity that includes pícaros, prostitutes, thieves, beggars, and at least one policeman. The violence that criminal enterprise used to maintain itself was not fictional. For two hundred years the worst neighborhoods of Seville will be the worst in Spain. In a rigid and stagnant society incapable of providing opportunities for the lowborn to climb the social ladder, numerous men of the lowest classes turned to crime—a highly competitive world where brave young men got ahead or died trying. It was crucial to maintain an overweening and extremely touchy notion of one's self-worth, and according to García Ferrero, a man backed up his bragging with a *navaja de santo óleo*, or holy-oils knife, so named because its use in a fight inexorably led to a priest being called to administer last rites to the loser.[41]

Seville was reputed to be the most vice-ridden city on earth, and Cervantes portrays crime there as an organized affair, a business sustained by equal amounts of violence and corruption. All this by the beginning of the seventeenth century. By the end of the century, the underground or underworld economy had grown enormously in importance because of contraband (the word itself comes from Spanish and was first used to refer to illegal trade with Spain's colonies). Spaniards' inordinate demand for cacao and especially tobacco had created a vast smuggling network throughout Andalusia that corrupted tax collectors and bureaucrats and provided full employment for bravos, guapos, jaques, and other tough guys. As might be expected, a ferocious competition broke out among them for control of the black market. And control, once obtained, had to be maintained through the same threatening postures and tough talk that guapos had always specialized in. As a result, the element of rivalry looms large in the many ballads that recount the exploits of famous homicidal bullies. The most famous of all was Francisco Estéban, the son of Galician emigrants who literally slashed his way to the top of the tobacco trade and had extensive dealings with governors, judges, and customs officials. Estéban's success spawned a host of imitators and rivals. Another ballad sings the praises of one Miguel de Arenales by denouncing all of his competitors, thus providing us with a vertiable "who's who" of seventeenth- and eighteenth-century Spanish outlaws:

Pedro Ponce fue una gallina	Pedro Ponce was a chicken
El Pelado fue vergüenza	El Pelado was a shame
Mateo Benet le respeto	Mateo Benet I respect
Corrales se colorea	Corrales turns color
Escobedo es un menguado	Escobedo is a has-been
Pedro Gil atrás se queda	Pedro Gil is out of it
Piquer fue muy corta pala	Piquer was small potatoes
Ganchet en guapos no entra	Ganchet wasn't even a guapo
Domingo Ribas es baba	Domingo Ribas is drivel
Miguel Aguilar no llega	Miguel Aguillar doesn't make it
Romero fue un mata moscas	Romero was a fly-killer
Juan de Lara fue una dueña	Juan de Lara was a duenna
Pedro Andrés no tuvo manos	Pedro Andrés couldn't fight
ni Cholvi el de Betjeléa	nor could Cholvi of Betjeléa
Leandro Escales fue un niño	Leandro Escales was a boy
Pedro Roxas no se cuenta	Pedro Roxas doesn't count
ni Don Agustín Florencio	nor Don Agustín Florencio
ni el guapo Francisco Estéban	nor the guapo Francisco Estéban
¿Qué vale Martin Muñoz?	What is Martin Muñoz worth?
¿Mosén Senén, que aprovecha?	What good is Mosén Senén?
Peñalver fue un pobrezuelo	Peñalver was a poor devil

y lo mismo Juan de Vera	the same goes for Juan de Vera
Robira fue un poco guapo	Robira was a little guapo
El Mellado ya flaquea	El Mellado is getting weak
¡Martín Alonso qué mandria!	Martín Alonso what a jerk![42]

We will see later on how crucial these elements of rivalry and one-upmanship are to the evolution of bullfighting. For now it can be pointed out that smuggling continued to be the mainstay of organized crime in southern Spain throughout the eighteenth and nineteenth centuries. Every rise in the official price of tobacco led to an increase in the number of smugglers, in flagrant competition and sometimes cooperation with the tens of thousands of tax collectors or customs agents deployed by the crown.[43] The guapos, jaques, and bravos of southern Spain, like barbarians, tough guys, and criminals everywhere, knew the importance of sharing the loot with their helpers; they simultaneously distributed their ill-gotten wealth and confirmed their hard-won prestige by sponsoring riotous orgies known as *juergas*.

Close contacts were maintained, in the meantime, with their "business partners"—the tough guys of the capital city of Madrid. The outlaw lifestyle had another important agent of transmission in the *gitanos*, Spanish Gypsies, a group that had always lived on the fringes of society, despised by many and romanticized by almost as many. Despite their marginal status, or perhaps because of it, the Gypsies followed a strict code of male honor, female purity, and blood revenge for any infraction of the first two. They quickly assimilated the violence and poses of the guapos while enriching underworld slang with innumerable words from *caló*. The stylistic and behavioral result of this collusion between the Andalusian underworld, the Gypsy subculture, and the Madrid underclass would eventually come to be known as majismo.

It may well be asked why the speech and manners of a minority of flashy hoodlums came to be admired and imitated by large numbers of lower-class but mostly law-abiding people. From a sociopsychological viewpoint, the process was not all that different from what was going on at the other end of the social hierarchy. In effect, eighteenth-century Spain was host to two great currents of imitation put in motion by a powerful minority above the law (aristocrats) and a powerful minority outside the law (the guapos we have been describing). The first served as a magnet for the incipient Spanish bourgeoisie, orienting their attention to the prestigious new modes of France. The second served as a magnet for the proletariat, mesmerizing them with swagger, swashbuckling, and easy money. What both minorities had in common, of course, was a certain mystique of autonomy. In decadent Spain, aristocrats often were a law unto themselves, protected by the loopholes of a subservient legal system; outlaws formed a kind of parallel or underground aristocracy—one that was far more functional and flexible than the other, it might be observed, since prestige was not derived from circumstances of birth but from an individual aptitude for aggression.

In any clime or country, most people will tend to imitate the lifestyles and the opinions of those who seem to be able to do what they want. In Spain, economic decadence and cultural backwardness predisposed the great majority of people, that is, the underclass, to take their cue from the lowest common denominator. And human nature being what it is, the lowest common denominator will always be the animal in us. The roughest, toughest, and meanest man, the expert practitioner of violence, will always seem more attractive to the masses than a cultivated man-about-town or dandy. Rambo over Oscar Wilde, in other words. However unsavory the above-mentioned hoodlums may seem, they were idolotrized by the unsophisticated Spanish proletariat. In a land of servitude and dependence, the guapos embodied a much-valued air of personalized power and autonomy. So it was not long before the lower-class neighborhoods of Seville and Madrid were full of men and women who had learned to strut, stare, talk smart, and dress provocatively. Few, however, proceeded to take up the licentious outlaw life in which the body language originated; even fewer rushed into the new forum for the social validation of personal power—the bullring.

The Joy of Bullfighting

In the last analysis, the body language of majismo would be (and often was) a silly posturing without the element of risk of life. At the heart of genuine majismo was an ethos forged in a primitive world where men got by or got ahead through crime and violence. As a direct consequence of their reduced life expectancy, outlaws and tough guys adopted a life of out-and-out hedonism. Any free time was to be spent carousing; any extra money was to be squandered in juergas. As we saw earlier, these orgies of wine, women, and song served a redistributive function and contributed to the maintenance of the tough guy's status.

Most early bullfighters retained this hedonistic and redistributive life-style, becoming "legends in their own time" as a result. Fernando Savater has attempted to account for the popular idolization of bullfighters by ref-erence to ancient myths of heroes who return from their cosmic confron-tations with telluric fertility gods to spread regenerated life among the needy masses—hence the successful matador's image as a hard-drinking, free-spending womanizer immersed in endless revel.[44] Hemingway em-ployed a more down-to-earth metaphor: "A shark rarely has more than four remoras or sucking fish that fasten to him or swim along with him, but a bullfighter, when he is making money, has dozens."[45] Juan Belmonte tells us that on numerous occasions he left his home to go to the café and was stopped by so many friends and admirers asking for money that he was cleaned out by the time he got to the café.[46] Belmonte, like all famous matadors before and after him, accepted the social obligations of wealth and popularity. As in other primitive or non-capitalistic subcultures, power on the planet of the bulls increased in direct proportion to displays of generosity.

One of the great modern historians of bullfighting looks back on its early social history with abhorrence. In the baroque style he often affected, Cossío writes almost as if the orgies had been held right next door:

> The irregular and boastful life of disoriented and impudent manliness, of clamor and noisy revel, was immune from even the most rudimentary requirements of decent sociability. The juerga with wine and women, the comradeship with the dregs of society, the celebration of any shameless audacity . . . before the risk of pistol or knife, governed by wine and the most improper and rash passions, were taken to be qualities of toreros in the vice-ridden environments they fre-quented, and the feats that were realized in service of such a concept of life were held to be the obligatory courtesies of the taurine profession.[47]

Cossío goes on to cite Pepe-Illo—the very bullfighter that García-Baquero et al. took to be an emblem of industrial rationality—as the incarnation of this lifestyle of primitive hedonism. Another historian sees Pepe-Illo in the golden glow of hero-worship that characterizes most taurine biographies: for Fernández y González, Pepe-Illo was the prototypical "man of the peo-ple"—naturally rustic, devoid of the slightest foreign contamination, un-educated but sharp-witted, jocular, generous to a fault, the life of any party, frank, impulsive, manly, irresistible to women, and so on.[48] Whatever perspective we take, Pepe-Illo must have been a little more civilized than some other early bullfighters. Consider José Ulloa, for example, alias

Tragabuches, who learned bullfighting from the great Pedro Romero and smuggling from his fellow Gypsies. When Romero retired and became a customs inspector, Tragabuches tried to kill him. Eventually he did manage to kill his own wife, a beautiful dancer nicknamed "La Nena," when he caught her in flagrante delicto with a fifteen-year-old altar boy.[49]

This story of a bullfighter killing a Gypsy dancer in a jealous rage sounds ever so much like the plot of *Carmen* and takes us dangerously close to *l'Espagne romantique*, the mythic image of Spain first created in the nineteenth century and unfortunately still with us today. As an antidote, we can ask if death is the appropriate punishment for adultery. As a stronger antidote, we can recall the ugly deaths of bullfighters that have nothing to do with romance and everything to do with the circles they moved in. Francisco Piñero Gavira, for example, who was shot down by a policeman in 1898, or Antonio Olmedo, alias Valentín, who died in a barroom squabble, or Juan Anllo, alias Nacional II, who was hit over the head with a bottle and died in jail a few hours later.[50] Another way to counter the temptation to mythify the lifestyle of early bullfighters would be to recall Hemingway's discussion of the two "occupational diseases" that afflicted the matadors of his day: tuberculosis and syphilis.[51]

Only when we have gone beyond popular mythology will we be in a position to account for it. The first step is to see through the romantic halo of bullfighters, and the next is to recognize all the same that the desire or the need to romanticize them as superhuman beings has been very strong and persistent in Spain. It would be grossly wrong to think that the popularity of bullfighters has been restricted to an inner circle of drinking buddies, prostitutes, and other parasites.

One of the historic ironies of bullfighting is that it has always had enthusiastic support among the same poor masses who would never have chosen bullfighting as a way to escape poverty—masses who, in other words, were either resigned to their fate or willing to hope that through hard work and daily sacrifice they could somehow find a better life, but who were willing, all the same, to deify those few who were neither resigned nor inclined to hard work. This paradoxical attitude, one of the secret wellsprings of Spanish bullfighting, was captured by Hoyos y Vinent in his portrait of a humble aficionado:

> In the ingenuous soul of the poor man, accustomed to the daily struggle, to the slow battle with the paltriness of life, to work, to savings, to fidelity, for whom the whole of existence was contained within a narrow confine of moral and

material obligations, there was an immense admiration for those valiant ones who triumphed at the risk of their lives, who knew how to look death in the face and afterwards squandered rivers of gold on wild fiestas, easy women, and adventures.[52]

The warrior primitivism of bullfighters, therefore, their paganistic or carpe diem philosophy of eat-drink-and-be-merry-for-tomorrow-we-may-die, stood in sharp contrast to the workaday reality principle of the majority. As Gil Calvo has pointed out, each lifestyle was rational in its own way. People always act in accordance with the degree of certainty they possess about the future; a high degree of certainty or predictability leads to long-term, stable, benefit-oriented investments of time and energy; if there is no certainty, the only rational course is to live life moment by moment, maximizing pleasure with no thought for the morrow.[53] The hazardous and unpredictable profession of bullfighting would clearly tend to make its practitioners adopt the second of these strategies. As Araúz de Robles has rightly affirmed, the profile of such individuals—rebels in a rigidly stratified society, nonconformists, violators of the general law of submission to circumstances, and idols of the underclass—would have great sociological value.[54]

On the basis of what we have seen so far, it could be hypothesized that something must have gone amiss in the socialization process of bullfighters or would-be bullfighters, some factor or factors that kept them from internalizing the workaday values of their elders, or, more exactly, led them to act out their society's taboo-breaking fantasy instead of the taboo-respecting reality. Something that enabled them (or compelled them) to prefer the risk of early death to a life of daily-wage drudgery. I will deal in depth with motivational factors in the next chapter. For now it can be pointed out that violation of one value system implies adherence to another. In their rebellious rejection of normal values and normal rewards, bullfighters have substituted a different code and a different mode of reinforcement. First the code: *vergüenza torera*. The word *pundonor* is often used as a synonym. Both terms possess a certain connotation of "touchiness" that descends quite directly from the oldest and most benighted tradition of Spanish honor obsessions. Simply put, *vergüenza torera* is a bullfighter's willingness to place his honor (or shame) ahead of his own life. This is not a mythical or romantic notion. It is a genuine code of conduct that has led time and again to the mythical or romantic exaltation of the bullfighters who succumbed to it.

Examples of *vergüenza torera* abound, unfortunately, but one will suffice to indicate its nature and consequences. On May 27, 1894, a Sevillian matador named Manuel García, alias Espartero, came up against a Miura bull named Perdigón in the bullring of Madrid. Espartero was rather graceless, and lacking in taurine skill. He was also lacking in fear, and for this he had become the idol of the masses, though not of the press. In the words of an exacting critic who observed Espartero on numerous occasions:

> There had been no exaggeration with regard to his much-exalted valor. As it happens, the greater part of the time it was not valor so much as a heedless and irreflexive temerity that erased all notion of artistic standards. With a blindness that irritated one, he would enter terrains that went beyond danger and bordered on suicide. Hence his twenty-odd gorings and frightful end.[55]

On this particular afternoon, Espartero was in great form. So was Perdigón: he managed to kill three horses in the first suerte. Willful and decisive, Espartero brought his formidable opponent under control with a dozen well-wrought passes; but as he drove in his sword at the "moment of truth," he was tossed high into the air and came down on his head. Espartero got to his feet, wobbly and pale, his men urging him to enter the infirmary. But to leave the bullring with the bull still alive would have infringed Espartero's *pundonor*. He gave the bull seven more passes, profiled, and went in with the sword in the slowest and most classic manner. It was a magnificent swordthrust, but the bullfighter was rewarded by a hornthrust to his own chest. Espartero saw his bull drop dead as he was being carried off to the infirmary where he died himself twenty minutes later. The public deified him overnight, and in the limestone walls of Madrid's bullring some unknown hand inscribed words to the effect that Espartero had been *vergüenza torera* personified.[56]

To conclude this chapter, let us briefly turn our attention to the system of rewards and punishments that keeps the taurine honor code in place. Episodes like the above make it clear that those bullfighters who best embody the values of *vergüenza torera* have been positively reinforced by the crowd—rewarded, as it were, for their appetite for punishment. Naturally bullfighters who stray from the code will get their share of negative reinforcement in the form of jeers, taunts, thrown objects, malicious reviews, and so forth. We have already discussed another aspect of the reward structure for a successful matador—the life of wanton pleasure that he can lead as long as he survives. Said pleasure need not be limited to low dives: as we saw earlier, a popular bullfighter can climb the social ladder in a way that other proletarians can only dream of. Finally, we must make mention of the fact that a bullfighter can achieve great pleasure not only after his work but during it.

When a bullfighter conquers or sublimates his fear, unsheathes his *ver-güenza torera*, and enters into combat with a deadly but cooperative animal, he is liable to achieve, at least momentarily, an ecstatic state. The exact nature of the sensations felt can only be approximated by vague metaphors of inebriation or sexual fulfillment. In describing a particularly successful *faena* or flannel performance, it is common for a critic to write that so-and-so "se emborrachó de torear"—"got drunk on bullfighting"—and it is something crowds respond to with great enthusiasm. El Cordobés reached such a state, apparently, during one of the best publicized faenas of the sixties. The bull he had drawn was unusually noble, and the young matador was determined to play him for all he was worth. According to his biographers, "No frantic warning, no plea for caution, could stop him. He was at that instant, he could later recall, 'crazy happy.' He was hypnotized by his own success with this animal, unable to think of anything else but that splendid, drunken feeling of power each movement, each pass of the bull, gave him."[57] (A hornthrust to the thigh soon brought El Cordobés back to reality.) According to Dr. Fernando Claramunt, a matador in the middle of an ideal faena can be hypnotized by the rhythm of the passes and arrive at a state of consciousness that paradoxically combines hyperlucidity with surrender to the most primary instinctual processes, accompanied by annulment of superego censure and indifference to blood and pain.[58] In a less scientific vein, Hemingway writes of one bullfighter who got so excited by his own dominance during a faena that he knelt down and bit one of the bull's horns.[59]

Some matadors describe the experience with patently erotic analogies. According to matador Juan Mora:

> When you are perfectly dominating a bull, if you reflect on what is happening to you at that moment, it is, at least for me, as if the bull were a woman and you were carrying out a coitus. Every part of you seems to stand on end and one enjoys it very much. If the faena isn't good, of course, everything collapses.[60]

Another bullfighter, Lázaro Carmona, corroborates his colleague's experiences:

> You are elevated, you forget everything. The bull excites you in such a way that you live him as something marvelous, especially when there is danger and it is

> dominated. The only thing you think about is to seduce and dominate the bull, and when you do it is a great pleasure, but I do not have *the other thing*.[61]

"The other thing" that the bullfighter is referring to is an ejaculation, something that numerous bullfighters have apparently experienced but do not wish to comment upon.[62]

It would be misleading, in any case, to take the sexual metaphor too literally or too explicitly. A faena is not a coitus, but the interaction of a man with a beast that he is getting ready to kill. This puts any eroticism present at an entirely different level, a level of excess, taboo violation, and sadistic fantasy of the kind explored by Georges Bataille.[63] Social scientists have yet to decide whether aggression or sexuality should be ranked first in the hierarchy of human impulses, but they undoubtedly intertwine in all of us. It is perhaps inevitable that a duel to the death between two different species should elicit all manner of unconscious associations and/or physiological responses. Personally, I believe it would be more helpful to picture the matador as a warrior rather than a sadist. The overpowering emotions that a matador occasionally feels can thereby be seen in terms of the ecstasy that old-time warriors achieved in their own duels to the death and orgies of destruction.

> This *furor*, as the Romans termed it, may be compared with the Celtic notion of *ferg*, the Germanic concept of *wut*, and the Greek idea of *ménos*; all these terms refer to the exalted state—the heightened prowess and the blind fury—which comes over the warrior and enables him to perform otherwise impossible feats. . . . Later on, as Rome developed into a major power, the idea of *furor* was played down, for it interfered with the discipline necessary to the successful functioning of the legions; single combat was superseded by a disciplined attack by massed infantry. Among the Germans and Celts, however, the emphasis upon single combat did not diminish and this aspect of their Indo-European heritage remained important.[64]

In bullfighting the emphasis has always been on single combat. During the nineteenth century—the so-called "Heroic Age" of bullfighting—tauromachy was seen not so much as a fine art as a martial art; matadors were identified as warriors or gladiators and their faenas as so many episodes of a grandiose popular saga. In his review of thousands of nineteenth-century newspaper chronicles, Francisco de Cossío discovers a constant concern for the "purity of the fiesta," which in practice meant the manner in which the matador was expected to execute the final swordthrust—"the very moment in which the dueling character of the bullfight is most in evidence."[65]

It is not necessary to assume that matadors represent the latest and possibly the last exponent of ancient Indo-European warrior ecstasy, although the thought is a tempting one. It would not be farfetched, however, to suggest that the invention of the modern bullfight was accompanied by a return to a most primitive mode of emotionality, one that served to reinforce a most primitive code of honor. In the last analysis, *vergüenza torera* represents an utterly atavistic warrior ethos, an ethos that requires its practitioners to make sport of bloodshed, to seek out death and mock it. It somehow seems appropriate that a profession that puts a man's tomorrow in such jeopardy should dispense such an intense degree of satisfaction today. By all accounts, the heady delusion of omnipotence that matadors experience, in combination with an understandable desire to play the hero, is quite addictive. In this sense, a retired bullfighter is like a reformed alcoholic, always on the verge of a relapse into his favorite vice. Sometimes death is the only sure cure. Consider Manuel Fuentes Rodríguez, alias Bocanegra, a brave but mediocre nineteenth-century bullfighter who managed to stay alive in bullrings for nearly twenty-five years. After his retirement he remained, naturally enough, a bullfight addict, and one bright June day of 1889 found him in the plaza of Baeza (Jaén) watching four apprentice toreros being terrorized by a bull named Hormigón. Although age, syphilis, and obesity had increased his natural clumsiness, Bocanegra jumped into the ring to save the day; he was instantly rewarded for his heroism with a tremendous hornthrust to the belly and died a day later.[66]

Unlike the guapos and bravos that preceded him, the majo/matador used his sword not on a human but on an animal rival, thus making him a public and socially acceptable hero. But as Cossío says, the bullfight's final act, the *suerte de matar*, is still very much like a duel. The time has come to turn our attention to the nature of the opponent. Although we have said much about the new breed of plebeian bullfighters, we have yet to mention the new breed of bulls that came about as the taurine spectacle evolved. Not that I am about to launch into a study of animal husbandry in Spain. As we will see, the social aspects of brave bull breeding are much more intriguing than the biological aspects. In the last analysis, the breeding of brave bulls is important because the bulls become the principal agent in the natural selection of men.

3. Brave Cattle, Brave Men

CONTRARY TO what some might have expected, the most resolute adversaries of bullfighting have always been Spaniards. There has never been a period of Spanish history, in fact, from the Middle Ages to the present day, that has not witnessed a clash between the apologists of bullfighting in one form or another and those who would abolish it for good. Outnumbered and outgunned, the abolitionists have failed miserably. Again and again they have marshalled their arguments and charged, like so many Don Quixotes, only to be bested at every encounter by the defenders of tradition, history, and the Spanish way of life.

The burden of proof has always been on the side of the attackers; the defenders have merely had to establish reasonable doubt in order to contain and neutralize the attackers and keep their opinions from spreading to the masses. And the bullfight has remained in place, century after century. Consider the cruelty argument, for example. For many it might seem obvious that the bullfight constitutes cruelty to animals and/or to humans; in practice, nevertheless, the charge of cruelty is hard to make stick and vulnerable to several modes of counterattack. One of the more eloquent refutations of the cruelty accusation was penned some years ago by a Jesuit priest, Father Julián Pereda, who derided it as "sickly sentimentalism" and the "misbegotten offspring of theosophical materialism."[1] Father Pereda argued that humans have been authorized by God to use animals for their own purposes, as stated in the Bible itself. Citing dogmas, encyclicals, and papal bulls, he meticulously removed any possible basis for thinking that there is something immoral about bullfighting. He even recalled the many Spanish preachers who used taurine terminology to explain the great mysteries of the faith.[2]

Throughout the past two centuries, the moral authority of the Church has never been brought to bear against bullfighting, and herein lies a major secret of its survival. As we saw in the previous chapter, the rise of bullfighting on foot was associated with the consolidation of casticismo, a conservative and traditionalist movement that renounced the Enlightenment

and all its works. It is not surprising, therefore, that a reactionary and bellicose Spanish Church would develop a remarkable tolerance for a *castizo*
spectacle like the corrida de toros. Bloody though it might have been, bullfighting did not interfere with the faith, it did not threaten established
hierarchies, it provided a safe outlet for pent-up frustration, and it even
upheld the manly virtues of old that Spanish priests and friars had always
been enamoured of.[3]

The most formidable arguments that have been arrayed against the bullfight have not been religious but social, economic, or political in nature,
and they have been formulated not from the right but from the left, if we
understand the left to include the progressive, secularizing, and reform-
minded members of the Spanish Enlightenment (Ortega's "men of quality") and their Regenerationist heirs of the nineteenth and twentieth centuries. The bullfight debate, therefore, can conveniently be seen against the
familiar gestalt of *las dos Españas*, "the two Spains" that warred against each
other, with words and deeds, through much of modern Spanish history.

The story of the thrusts and counterthrusts of Spanish taurophobes and
taurophiles is varied and fascinating, and has been dealt with in detail by a
number of scholars.[4] By way of simplifying this complex terrain, it can be
shown that most of the acccusations have a common ambition. Time and
again they have sought to show that the bullfight is related in some way to
their country's sorry economic and political condition. A few, like Eugenio
Noel, rashly concluded that bullfighting was nothing less than the *cause* of
Spanish decadence. Most, however, have stuck to a more moderate line of
attack and have diagnosed the bullfight as the most telling symptom of a
disease that afflicts the nation as a whole. It is here, finally, that the proponents of bullfighting have been forced to retreat and regroup, for it
would seem undeniable that Spain has been so afflicted.

In this century such arguments were given a boost by Ortega y Gasset's
dissection of the Spanish nobility. For Ortega, the institutionalization of
bullfighting on foot in the eighteenth century was a crucial event, one that
helped to make the class system of Spain different from that of any other
European country; when the aristocrats backed away from the ideals of the
Enlightenment and started to ape plebeian styles and plebeian sports, it
was tantamount to their abdication of social responsibility. Result: an in-
vertebrate and directionless Spain collapsed upon itself, to writhe in economic backwardness and sterile civil wars throughout the nineteenth century.[5] The philosopher's idea that bullfighting had greatly contributed to
the inversion of the Spanish class system clearly reflected his own efforts to
shock the Spanish ruling class into action. Ortega, to be sure, was neither

a fan nor an opponent of the bullfight; he simply used the bullfight, and casticismo in general, as a whip with which to flail the aristocracy for its failure to live up to its position and supply Spain with a much-needed backbone.

Other scholars have echoed and amplified the dark tenor—and implicit elitism—of Ortega's views. Pérez Delgado, another sociologist, associates the growing plebeianization of seventeenth-century bullfighting with anti-Semitic massacres, miraculously bleeding icons, long processions of hysterical monks, and other signs of social chaos.[6] Araúz de Robles argues that eighteenth-century nobles resting on their laurels were fascinated by the plebeian "mirage," blinded by the flashy acts of bravery protagonized by their servants, and deluded into thinking that somehow something good could come from the lowborn.[7] All of these scholars, Ortega included, remind us of the seventeenth- and eighteenth-century observers of corridas who perceived social evolution in terms of pollution or contamination. Such observers spoke with alarm about the dangerous mixing of men with women and one social class with another; they claimed that the rise of bullfighting on foot was accompanied by "anarchy" and "promiscuity." The most noteworthy attacks were penned by an author who hid his identity under the pseudonym of *el Pensador matritense* ("the Thinker of Madrid"). This writer was obsessed with the numerous possibilities for indecency that bullrings occasioned, where women offered fleeting glimpses of their legs as they climbed up the bleachers and where both sexes took advantage of the crowded conditions to press against one another in "suspicious" ways. The Thinker considered the worst offenders to be "those who are called majos and majas and other libertine and dissolute people" for whom bullfights were an excuse for joy, drinking, profanity, noisemaking, and general licentiousness.[8]

Like the anonymous "Thinker of Madrid," Ortega and his disciples take for granted that in order for a society to work it must have a fluid, functional aristocracy and a populace that knows its place. There is, in addition, an element of puritanism involved: bullfights are sinful not only because they put one sex into close physical proximity with the other but also because both sexes should be out there working instead of living it up at the fiesta de toros. In a careful examination of Ortega's position, Gil concludes that the great philosopher had essentially reproduced the old Regenerationist claim that the Spanish love of bulls was the major component of the wasteful, gratuitous, and economically ruinous hedonism that kept Spain from making genuine material progress:

It is almost as if Ortega glorified in decadence, entertained himself with degradation, and congratulated himself for impotence: happiness in social nihilism—
that is what it implies to hold a fiesta de toros in a space made empty by the lack
of social leadership.[9]

For the sake of argument, nevertheless, let us agree to overlook the
element of elitist moralizing in Ortega and those who draw their inspiration from him. We can then admit that their basic argument possesses a
certain surface plausibility. We already confirmed in the previous chapter
that a substantial amount of prestige and even moral authority passed
from the nobles to the common people in the eighteenth century. In general, the rise of casticismo, majismo, popular theatres, and bullfighting on
foot would seem to suggest that a true social revolution had taken place.
Unfortunately, however, the ancien régime aristocracy was never really un-
seated. As soon as we look more closely into the social background of bullfighting, we begin to suspect that Ortega's obituary on the nobility was, to
say the least, premature.

A Strategic Retreat

To begin with, the same scholars who castigate the Spanish nobility for
their lack of moral prestige or civic responsibility in the eighteenth century
are quick to acknowledge that the nobles retained every bit of their legal
and economic preponderance. They continued to benefit from centuries-
old systems of tribute, rights of inheritance, feudal jurisdictions, and so
forth, and above all they continued to possess the vast quantities of land
upon which all their other privileges were based. According to a census
taken in 1797—at the very end of the "revolutionary" inception of the modern corrida—the Spanish nobility owned 15 cities, 267 towns, 400 game
preserves, 430 *despoblados*, or uninhabited regions, 612 farms, 671 villages,
and 2,286 hamlets.[10] The three percent of Spaniards who occupied the top
of the social pyramid possessed something like 97 percent of the Iberian
peninsula.[11] There was, therefore, no "collapse" of the aristocracy in
eighteenth-century Spain, certainly not in the all-important economic terrain. Moreover, ownership of huge estates went hand in hand with ownership of vast herds of livestock, especially of the species *bos taurus* that roamed
over the vast plains of the southern and western areas of the country.
Such statistics could well lead us to reinterpret the significance of the

end of the knightly bullfighting on horseback and the beginning of the plebeian bullfighting on foot that we discussed in detail in the last chapter. As we saw, the respect owed to the new Bourbon monarch was the initial stimulus. Felipe V disdained bullfighting and courteous aristocrats were not inclined to contradict him. But a passion that had been so closely identified with the glory days of Spain and the martial valor of their own lineages could not really be expected to evaporate overnight. It is entirely possible, in fact, that in abandoning the urban corridas to the plebeians, the aristocratic class was really carrying out a kind of strategic retreat. Naturally the nobles most closely associated with or dependent upon the Bourbon monarchy would go the farthest in adopting a refined Gallicized lifestyle. But those sectors of the nobility whose status and power were based on their control of the rural land mass (and the rural masses on the land) would remain partial to equestrian and taurine traditions, bide their time, and eventually secure for themselves a crucial role in the newly plebeianized corrida de toros. Though no longer the protagonists of the bullfight, the agrarian-based nobility would reassert themselves in three ways: (1) by constructing and managing the new public buildings known as bullrings; (2) by using their influence to promote and protect the first great bullfighters; and, above all, (3) by breeding the kind of bull that the new bullfighters and their fans required for their spectacles. It is in the origins of brave bull breeding that we can most easily appreciate the long-term significance of the aristocrats' "strategic retreat." Here we discover a number of fascinating ideological and psychological aspects that have shaped Spanish bullfighting, and Spanish society itself, to this very day.

Before the eighteenth century, Spanish bulls bred themselves with no interference from the human species. As the reader will recall from the first chapter, Iberia had been home to enormous numbers of wild bulls for thousands of years. Their numbers were never depleted by Bronze Age hunters, Roman conquerors, Moorish invaders, or Christian re-conquerors. No one even tried to count the bovids until 1768, in fact, when the Royal Council of Castile sent its agents out into rural Spain to take a survey. The project failed miserably. The peasants suspected that the official survey was the first step in a secret plan to prohibit their beloved fiestas de toros; so they lied about the actual number of bulls. The people of Ronda (Málaga), for example, reported to the authorities that there were 4,400 cows but only seven bulls in their area.[12] We know, nevertheless, that *torradas*, or herds of wild bulls, were plentiful throughout Spain, grazing, cavorting, and breeding, and acquiring special *bravura* (aggressiveness) in the marshes of western Andalusia and along the banks of the Tajo and

Jarama rivers. Numerous accounts written by foreign travelers of the seventeenth and eighteenth centuries testify to the existence of enormous herds of brave cattle, roaming freely over the vast properties of the titled nobility.[13]

When knightly bullfighting was in flower, the nobles would either send their peons into the country to round up and capture as many bulls as they could or buy them from one of the many towns or villages that specialized in providing bulls for the grandiose spectacles of the elite. But as taurine historians point out, there was never any guarantee that the merchandise would meet specifications; not every wild bull had the right amount of bravura to make the aristocrat look good with his lance. Thus, a large number of bulls was supplied in the hopes that enough of them would act out their roles convincingly. Those that did not were harassed and worn down by packs of dogs and gangs of *desjarretadores* who sliced the tendons in the bull's hindquarters and ignobly finished him off with a knifethrust to the spinal cord.[14]

As bullfighting on foot became ever more popular in the eighteenth century, the demand for bulls increased accordingly—especially for bulls that could be counted on to charge and not to flee. Until recently it was assumed that progressive and scientifically minded members of the Spanish bourgeoisie deserve the credit for introducing systematic methods of brave cattle breeding to supply the increased popular demand. It now appears, however, that this assumption was wrong. Pedro Romero de Solís has demonstrated in a most convincing way that the credit belongs almost entirely to the aristocracy. And most ironic of all, the nobles achieved success not through science but through the same techniques of selective breeding that they had practiced on themselves for centuries.

Here in brief is the new paradigm. The celebrated *toro bravo* of Spain can be seen as the end result of the projection of a feudal ideology onto a wild animal species. At the root of this ideology lay the idea of consanguinity. For centuries, the noble families of Spain (and elsewhere) had based their alleged superiority and right to rule on the purity of their blood. An almost permanent state of warfare had functioned as a kind of natural selection, a true survival of the fittest; mounted warriors proved the quality of their own blood by spilling the enemy's; landed estates were the coveted rewards for this hazardous testing. This combined with another form of selection through marriages—marriages that had nothing to do with love and everything to do with the nobles' desire to reproduce themselves within a limited circle and maintain the continuity of their battle-tested traits. When the historical occasion was ripe, the landed aristocrats

of Spain reproduced this same ideology, the only one they could understand, in their cattle-breeding techniques: first they tested the bravura of
the bulls with a procedure known as the *tienta* (similar to a piccing but
without actual wounding) and then they perpetuated the blood of the
bravest through consanguineous mating.[15] In other words, the same two
selection techniques that had produced noble people served to produce
noble bulls. Whether or not we think that aristocrats were a superior species, it is unquestionable that the animals they came to breed were amaz-
ingly consistent in their power, size, and aggressiveness.

Romero de Solís clinches his argument by pointing out that the progressive, scientifically minded bourgeoisie of the Enlightenment sub-
scribed to a completely different theory of how both human and animal
races were to be improved. According to the French naturalist Georges
Louis Leclerc de Buffon (1707–1788), breeding progress lay in breaking
down the closed wall of consanguinity and incorporating new bloodlines.
This theory was enthusiastically embraced by the bourgeoisie because it fit
in so well with their own ideology of love, marriage, social mobility, and
individual freedom. Marvelous as this ideology has been for human breeding, however, it could have negative results for animal breeding: Spain's
native population of purebred horses was hybridized out of existence with
techniques á la Buffon.[16]

Speaking of horses, Gil Calvo has pointed out that what Spanish aristocrats did for bulls has an exact parallel in what British aristocrats did with
their stallions, that is, developing a purebred species through artificial
methods of selection based on their own class ideology. He then uses this
parallel to rebut the Regenerationist critics who claimed that bullfighting's
wasteful hedonism had kept Spain poor. Since England's extravagant and
unproductive cult of the horse did not keep the country from economic
development, asks Gil Calvo, how can Spain's extravagant and unproductive cult of the bull be blamed for its economic failures?[17] In this context
we ought to mention another feature of the aristocratic lifestyle in England—the fox hunt. The fox hunt can be defined as a showcase ritual for
the riding skills of a social elite that involves great fanfare, excitement, and
animal killing. Although there are a few points of similarity between the
fox hunt and the bullfight, it is here that the parallel between the British
and the Spanish elite breaks down. The fox hunt is a badge of class prestige,
as self-consciously exclusive as yacht racing or polo. But the bullfight is an
interclass affair, a de facto partnership of the highborn and the lowborn.
In Spain, aristocrats remain in the background and offer up their own care-

fully bred animals to be killed by brave commoners, for the amusement of every social sector in between.

If we bear in mind all of the foregoing, we have no choice but to qualify Ortega's portrait of a failed and listless Spanish aristocracy. It would seem, in fact, that the nobles found a perfect way to vindicate their ideology and their very existence in becoming brave cattle breeders. They certainly re-covered some of their lost prestige, at least in the eyes of the people, by providing exemplary purebred beasts for the *fiesta nacional*. And very few things in the history of Spain have made Spaniards as happy as the bull-fight, as Ortega said himself.[18] For a long time, the brand of the bulls to be fought occupied a more important place on bullfighting posters than the names of the fighters themselves, proof of the importance people assigned to the nature of the beasts under development.[19] After all, it is no small feat to turn a wild animal into a domestic one. This point is emphasized in the strongest terms by Romero de Solís, for whom today's toro bravo is not a natural but a cultural product, the result of a conscientious process of cul-tivation. Modern tauromachy would be utterly impossible, he argues, if the aristocrats had not submitted the untamed and unpredictable bull to a de facto process of domestication.[20] As it happens, one of the more pow-erful arguments currently being made by apologists of bullfighting is the ecological one. The Spanish bullfight, they say, is nothing less than an eco-logical preserve. Without it, a valuable and beautiful animal species would not even exist.

Hundreds of brave cattle ranches are now in existence to supply the roughly twenty-five thousand bulls killed every year by Spanish matadors. Interestingly, however, the brave bulls that constitute the indispensable raw material for today's corridas descend from only five different *castas*, or bloodlines: *jijona*, named after Don Blas Jijón, who achieved renown in the latter part of the seventeenth century for his prestigious, reddish-colored bulls; *navarra*, developed by nobles like Don Miguel Sesma or the Duke of Granada (and sketched for posterity by men like Goya); *vistaher-mosa*, the caste from which the majority of modern bulls descend, founded by the Count of Vistahermosa in 1772; *vazqueña*, originally developed by Don Gregorio Vázquez of Utrera, owned at one time by none other than the nightmare of Spanish liberals, King Fernando VII, and eventually ac-quired by the Duke of Veragua; and *cabrera*, a caste characterized by giant horns, long bodies, and fine silky hair, founded by Don Luis Antonio Ca-brera in the first part of the eighteenth century and eventually acquired by Don Eduardo Miura.[21]

In fairness to Ortega, however, we must still entertain the possibility that the aristocrats' skill in breeding brave bulls may not redeem them in the eyes of history. It does seem lamentable, for example, that the prestige of an aristocrat's bulls was largely based on the number of horses, toreros, or innocent bystanders that they had killed or maimed. In the eyes of bull-fighting history, of course, the names and deeds of notorious bulls occupy a place of honor. The process of selection begun by the aristocrats of the eighteenth century begot some spectacular exemplars in the nineteenth, bulls like Saltador, of the Veragua ranch, who disabled seven picadors on October 27, 1841; or Caramelo, of the Suárez Jiménez ranch, who triumphed over a lion and a tiger in the bullring of Madrid on August 15, 1848; or Soberbio, a bull of Hernán Rozalén, who killed twelve horses in Palma de Mallorca in 1869. In the same year, a López Cordero bull named Gordito killed twenty-one horses; the public, deeply moved by Gordito's nobility, intervened to save his life just before banderillas were to be placed. On the eve of Good Friday, 1877, a bull being shipped to Madrid escaped from his railroad crate to fatally gore six people and trample numerous others. The following year, a Linares bull named Morriones killed seven horses and gored two picadors in Granada; his life was spared as a reward. When the same bull was trotted out again on August 20, 1882, now eleven years old, he managed to kill another six horses.[22] These examples can be multiplied almost ad infinitum. Cossío lists hundreds of *toros celebres*, or celebrated bulls, in his encyclopedia.[23]

Hemingway deals with the same topic in *Death in the Afternoon*.[24] As is well known, Hemingway went to Spain to observe bullfighting before 1929, when the military government of Miguel Primo de Rivera ordered the picadors' horses to wear protective padding. With the candor that characterized him, Hemingway writes of the humorous aspects of bulls killing horses:

> There is certainly nothing comic by our standards in seeing an animal emptied of its visceral content, but if this animal instead of doing something tragic, that is, dignified, gallops in a stiff old-maidish fashion around a ring trailing the opposite of clouds of glory it is as comic . . . as when the Fratellinis give a burlesque of it in which the viscera are represented by rolls of bandages, sausages and other things. . . . I have seen it, people running, horse emptying, one dignity after another being destroyed in the spattering, and trailing of its innermost values, in a complete burlesque of tragedy. I have seen these, call them disembowellings, that is the worst word, when, due to their timing, they were very funny. This is the sort of thing you should not admit, but it is because such things have not been admitted that the bullfight has never been explained.[25]

Hemingway goes on to explain that when people truly empathize with the whole well-ordered ritual tragedy of the bullfight, they are not distracted by the incidental comic-tragedy of the horse.[26]

In the context of aristocratic cattle breeding that we have been dealing with, horses are indeed only a part of the general picture. During a lengthy period of bullfighting history, horses were only a means to an end, to be consumed in the demonstration of a bull's bravura and nobility. The bull himself, in turn, had been purebred by the aristocrats to be consumed in the demonstration of the matador's valor and artistry. This leads to a crucial point. Just as the bull has undergone a long process of intense selection to bring out certain traits, the bullfighter has been subjected to a similar, but much harsher, breeding process. Naturally I am not referring to a deliberate or conscious attempt to alter genetic characteristics. I am referring, instead, to a true survival of the fittest in the Spanish social environment, where thousands of men have been used up and discarded in order to produce a very rare breed indeed—the *matador de toros*.

Natural Selection

The popular image of a matador (both in and out of Spain) is usually that of a smiling young man in a glittering suit of lights, facing a murderous bull with haughty resolve, finishing him off with a well-placed sword-thrust, and then bathing in the acclamations of a cheering, carnation-throwing public. This is also the image that every bullfighter or would-be bullfighter himself aspires to embody, of course. But for every successful matador being carried out on the shoulders of his fans, we can well imagine that he is being supported by an invisible army of forgotten young men who tried and failed. Or, to vary the metaphor, we can compare the entire history of bullfighting on foot with those marine species that give birth to hundreds of thousands of young in the hopes that a few will reach maturity. As Francisco de Cossío has pointed out, one needs only to review the biography sections of his uncle's great taurine encyclopedia to appreciate the incredible sacrifices that have been made. (The biographies fill over 2,200 pages of very small print in three different volumes.)

> Every bullfighter began by being a mere promise; only a few managed to become a reality, and very few were able, with the passage of time, to become myths or legendary figures. . . . The most modest bullfighter—he that appeared only once on a bullfight poster of some third-rate, fourth-rate, or fifth-rate

plaza—paid a high price for his contribution, in physical risk and hardship, in order to wear the suit of lights one day, only to fail. Without this enormous sum of failures, we would not be able to attend a corrida de toros today.[27]

In the case of bullfighting, we can cite a number of environmental factors, each harsher than the last, that have effectively eliminated the overwhelming majority of Cossío's "promises." First and foremost, of course, is the toro bravo—himself a product of an intensive process of selection. What the bull's horns can do, and might do, and have done innumerable times, can be counted as the most basic, physical agent of the selection process. Gorings eliminate bullfighters or would-be bullfighters in ways both gross and subtle: anything from death or a crippling mutilation to an invisible but equally disabling loss of will. Although the subject is not particularly pleasant, we would do well to acquaint ourselves briefly with gorings, for they constitute an agent of selection that is operative from the very beginning to the very end of a bullfighter's career. For many young Spaniards, of course, the beginning *was* the end. From 1747 to 1962, at least 153 young aspirants were killed by bulls (as well as 132 banderilleros, 60 picadors, 51 full matadors, and 2 comic bullfighters). The most tragic bullring was far and away that of Madrid, the most dangerous month was August, followed by September and June, and the most fatal cattle brands included Anastasio Martín, Veragua, Concha y Sierra, and Miura. The historian who compiled these statistics acknowledged that they were incomplete and did not include other victims like ring attendants or town fools, nor bullfighters killed during ranch tests or private parties or in the open field.[28] Nor, for that matter, do they include capeas, which have arguably been festal Spain's major device for maiming young bodies and crushing hopes.

In no other country can a medical student specialize in the lucrative field of *taurotraumatología*, or horn wound surgery. Practitioners must know everything that can be known about the symptomatology of gored bullfighters, traumatic hemorrhage, shock, exploration of the wound or wounds, and so forth.[29] Gorings can be very complex, depending upon the area of the body in which they occur, the route or trajectory the horn may take once inside the body, and the movements that a bullfighter may make in attempting to free himself. Hemingway, in training and vocation a keen observer of gore, writes of seeing horn wounds that looked minor on the outside but "when probed and opened inside had as many as five different trajectories, these being caused by the man's body revolving on the horn and, sometimes, by the end of the horn being splintered. All of these inner wounds must be opened and cleaned and at the same time all incisions in the muscle must be made so that it will heal in the minimum of time and with the least possible loss of mobility."[30] Surgical techniques have progressed since Hemingway's day and there have been major advances in antibiotics and painkillers. The horns of bulls have remained much the same, of course, and continue to exact their toll from those who place themselves in front of them.

Since the likelihood of a *cornada*, or horn wound, increases with the frequency of exposure, top-of-the-line matadors with numerous contracts are logically the most vulnerable. During the season of 1989, in fact, the number of famous matadors gored reached epidemic proportions, although fortunately there were no fatalities. In May the Maestranza, Seville's beautiful bullring, witnessed its worst goring in years when Pepe Luis Vázquez was gored by Estudiante, a Gabriel Rojas bull weighing a mere 474 kilograms. Somehow the bull was able to penetrate the thigh and go up into the abdomen, destroying arteries and affecting ilium, intestines, bladder, and rectum.[31] Ironically, it was Curro Romero, a bullfighter (in)famous for his caution, who received one of the more severe gorings of the season: on June 9 in the picturesque plaza of Aranjuez (Madrid), the Sevillian matador suffered a cornada in his inner left thigh with an upper trajectory of ten centimeters and a lower one of twenty centimeters, along with a third wound in the scrotum that eviscerated a testicle. He was also severely bruised from being stepped on by the bull.[32] Two days later, José Luis Parada was gored in the scrotum and the abdomen, with partial disemboweling of the large intestine, by a bull in Barcelona.[33] In Tarragona on August 13, a bull left José Luis Palomar with a five-centimeter hole in his abdomen and a ruptured rectum.[34] The next day in Málaga an up-and-coming novillero called Finito de Córdoba was gored in the thigh, with twelve and eighteen centimeter trajectories, just as he drove a sword into his second novillo; with the foolhardy pride that characterizes bullfighters, Finito pressed his own hands to the wound and waited for the bull to drop before going to the bullring infirmary.[35] There was more of the same two days later, as the brilliant Joselito made a triumphant promenade around the plaza of Málaga with a bull's ear in his hand and a hemorrhaging twelve-centimeter cornada in his leg, the crowd watching in awe as the matador's pink stocking slowly turned red.[36] The worst mishap of all occurred toward the end of the season, and it was not a goring but a tossing. On September 10th, Christian Montcouquiol, alias Nimeño II, considered to be France's number one matador, was thrown high in the air by a Miura bull in Arlès, landing on his neck. Totally paralyzed, he was rushed by helicopter to a hospital in Marseille. By the following summer the French matador had managed to recover some mobility in his arms and legs; but then on August 13, 1990, a Spanish matador named Julio Robles suffered precisely the same injury in the French plaza of Béziers—before the very noses of the local Nimeño II fan club as cruel fate would have it. As the Spaniard lay paralyzed in the hospital of Montpellier, Brigitte Bardot complained that the bull that had tossed him "should have been spared for having proved himself stronger than the torero."[37]

The above chronicle is by no means a complete listing of the damage done by bulls in 1989 and 1990. There were many other cornadas and tossings in plazas the length and breadth of Spain and southern France. In most cases prompt medical care was available for wounded toreros. It is a fact, nonetheless, that the quality of the care increases or descends along with the size and importance of the bullring. In the old days, small-town bullrings were notorious for their deficient infirmaries. And in the not-so-old days as well. On September 26, 1984, the enormously popular Paquirri was gored in the third-rate plaza of Pozoblanco. He received emergency treatment in the bullring infirmary but several hours later he was dead on arrival at the Hospital Militar in Córdoba. The videotape of a calm and smiling Paquirri lying in the decrepit Pozoblanco infirmary still haunts Spaniards. The attending physicians had promptly ligated the femoral artery and everything else that they could see bleeding, but unseen and uncontrolled internal bleeding and the long journey by ambulance to Córdoba induced hypovolemic shock. According to Dr. Bartolomé Beltrán, Paquirri's life would have been saved by helicopter transport, adequate supplies of plasma, a decent operating room, and an abdominal incision to allow suturing of the iliac veins that the bull's horn must have severed in one of the upward trajectories. As it was, the bullring infirmary was only required by law to have one liter of plasma on hand, and it is likely that Paquirri lost almost that much just as he was being carried from the ring. That the matador was succumbing to hemorrhagic shock on the way to Córdoba was evidenced by his own words, "Me ahogo" ("I'm suffocating")—precisely what the great Manolete said shortly after his fatal goring in Linares in 1947.[38]

If adequate medical treatment has sometimes been lacking in the tragic deaths of famous and well-paid matadors, we can well imagine that an even graver state of affairs has prevailed in village capeas. We do not have, nor will we ever have, reliable statistics on the number of apprentice bullfighters who have been maimed or killed in the capeas. The sheer number of such fiestas, the isolation and backwardness of the places that celebrate them, a general acceptance of tragic death as part of the order of things, the lack of hospitals and doctors—these factors in themselves would effectively prevent the recording or even communication of mishaps. In addition, the marginal status of the maletilla—a hungry little nobody from nowhere, in the eyes of many locals—must have made it hard to see any possible transcendence in his injury or death. In the worst cases, the bloodshed of the folk festival was accompanied by the barbarity of folk healers called *curanderos* or *curanderas*. One of Eugenio Noel's most moving pieces was devoted to a description of a clumsy, grandmotherly curandera trying to keep a boy named Tarugo from bleeding to death, prostrate under the sun, surrounded by flies and morbid onlookers.[39] Collins and Lapierre cite the case of Robustiano Fernández, a scrap metal scavenger with big dreams who was gored in a remote village of Extremadura on May 15, 1964. The local midwife applied a tourniquet made from a dirty sheet and he was taken by taxi to Badajoz. When gangrene inevitably set in, he was loaded on a delivery van and shipped to Madrid to have the leg amputated.[40]

If we were to put ourselves in the place of the "Thinker of Madrid," or any other thinker for that matter, we would surely make a rational recommendation: if people cannot count on adequate medical treatment for horn wounds, they should either stay away from bulls or do away with their hazardous blood sport altogether. Unfortunately, the fiesta de toros is not a product of rationality. It is built on the volatile terrain of passion and subject to the blind workings of chance. Somehow it seems appropriate, albeit grotesque, that an almost third world medical infrastructure has served to compound the process of selection by which incompetent and unlucky would-be toreros are eliminated. The incompetent but lucky ones survive to fight another day, hopefully learning from their mistakes and becoming more competent as time goes by and their luck holds out.

In reality, several kinds of testing are going on at the same time. Bulls' horns are there to eliminate those who are not tough enough, agile enough, smart enough, or, naturally, brave enough. It is widely held by taurine experts that the way a bullfighter reacts to his first serious horn wound is crucial to his later success as a matador. When an apprentice bullfighter recovers from his first goring and reappears in the ring, his manager anxiously watches for any sign that his valor or his determination has been compromised. But even if the young man's willpower is intact, and even if he grows in toughness, agility, and intelligence, the powerful element of luck will preside over his career. Luck, above all, in the form of the bull, whose behavior in the ring is never predictable (despite two centuries of breeding); to be successful, a man must meet the right kind of noble, cooperative bull at the right moment of his career. And even that is not enough: he must also have *padrinos*, or godfathers, a good manager, opportunities, a crowd-pleasing personality, grace, flair, and a whole series of other qualities that are hard to isolate but that nevertheless mean the difference between glory and mediocrity.

We can learn a great deal about what it takes to be a bullfighter by studying the careers of the great ones. But we stand to learn even more by examining the failures. The best-selling biographies of successful bullfighters make it easy to forget that the general rule of bullfighting is not success but failure. Moreover, the contrast between the failed bullfighter and the successful one can be very instructive. Everyone, for example, has heard of Manuel Benítez, alias El Cordobés, unquestionably Spain's most famous bullfighter of the past quarter century. But no one has heard of Juan Horrillo, although for years the careers of the two men were almost indistinguishable. Or rather, the two boys. Benítez and Horrillo hailed from the same Andalusian town, Palma del Río (Córdoba); unwanted sons of *jornaleros* or landless day laborers, they both grew up in misery. As Pozo and Bardón relate, the two lads became inseparable: too wild to study and too restless to work in the fields, they became juvenile delinquents; stole tomatoes, chickens, and whatever they could get their hands on; and suffered numerous beatings at the hands of the local Guardia Civil. They were both infected with taurine fever at an early age, as Andalusian ne'er-do-wells often are; they became maletillas and for years they went from one capea to the next, getting gored, starving, begging, jumping fences to fight bulls at night for practice and then jumping freight trains to escape. Two decades after the Civil War, Spain had yet to recover from its devastation. Life was harsh for many, but the two young Andalusians seemed to have a special appetite for hard knocks. Wandering like hobos all over the country, "one was the shadow of the other."[41] They were indistinguishable, then, until one day in May 1960, when they finally got the big break they had been waiting for—a novillada without picadors in their own home town of Palma del Río, featuring a gigantic seven-year-old brave cow named Almendrita. When the moment to prove themselves came, only one of them was able to rise to the occasion. As Horrillo later recalled:

> I was paralyzed. I trembled all over. Those insults kept coming out, and still I couldn't take a step. They began to throw stones and bottles at me. They started to yell "*Fuera, fuera*"—out, out. God, I hated it. And there was Almendrita in the middle of the ring staring at me with those murderous eyes of hers. Suddenly it happened. She came for me. I did a terrible thing then, an unforgiveable thing. I dropped my muleta and ran. I ran as fast as I could for the barrera, as

fast as I ever ran from the Guardia Civil. When I got there, I jumped the barrera and fell into the callejón. As I lay there, shaking, they spat on me. I could hear them all screaming, whistling. It was horrible. I don't know how long I lay there listening, but I know one thing: for me, everything was finished. I could never put on the suit of lights again.[42]

By contrast, Horrillo's friend responded to the same situation with the suicidal courage that would one day make him the legendary (and much-gored) El Cordobés.

Equally instructive is the case of two brothers, the sons of a man who had once dreamed of being a bullfighter and had even managed to debut as a novillero in Madrid's Monumental in 1941, but had ended up working, appropriately enough, in the slaughterhouse of Barbate (Córdoba). Like many other frustrated bullfighters, Antonio Rivera hoped that his sons could succeed where he had failed. He lavished time and taurine lessons on his firstborn, José, taking him to ranches and *tentaderos*, helping him, egging him on. Francisco, the secondborn son, tagged along on these outings, burned with envy, and tried to copy his brother, but did not seem to have any particular aptitude. To make a long story short, José adopted his father's old nickname of Riverita, managed to become a mediocre matador, and eventually settled down as a junk dealer. It was the ignored younger brother Francisco who went on to become a superb and immensely wealthy bullfigher under the name of Paquirri. It was precisely what Paquirri had and Riverita lacked—rivalrous self-affirmation and passionate one-upmanship—that kept him from retiring with his life intact. With the memory of Paquirri's tragic death still fresh in Spaniards' minds, cynical entrepreneurs had no trouble in persuading his brother José to return to bullfighting in a much publicized corrida in Málaga. When asked if he considered himself a better bullfighter than Paquirri, José glibly responded, "I am no better and no worse; I would just say that I have another way of fighting bulls, another style."[43] It is entirely possible that the two brothers were comparable in knowledge of bulls and bullfighting techniques, but many other factors go into the equation. In the case of the Rivera family, the father's favoritism toward the elder son helped to make the younger one a much fiercer competitor than he might have been otherwise.

For more insight into the dynamics of failure and success we can turn to regional histories of bullfighting—books that seek to mention every single bullfighter from a given area by way of demonstrating that area's heroic caliber and appetite for glory. Among the most complete is Sánchez Garrido's chronology of novilleros and matadors of Córdoba province, some of whom achieved great renown (Lagartijo, Guerra, El Cordobés, and others) and most of whom fell short of the mark for one reason or another. Sánchez has chapters with such suggestive titles as "Two Undistinguished Toreros," "Three Promises," "Another Unfulfilled Hope," "The Ones Who Could Have Been," "The Ones Who Could Not Have Been," and "A Luckless Foursome."[44]

The actual case histories of the luckless and the undistinguished prove once again that truth is stranger than fiction. Consider Serranito, for example, who grew up on a brave cattle ranch owned by a famed matador named Machaquito and who strove to achieve the same success in the same way. Serranito had the right "godfathers" or connections and was very good with the sword, but somehow his career never caught fire and he ended up as a telephone company operator. After years away from the bullrings he made a comeback attempt on the Feast of Santiago, 1929, and it literally cost him an arm and a leg.[45]

A fate worse than death was reserved for Paco Asensio. Born in Córdoba in 1946, he killed his first brave calf at age sixteen and was killing novillos (young bulls) by 1965. His career floundered in the following years, however, and when he was all but forgotten he decided in desperation to *tomar la alternativa* (take the alternative), that is, graduate from being a novillero to a full matador in a special bullfight organized for the purpose. It is crucial for a bullfighter to be good on this all-important ritual occasion, but Paco was not, to the point that his appointed bull left the bullring in perfect health and Paco was left in shame too terrible for most of us to imagine. He was finished as a matador before he even started.[46]

Antonio Porras was a more talented and promising novillero who in order to make up for a rather bland personality decided to resuscitate a long-forgotten maneuver called *el salto de la garrocha*—last seen in Goya's engravings. This spectacular suerte calls for the torero to pole-vault over the bull's horns as he charges, landing safely on the ground at the other end of the animal. The public loved to see Porras perform this stunt; on the wings of his popularity (and against the counsel of the critics) the novillero "took the alternative" in Madrid in 1972 and became a matador de toros. Porras managed to fight in twenty-eight corridas before he was seriously gored by a bull he was trying to pole-vault. After two years of convalescence he reappeared in the bullring of Moraleja (Cáceres) and had a brilliant afternoon, cutting three ears. He immediately retired from bullfighting, wisely deciding to do something bullfighters almost never do—quit while they are ahead.[47]

Antonio Benete, a friend of Porras and fellow novillero, could not do the *salto de la garrocha* but he found a different gimmick. By way of communicating to the world just how promising a novillero he thought he was, he adopted the alias of El Mesías—The Messiah. Unable to deliver, however, The Messiah soon found his career adrift. Knowing himself to be on the verge of oblivion, he arranged to be anointed as a full matador in the great plaza of Valencia; but then fate intervened, as it often does on the so-called planet of the bulls, and the bullring veterinarians rejected the bulls that were supposed to be fought. "From that very moment," Sánchez notes dryly, "the sobriquet of 'The Messiah' disappeared from the taurine map."[48]

The case of Fermín Vioque Ruiz illustrates yet another way to disappear. Vioque had acquired valuable experience by traveling through Spain with comic bullfighting spectacles like "The Fireman Torero" and "Cantinflas and His Midget Gladiators." As a novillero in the early 1980s he found himself on the fast track, fighting more corridas every year despite his numerous gorings. (The gorings were attributed to his blind ambition and temerity.) He took the alternative in Córdoba in 1984 and gave a brilliant performance. Then fate intervened—in his favor. A bullfighter who had been scheduled for the next day's corrida had gotten himself gored, and Vioque was called upon to take his place. The bulls were perfect and the new matador gave a stunning performance, enough to earn him the Manolete Award for overall performance and the Machaquito Award for best swordthrust. Dazzled by his success, Vioque decided he didn't need a manager. Result: the contracts dried up and his career came to a screeching halt. As Sánchez observes, bullfighters who "miss their train" find it next to impossible to catch it on the run.[49]

These are just a few examples from the lesser known side of bullfighting in Córdoba; the same story could be told, indeed has been told, for many other Spanish provinces.[50] In reality we are speaking of several thousand young men who left their homes with dreams of glory and came back home lucky to be alive but rejected, dejected, ashamed, and often mutilated. Francisco de Cossío has aptly summarized the general pattern:

> An infinite number of toreros had, at least once, an important triumph, sometimes more than once; they listened to the applause of an ardent public, they were carried out on shoulders—only to see all of their illusions vanish, without ever understanding the cause; even those who managed to remain active and fight a more or less modest number of corridas over several years ended up their careers in oblivion. To triumph again and again and sustain oneself at the top has been a very difficult privilege to acquire in every epoch of bullfighting. To endure in the memory of aficionados, it was essential in some cases to have valor

and in others to have exceptional artistry, and, in either case, an extraordinary personality. Sometimes such a vivid personality that the triumphs made people forget the numerous failures.[51]

If there is a lesson for us all in the tales of failed bullfighters, it would be something like "pride goeth before a fall and a haughty spirit before destruction." Many young men were led into disaster by their overweening egos or their unwillingness to acknowledge their own defects and inadequacies. In recounting a given novillero's comeuppance, Sánchez himself often adopts a fatherly/judicial tone of "it's your own fault because you were so vain." Not knowing how to fight bulls should obviously not mean the end of the world for anyone; in fact many taurine failures went on to be wise, reality-chastened, more mature individuals. Many others, unfortunately, never saw the error of their ways and spent the rest of their lives making excuses, blaming this padrino or that cattle breeder, hoping against hope for a comeback opportunity, never having actually learned their lesson or matured. Maturity might not have been all that easy to obtain, at any rate, under a sociopolitical system that gave such incredible rewards to a finite number of foolhardy men with agility, good wrists, and what Stanley Brandes terms "testicular willpower."[52]

As it happens, the process by which men fail at being matadors is much the same process by which men become *peones*, that is, subordinate members of the bullfighter's *cuadrilla*, or crew. Surely one of the great ironies of bullfighting on foot is that, plebeian invention that it is, cuadrillas replicate the rigid hierarchical mentality of ancien regime Spain. The very order in which they promenade into the bullring is significant. The matador is the boss, the *jefe absoluto*, the caudillo; he comes first, followed by the men who failed to make it as matadors and who perform a variety of supporting roles during the corrida; they place banderillas, they finish off a dying bull, they pick up the carnations and other offerings the public throws to the triumphant matadors. The matador's assistants are euphemistically known as "men of silver," the better to contrast them with the matador, who alone may wear golden adornments on his suit of lights.

A number of twentieth-century Spanish authors have explored the small-group dynamics of cuadrillas and the plight of the peón, who is constantly reminded of his subordinate status. As the cuadrilla travels from one bullfight to another, writes Cela Trulock, the peón is always the one with the worst seat in the car; no one ever laughs at his jokes; at the end of the journey he has to unpack everything and sleep in a inferior room, never daring to take seconds in the hotel dining room, and so on.[53] The final irony: statistics show that it is almost three times as dangerous to be a banderillero as a matador.[54] If they meet with death in the bullring, however, banderilleros or other peones may be mourned, but they have never been mythified like martyred matadors.

In all of the proceeding it has been apparent that the major device of selection has been the bull, not only for the physical but for the psychological damage that he can do to apprentice toreros. Yet there is another factor of selection that has been every bit as powerful and effective in weeding out the incompetent, the unlucky, and the mediocre—bullfight spectators. For the purposes of this chapter, bullfight spectators can be divided into two groups: (1) those for whom bullfighting is a pastime, a predilection, or a passion; and (2) those for whom it is a profession and a source of income. The first category comprises the great majority of observers, ordinary people who express their approval and disapproval on the spot in the most vocal way imaginable. The second category is comprised of a tiny but highly influential minority of bullfight critics, people who express their approval or disapproval with somewhat less passion and somewhat greater finesse. Taurine journalism is a very old profession in Spain, and quite broad in its scope; it combines basic reporting with literature, sports commentary with art criticism, and straightforward bullfight chronicles with history, politics, philosophy, or aesthetics.[55] More will be said in the next chapter about the elitist bias of many critics, their partisanship, and their occasional venality. More will be said, as well, about the mass psychology of the ordinary spectators that taurine critics have always looked down upon. For now it is enough to underline the role of journalists in the selection process we have been describing. It is no exaggeration to say that the pen of a hostile critic can do almost as much damage to a bullfighter's aspirations as the horn of a raging bull.

The most important English-language taurine critic, and one of the most demanding and outspoken ones in any language, was the American Ernest Hemingway. In *Death in the Afternoon*, Hemingway makes it clear that his sympathies are not with the bullfighters but with spectators like himself who have purchased their tickets and therefore have a right to see a man perform with integrity and style in front of serious bulls.[56] Hemingway looked around himself and saw "seven hundred and sixty-some unsuccessful bullfighters still attempting to practice their art in Spain; the skillful ones unsuccessful through fear and the brave ones through lack of talent."[57] Readers can still find amusement in some of Hemingway's descriptions of toreros, unfortunate fellows like Domingo Hernandorena, "a short, thick-ankled, graceless Basque with a pale face who looked nervous and incompletely fed in a cheap rented suit" and whose "effort to be statuesque while his feet jittered him away out of danger was very funny to the crowd," or José Amorós, "who has a peculiar rubbery style, seeming to stretch away from the bulls as though he were made of elastic bands, and is completely second-rate, except of course in his unique rubberyness," or Chucho, considered by Hemingway to be brave and highly competent but berated for "a sort of apologetic, slinking, faulty, hump-backed way of carrying himself when he is not directly involved with the bull."[58] Hemingway is at his most merciless when it comes to *fenómenos* or one-triumph bullfighters:

> Five years from now, eating only occasionally but keeping their one suit neat to wear to the café, you will be able to hear them tell how, on their presentation in Madrid, they were better than Belmonte. It may be true too. "And how were you the last time?" you ask. "I had a little bad luck killing. Just a little bad luck," the ex-phenomenon says, and you say "That's a shame. A man can't have luck killing them all," and in your mind you see the phenomenon, sweating, white-faced and sick with fear, unable to look at the horn or go near it, . . . cushions sailing down and into the ring and the steers ready to come in. "Just a little bad luck killing." That was two years ago and he hasn't fought since except in bed at night when he wakes up with sweat and fear and he will not fight again unless hunger makes him and then, because everyone knows he is a coward and worthless, he may have to take some bulls that no one else will take and if he nerves himself up to do something, since he is out of training, the bulls may kill him. Or else he may have, "Just a little bad luck killing," again.[59]

Few passages are more revealing of Hemingway's style and obsessions than this one, except perhaps for those in which he adulates the handful of bullfighters who are "honorable" enough to give spectators their money's worth of suicidal valor.

In all fairness to Hemingway, however, it must be pointed out that he came much closer than most critics to approximating the sentiments and perspectives of the masses. It was precisely Hemingway's identification with the broad public that irritated some elitist critics.[60] But it is well to remember that it is the masses, after all, who make or break a bullfighter with their applause or their indifference; influential as some critics have been, the majority rules in Spain's taurine "democracy." And in every age, the majority has applauded bravery much more fervently than art. That is why the professional critics, who generally favor art over bravery, were so irritated with the success of the artless but insanely valiant El Cordobés. In the final analysis, the critics and the public represent two sides of the same coin. Both contribute in their own way to the cruel process of selection that has ground up the bodies and aspirations of thousands of men to produce a handful of mythical figures.

The Forging of a Masochist

In view of the bloody selection process discussed above, it might well be asked why any young man in his right mind would want to be a bullfighter. Bullfighters themselves have answered this question in many ways, but no answer has had the resonance of the one given by the famous nineteenth-century matador Espartero. The victim of numerous gorings, Espartero was asked why he kept on. His laconic response has been cited ever since, by taurophobes and taurophiles alike: *"Más cornás da el hambre"* ("Hunger gives more cornadas").[61]

At first glance this answer would seem to be the sad incontrovertible truth. In the past two centuries the overwhelming majority of bullfighters have come from the bottom of the social heap. A sociologist like Pérez Delgado does not hesitate to cite the Espartero quote in support of his view that poverty is the "social cause" of bullfighting.[62] For a number of historical and economic reasons that need not be gone into here, large portions of the Spanish population have been condemned to poverty, illiteracy, and lack of opportunity. This much is unquestionable. Harsh as they have been, however, these necessary social conditions are not sufficient in themselves to explain matador motivation. They obviously would not tell us why bullfighters who were already immensely wealthy—like Espartero or Belmonte or Paquirri—remained in the plazas. And they are even insufficient as initial motivation. As Pérez de Ayala pointed out when glossing Espartero's famous line, hunger would logically lead men to rob and to kill but not to dedicate themselves to the profession of receiving constant cornadas; otherwise, there would be as many million bullfighters as there are poor people in Spain.[63] Scores of men who had found or could have found regular employment wanted only to fight bulls. Clearly we must seek out additional motivational factors to explain why only a relative minority of poor young Spaniards have reacted to poverty in a way unlike that of everyone else sharing the same fate, actually preferring cornadas to hunger pangs or hard work in fields and factories.

A number of studies have confirmed what we might well have expected: bullfighters have masochistic tendencies. In an often cited study carried out by a team of doctors at the University of Pamplona in the 1960s, some four hundred toreros were given the Szondi test and were found to rate much higher on the masochistic side of the sadomasochistic scale. Phobic and obsessive-compulsive traits were also present, undoubtedly related to the numerous superstitions and rituals bullfighters are known to engage in.[64] Delgado Ruiz cites a more recent study that showed bullfighters to harbor strong albeit indirect tendencies toward self-destruction: Drs. Cruz and Corominas of the Facultad de Medicina of the University of Barcelona gave toreros the Minnesota Multiphasic Personality Inventory and found important suicidal tendencies among them.[65]

It is easy to find passages in taurine biographies that corroborate these findings. Consider, for example, Juan Belmonte's statement:

> I have the knack of fervently desiring, with all the powers of my soul, that which can do me the most harm. Only in this way can I hope to exorcise evil. It is as if I wanted to grab Destiny by the horns. I have already said that the ideal faena I dreamed of when I wanted to become a bullfighter invariably ended with the bull giving me a cornada in the thigh.[66]

Belmonte, incidentally, is considered to be the father of the modern style of bullfighting; when he introduced his revolutionary style of working close to the bulls in the second decade of this century, the public and the critics rushed to see him, certain that his death was only a matter of time. It is hard to believe that his own self-confessed fantasies of self-destruction did not play a large role in his success.

The biography of another famous bullfighter, El Cordobés, could almost be titled "The Forging of a Masochist." Born two months before the outbreak of the Spanish Civil War, Manuel Benítez had such a dirty, half-starving, chaotic babyhood that by the age of three, his sister says, he had already forgotten how to cry. Subsequent years of chronic malnutrition "burned his body down to muscle, bone, and skin." When instead of working or studying he preferred to trespass onto ranches and play with brave cattle by the light of the moon, his sister beat him as hard as she could: "He'd never cry or say he was sorry." That was nothing compared to what the bulls themselves gave him, or savage guard dogs, and even the animals were bested by the Guardia Civil: Manuel and his inseparable pal Juan Horrillo were bludgeoned every time they were caught in the fields, and sometimes "the Guardia Civil didn't even bother looking for some sign of their nocturnal corridas. They gave them a beating anyway, convinced of its therapeutic value."[67] At one point the beating was followed by a ten-day stint in a stable where they were forced "to eat like animals, scooping their oats from the horses' troughs by the fistful. For drinking water, they plunged their mouths into the same rusty buckets used by the horses."[68] When they were finally thrown out of Palma del Río, they did what taurine ne'er-do-wells from all over Spain did and hopped a freight train bound for the capital. As El Cordobés later recalled:

> My first memory of Madrid is being kicked in the ass by a cop. We were half asleep in a doorway, where we had lain down to get out of the cold. I felt this terrific pain. Then I heard a voice yelling, "Get up, get up." I rolled over and caught another kick—in the ear. . . . He made us go with him to the police station. . . . I explained that we were toreros looking for an *oportunidad*. I waited for the beating to start. That's the way it would have been in Palma, a beating, and then they'd lock us up for a while. What I didn't realize was that in Palma there was no one else like us. In Madrid there were hundreds. The police didn't have time to bother with us. They yelled "Anda!" and threw us out of the station. We went back to our doorway and went back to sleep.[69]

It is clear from the above that besides being a glutton for punishment, Manuel Benítez forged his identity through defiance, persisting in the very acts for which he was being punished so harshly. It might well be conjectured that the masochistic tendencies revealed by studies and biographies of bullfighters are closely related to an untamed and untamable will to have one's way at whatever the cost. Manuel obstinately resolved to be a bullfighter precisely because the whole universe seemed to be against the idea; the more beatings he got, the more he became convinced of the value of his quest. In other words, his desire was a function of the obstacles placed in his path. To better understand El Cordobés and numerous other matadors, it behooves us to look more closely into the relationship betwen masochism, desire, authority conflicts, and the dialectical or mimetic rivalry that sets everything else in motion.

Rivalry, to begin with, is nothing less than the nucleus of bullfighting, both structurally and historically. Structurally, we have the basic competition between man and bull, a plot that has remained fixed for centuries. Historically, as we saw earlier, the institution that showcases this primary rivalry was itself the object of a prolonged class rivalry: the proletariat eventually wrested control of the taurine spectacle from the aristocrats. Subsequently, intense rivalries between matadors of different "schools" or styles provoked passionate partisanship in the masses year after year and decade after decade.[70] And yet a fourth type or degree of rivalry must be mentioned, one more metaphysical than the previous three—the sense of competition with great idols of the past. Claramunt refers to the keen envy that Ignacio Sánchez Mejías felt for Joselito, who had been fatally gored in 1920 and deified by the masses and was distressingly out of reach.[71] A similar phenomenon has been recorded among other men obsessed with insurmountable role models: the foremost expert on nineteenth-century *bandolerismo* spoke of the "magic and prestige" that legends of celebrated bandits held for their unsung successors and the resultant inferiority complex that more than one labored under.[72]

As we saw in the last chapter, the bandits, guapos, bravos, and assorted tough guys that populated eighteenth-century Spain had a keen and touchy regard for their reputations and rarely missed a chance to settle their rivalries through violence. Their sense of honor, in other words, was exaggerated enough to supplant the survival instinct itself. This is the beginning of *vergüenza torera*, also called *pundonor*, the code of honor that tough guys took with them when they replaced the patriciate in the bullrings. Caro Baroja relates all of this to the tragic flaw of hubris and shows how it fits into the closed, cyclical, and fatalistic world of popular romance.[73] Unlike professional swashbucklers, matadors use their swords on the bull, not on each other; and crowds idolize them when their swordhandling skill is accompanied by *vergüenza torera*.

For the purposes of this chapter, we can redefine *vergüenza torera* as metaphysical desire, that is, the willful, envious, and potentially pathological spirit of self-affirmation elicited by rivals and/or other sorts of obstacles.[74] This should enable us to account not only for the historical or mythic dimensions of taurine motivation but its ongoing psychological dynamics as well.

The case of Paquirri illustrates how envy and rivalry engendered in childhood can mean the difference between a great matador (like Paquirri) and a mediocre one (like his older brother, or, for that matter, his father). As the reader will recall from the previous section, Antonio Rivera's partiality toward his elder son spawned an irrepressible and eventually fatal spirit of competitiveness in the younger one. The Rivera family romance was hardly exceptional; as Claramunt notes in his review of torero motivations, the transmission of taurine desire from fathers to sons, or from uncles to nephews, is extraordinarily frequent.[75] It is common for men who have failed as bullfighters to fill their sons' heads with fantasies of glory and set in motion a complex dynamics of identifications and counteridentifications. How is a son to know, for example, if his father really wants him to succeed where he didn't or fail and be *just like* father? In any country, the son can be confused when the person ordering the son to outdo his father is the father himself. In an old-fashioned God- and father-fearing country like Spain, and in the context of a patriarchal and oedipally charged affair like animal-killing, father-son relations can be unusually intense and contradictory. As one matador told Claramunt, "By no means did I wish to achieve what my father was incapable of. That would have been a sign of a bad son. What happened is that as soon as I could I told him to keep his nose out of my business because when I was fifteen years old I knew a lot more about bulls·than he ever did."[76] One of the elder Cossío's favorite anecdotes had to do with an apprentice torero of Valladolid called El Besuguito, whose clumsiness made crowds laugh but who stayed in bullrings at the behest of his father. As the son did what he could with a given bull, his father would watch intently with cane in hand. One afternoon El Besuguito was performing miserably against a particularly difficult bull; from behind the barrera his father brandished his cane and shouted, "You're making me look ridiculous in front of everybody! I'm going to beat you to death as soon as you get home! Get close to that bull once and for all!" Trapped between the bull and his father, El Besuguito decided to confront the latter: "Father, forgive me for paying no attention to you, but here you're just a spectator like everybody else."[77] Such a reply may strike us as mild, but in the context of provincial Spain it was tantamount to blasphemy.

Oedipal rivalries of the type described above can easily give way to or combine with sibling rivalry, and once unresolved conflicts go underground, in a person's unconscious, they can be endlessly projected onto other people. Matadors are no different in this from anyone else. As Arévalo and Moral relate:

> Paquirri was born into bullfighting in competition, an intimate and familiar competition that had an archetypal referent: the big brother. Bullfighting for him was a challenge to affirm himself vis-à-vis his brother and everyone else who initially thought he was less gifted. Later on, when he had already distinguished himself as a matador, his own cuadrilla observed a strange envy in him on days when he performed with important figures. Camino's art, for example, unhinged him. And then he would overwhelm [his competitors]. Bullfighting is a struggle with the bull, but bullfighters challenged Paquirri even more.[78]

What makes matadors very different from other people, of course, is the way in which old psychological traumas can propel one into real, physical traumas. The biographers go on to relate how Paquirri's "strange envy" led him to triumph again and again over renowned matadors and to receive a

series of cornadas that a more prudent (and therefore less popular) matador would have avoided.

Paquirri's envy was certainly not strange in the sense of "rare." Any
number of Spanish authors could be cited to testify that the planet of the
bulls is shot through with envy, rivalry, resentment, one-upmanship, and
pure, unmitigated hatred. It could hardly be otherwise in view of the harsh
process of appraisal and elimination that we have reviewed above. With an
activity that has been one of the only means of advancement in a rigidly
stratified society, whose wellspring is passion and whose lifeblood is the
ritual combat between two animal species, where a lucky and skillful few
succeed where so many hundreds fail, where so many frustrated men
hound their sons into bullrings to avenge their own defeats, where critics
dip their pens in poison and crowds go from mockery to adulation in a
second, we will find every necessary and sufficient condition for the most
corrosive kinds of envy. When one of the twentieth century's top matadors, Marcial Lalanda, was asked why he had kept his seven sons completely out of bullfighting, he responded:

> This is a contagious profession, and if one son becomes a figure—making
> money and living better—envy is born and an atmosphere is created that can
> ensnare the others. Of course not everyone can become a figure, but they put
> away their books, try their luck, and very probably in the end they will become
> bitter, desparing, and wreck their lives.[79]

The themes of envy, resentment, and hate are present in taurine biographies (beginning with Pepe-Illo) and abound in taurine novels as well,
whose format has permitted some authors to explore the psychological
consequences of rivalrous envy with great subtlety. In *Arcángel* by J. V.
Puente, Envy, Resentment, and Hate are personified in the manner of a
medieval allegory and shown plotting the destruction of the great Manolete.[80] In a more famous novel, *Currito de la Cruz* by Alejandro Pérez Lugín, bullfighters vie for supremacy in an atmosphere of jealousy and rancor
of suffocating proportions.[81] Numerous other titles could be cited from the
nineteenth and twentieth centuries, but it is important to understand that
envy is a very real phenomenon in bullfighting. Truth certainly beat fiction
on May 18, 1968, in Madrid's Monumental bullring. El Cordobés was in
the middle of a faena with a large bull when suddenly a man leaped into
the ring, ran up to the bull, grabbed its horn, caressed its snout, and embraced it (the bull made no objection). The man was none other than Miguelín, a second class bullfighter who deeply resented the popularity and

power El Cordobés had acquired and whose gesture was intended to show that the toro being fought was not bravo but, in the words of Miguelín, a "she-ass." Miguelín was hauled off to jail and the incident provoked an upheaval in the press. In the same month that Paris was being shaken by the great student uprising, writes Lyon, the envious torero's gesture was debated interminably in Generalísimo Franco's Spain.[82]

Miguel de Unamuno, one of the great minds of the twentieth century, considered envy to be "the intimate gangrene of the Spanish soul."[83] In a number of writings he attempts to explain how a universal human flaw that made its first nasty appearance in Cain's murder of Abel came to acquire a peculiar power in Spain, a land of passionate internecine conflict for much of its history. In his novel *Abel Sánchez*, Unamuno transplants the biblical story of Cain and Abel to Spain in order to explore the dialectical relationship between the envier and the envied; he shows how each needs the other for purposes of self-affirmation and how one is no guiltier or more innocent than the other, although the envier is the one who struggles and suffers the most.[84]

In recent years, René Girard has profoundly explored the dialectics of envy, and his conclusions illuminate the world of Spanish bullfighting. To battle for prestige or honor, says Girard, is literally to battle for nothing. Rivals model themselves on each other in pursuing an object that is not physical or tangible; in more advanced stages, this "metaphysical" desire becomes the desire *to be* the envied rival, the supreme model that others slavishly imitate. But if the rival/model was the obstacle before, now any obstacle can become a model, and this is how metaphysical desire leads inexorably into sadomasochistic behavior patterns. The obstacle is absolutized, so to speak; its value is a function of its resistance to appropriation. Once a person is caught up in the pattern, it is not suffering per se that he or she aspires to but the quasi-divine superiority of the obstacle/model whose resistance is precisely what stimulates pursuit. Thus, violence becomes identified with fullness of being. The slave needs the master to struggle against and the persecuted one longs for the persecutor, just as the envier glamorized the envied one at the beginning of the cycle. Winning or losing, brutalizing or arranging to be brutalized, the subject keeps the fantasy of omnipotence alive. Like Unamuno, Girard posits that the dynamics of the whole process is best understood in understanding the one on the bottom, Cain, the envier, the metaphysical masochist.[85]

One brief anecdote will help the reader grasp what all this has to do with bullfighting. On August 9, 1914, a rather obscure matador called

Corchaíto was fighting a rather ignoble bull named Distinguido in the ring of Cartegena. When the "moment of truth" arrived, Corchaíto's sword glanced off one of the vertebra between the bull's shoulder blades; the bull simply sat down. In a display of *vergüenza torera*, the torero ordered his cuadrilla to get the beast on his feet. Corchaíto profiled once again, again the sword bounced off, Distinguido sat down again, and again the matador insisted that his men make the bull stand up. On the third try, Corchaíto achieved a magnificent swordthrust but was tossed high into the air. When he came down, he was gored in the groin and the heart and died instantly.[86]

If this sort of incident sounds familiar to the reader, it should. We have already spoken of the death of Espartero, of Paquirri's "strange envy," of the bloody consequences of *pundonor* or *vergüenza torera* in bullfighters great and mediocre. The logic of taurine "honor" is that of metaphysical desire; and the logic of metaphysical desire is one, says Girard, with the logic of betting: "Beyond a certain degree of bad luck, the unlucky player does not renounce, but only places ever larger sums on ever weaker chances. . . . Pursuit of failure becomes ever wiser and more expert, without ever understanding itself as pursuit of failure."[87] Bullfighters are not gored by the bull, say Arévalo and Moral, but by "their need to do the impossible."[88]

The important thing, perhaps, is not the specific suicidal incident so much as the spirit in which it is recounted. Every taurine chronicle or biography that I have seen narrates the gorings of brave matadors with respect, admiration, or outright hero-worship. Hemingway idolized masochistic matadors with an almost adolescent enthusiasm.[89] If we adopt a more mature perspective, however, it becomes apparent that men like Corchaíto and Paquirri were in the grip of pathology. In many ways they were like compulsive gamblers who give in to their buried fantasies of grandeur, throw moderation and caution to the winds, and unconsciously play to lose all. The observations of a noted psychologist of gambling:

> The unconscious driving force behind the gambler springs from the inner revival of his illusion of omnipotence, with all its neurotic results. At bottom, the gambler is a naughty child who expects to be punished for having aggressively broken the rules. The pleasurable part of the tension he feels comes from the gratification of exercising his alleged magic power—an act which is in itself an attack on the authority of his parents. . . . It is the masochistic component in the gambler's psyche that guarantees he will be a loser. His unconscious aim of

masochistic pleasure cannot be achieved if he wins. Consciously, it is true, he plans and desires to win, but his conscious wish is not dynamically effective.[90]

It will come as no suprise to the reader to learn that the masochistic El Cordobés was obsessed with poker, unable to stop playing in all-night juergas until he was bankrupt.[91] Bullfighting could easily be seen in this light. Incapable of abandoning the illusion of magic power that was created and fed by metaphysical desire, the most ambitious toreros get caught up in a potentially fatal game that might well be termed "Spanish roulette." This is a non-romantic, but surely more accurate, view of *vergüenza torera*.

Nevertheless, we must guard against seeing the bullfighter's metaphysical desire as his individual hang-up and gorings as the wages of his personal folly. Unlike average gamblers, bullfighters go for broke in front of huge crowds of people egging them on. In the last analysis, *vergüenza torera* belongs to the province of social psychology. One cannot discuss the possible pathology of the torero without mentioning the possible pathology of the public in the same breath. Girard himself points out that the people most susceptible to metaphysical masochism are those whose livelihoods depend on the arbitrary mass "other"—the crowd.[92] Countless bullfighters have confessed to fearing the crowd's reactions more than the bulls themselves. Mass desire is as potentially sadomasochistic as individual desire. It tends to polarize around any expert manipulator of violence, seemingly autosufficient and untouchable in his charisma (or his majismo, to use the Spanish term). The supercharged emotional bond that unites idols and idolizers can have comic and highly revealing consequences, as shown by some of the anecdotes Belmonte told of his fans—how they mobbed him on every occasion, how they sought to parade him around on a platform like a patron saint, how their moods of elation or despair were totally synchronized with the matador's luck on any given afternoon.[93] The dramatic death of a matador in the line of duty (caused, most often, by his socially sanctioned *vergüenza torera*) and his subsequent deification in popular lore simply carry this whole idolatrous process to its logical conclusion.

In the next chapter we will probe more deeply into the sociopsychological mechanisms of spectators—including critics—who unwittingly encourage and reward suicidal behaviors. In order to do this, however, we must first draw back and get the larger social perspective. We must get a better picture of how bullfighting as spectacle fits into Spanish political life, what each gets from the other, how one might mirror the other.

The final moments of tension before the parade into the ring (Bilbao, 1972). Photo by Rosario Cambria.

A calm, classical *verónica* by El Viti (Caracas, 1966). Photo by Rosario Cambria.

The dramatic *chicuelina* by a master: Paco Camino (Madrid, 1967). Photo by Rosario Cambria.

The matador himself citing for the placing of the sticks: Angel Teruel (Bilbao, 1969). Photo by Rosario Cambria.

A close *derechazo* by Diego Puerta (Madrid, 1967). Photo by Rosario Cambria.

The perfect execution of the left-handed *natural* by Paco Camino (Linares, 1969). Photo by Rosario Cambria.

The danger is real. Raúl Aranda in a dramatic moment (Bilbao, 1974). Photo by Rosario Cambria.

César Girón is preoccupied as he prepares for the "moment of truth" (Caracas, 1965). Photo by Rosario Cambria.

Younger brother Efraín Girón entering the "cradle of death" (Madrid, 1967). Photo by Rosario Cambria.

Ruiz Miguel in an honest and successful *estocada* (Madrid, 1986). Photo by Rosario Cambria.

The final gesture by a master of the pose: Curro Romero (Alcalá de Henares, 1967). Photo by Rosario Cambria.

José María Manzanares in a moment of triumph: two ears (Gijón, 1972). Photo by Rosario Cambria.

The Sepulcher of Joselito in Seville's San Fernando Cemetery, sculpted in marble and bronze by Mariano Benlliure in 1920 and described by Noel as "an absurd deification" that nevertheless communicated "feelings of heartfelt pain—of that immense pain that Spain is for every Spaniard" (*Escritos antitaurinos*, p. 144). Nearby are the tombs of Espartero, Pepete, Montes, Chicuelo, and now Paquirri. Photo by Sara Paulson.

4. The Fiesta Nacional

UP TO NOW we have devoted a good deal of time and space to the social background of bullfighting on foot, with particular attention to the eighteenth century. Although a few scholars consider Spain to have been a cultural wasteland during this century, it is clear from our review that there was an enormous amount of ferment and innovation. Whole realms of popular culture that were forged in this period constitute Spain's identity signs even today—with the bullfight, naturally, as the prime example. Unfortunately, there was little or no progress in other areas. A major twentieth century Spanish author has passed judgment on the period with splendid irony:

> At the same time as the American colonies were breaking their dependence on the English sovereign to search out, establish, and proclaim the laws of democracy, and the citizens of France were challenging the ancien régime aristocracy to conquer liberty for the people and the equality of the rights of man, for their part the good and brave Spaniards were separating themselves from royal traditions and from chivalric and aristocratic customs of horse and lance in order to search out, establish, and proclaim taurine democracy, and conquer liberty for the bullring, and enunciate the inalienable canons of the art of bullfighting on foot. As durable as the American or the French revolutions was our revolution in tauromachy.[1]

The above passage would be stirring and patriotic if it could be taken at face value. But it cannot. Pérez de Ayala was only too aware that the revolutionary art of bullfighting on foot was a poor substitute for the kind of political revolution that had profoundly transformed other nations to make them free and powerful—just the type of transformation that Spain had so sorely needed. The laws of democracy were never established in eighteenth-century Spain, and in the following two centuries, the growth of liberal parliamentary institutions was to be far more traumatic than in other nations of the West.

All of this leads to questions that are simple enough to express but mind-boggling in their possible ramifications: Can a solid connection be established between the rise of modern bullfighting and Spain's social and political backwardness? Did Spain's taurine "revolution" subvert or impede the real kind? Did Spain's taurine "democracy" somehow slow down the progress of the genuine article?

Pan y Toros

By way of setting the stage for a more sophisticated exploration of the connection between bullfighting and the social order in Spain, let us briefly consider a less sophisticated but quite persistent answer to the above questions. During the past two centuries, a number of different thinkers have advanced the idea that the Spanish ruling class stayed in power by cannily distracting a restless populace with exciting bull-baiting spectacles. In the same way that Roman emperors kept the restive Roman mob supplied with *panem et circenses* (bread and circuses), it is said, Spain's monarchs or oligarchs mollified their subjects with *pan y toros* (bread and bulls).² The assumption is that violent spectacles effectively drained away the aggressive energy that could have been applied against the powers that be. This seems to have been the strategy adopted by at least one autocrat: in a futile effort to strengthen his power, King Joseph Bonaparte not only authorized public bullfights but actively involved his government in their finance and organization.³

A modern version of the *pan y toros* argument might run something like this: in a bullfight, the symbol of the aristocracy (the noble bull) is dominated and killed by the symbol of the proletariat (the matador). Without delving too deeply into depth psychology, we can surmise that the spectacle of a noble symbol being slain by a commoner must have been quite gratifying for members of the oppressed and abused lower classes—the majority of Spaniards. This symbolic killing has both a dimension of class struggle and an oedipal dimension. Conrad asserted some years ago that the bullfight "may be thought of as a culturally sanctioned ritual through which culturally produced but repressed fears and frustrations find release and expression in displaced aggression against the bull as a symbol par excellence of power and authority."⁴ As the matador dominates and dispatches the bull, Conrad affirmed, Spaniards unconsciously fantasize that their fathers, kings, bishops, and lords are all being done away with in the arena.⁵ But if this were the case, it might be asked, why would aristocrats be so willing to participate? Why would they painstakingly breed four-footed symbols of themselves to be slaughtered by their social inferiors? The answer is obvious: it is far better to have a symbol of yourself killed than for you to be killed yourself. By permitting and even facilitating a confrontation with and "massacre" of the representatives of their social class, the aristocrats might well have avoided the fate of their cousins in France. Herein, perhaps, lies the secret triumph of the nobility's "strategic retreat" from the corrida de toros. For after all is said and done, the wave of plebeianization that swept over Spanish cultural life in the eighteenth century did nothing to alter the legal and economic balance of power. The nobles remained at the vertex of the social pyramid. Spain's aristocrats may have been a sorry lot, certainly they were for Ortega, but at least they were smart enough to save their own necks by offering their bovid stand-ins to be sacrificed in their place. This, at least, is a conjecture that can be made.[6]

In its most radical formulation, the *pan y toros* argument held that, thanks to bullfighting, the Spanish status quo remained in place, as oppressive and unjust as always. This strikes us as rash and simplistic, for numerous other factors were on hand to preserve outmoded social structures and mentalities in Spain. But to the degree that it served as a safety valve for pent-up frustrations, bullfighting could certainly be considered an accomplice of the status quo and an agent of inertia. For when all the shouting and cheering and make-believe parricide is over, nothing has really changed. Ironically, the very thing that the proponents of the "bread and bulls" argument detested was celebrated by some conservative upholders of the status quo. Consider the words of Father Pereda, the staunch defender of bullfighting that we met earlier:

> It is necessary to educate and cultivate the public with patience and paternal authority. This explosion [of enthusiasm at bullfights] can be, at times, a good safety valve, an escape mechanism to get rid of bad moods and worse ideas. It is impossible to imagine that people could leave a good corrida de toros with an inclination for political rallies or social disturbances; they have unburdened themselves, they have shouted, they have laughed, they come away happy![7]

Thus, social reformers and reactionaries alike could ascribe to the same basic postulate—that bullfighting is a cathartic escape mechanism, with one side's ammunition serving as the other side's comfort. Even if the bullfight did exercise some cathartic effect, however, it was apparently not enough. Spanish history of the nineteenth and twentieth centuries demonstrates that the people had plenty of energy left over for uprisings, coup attempts, socialist or anarchist agitation, and civil disorders of all kinds. If indeed it ever existed at any level of government, the *pan y toros* strategy was a failure.

Still, it would seem difficult or impossible to turn around and argue that bullfighting actually *helped* to bring about progressive social change of any kind. But this is precisely what has been advanced—and in a most persuasive way—by Spanish sociologist Enrique Gil Calvo. In *Función de toros* (1989), Gil concludes that bullfighting played a major role in fomenting modern ideas of democracy and fair play in Spain. Let us proceed at once to an analysis of his case, for it represents the most ambitious and well-reasoned attempt ever to vindicate bullfighting as a socially useful phenomenon.

Gil actually begins where Ortega left off. As the reader will recall, Ortega was the first intellectual heavyweight to affirm that the history of Spain could not be understood apart from the history of bullfighting; he underscored the importance of the eighteenth-century revolution in popular culture and the plebeian styles and art forms that took Spain by storm. Here Gil agrees: for him, the social norms that emerge in the eighteenth century had all the vitality, rationality, and initiative that had been lacking in the rigid and melancholy Spain of previous centuries. But Ortega was not exactly a friend of the common man: he saw casticismo as an undesirable inversion of the Spanish class system and a veritable black mark on the record of the do-nothing nobility. The Enlightenment failed to make sufficient headway in Spain, Ortega was convinced, because too many men of quality abdicated their responsibilities and spent their time aping plebeian lifestyles and mannerisms.

Here is where the sociologist parts company with the philosopher. According to Gil, it is essential to distinguish between the "official" Spain of the eighteenth century and the real one. Official Spain, misruled by a Baroque absolutist Bourbon monarchy and its swollen, hidebound, otiose, and inefficient bureaucracy, was indeed a calamitous failure in its attempt to impose modernization from above. In the meantime, however, outside the institutional framework, an informal and extraofficial modernization was being carried out, stimulated by new social forms that were far more creative and productive than those of Spain's official Enlightenment.

This is the authentic inversion of the Spanish social structure that Ortega referred to, even though his interpretation of it was equivocal. In his elitism he feared that the masses had supplanted the nobility. What was happening, in reality, is that new ways of acting were supplanting the old Baroque impotence, new ways protagonized as much by the people, including the meager bourgeois faction, as by the nobility—the social segment that benefits the most from this spectacular turnabout. . . . By the route of fait accompli, therefore, and preceding the formal collapse of the Baroque seignorial empire by many decades, and under the leadership of a landholding obligarchy composed almost entirely of aristocrats, Spanish society was carrying out on its own the dizzying adventure of the modernizing Enlightenment.[8]

In the institutionalization of bullfighting on foot, argues Gil, we can find the happy union of two different types of initiative. The first is the economic initiative that logically belonged to the many nobles that had thrown off the anti-commercial prejudices of their ancestors to become successful capitalistic cattle breeders. The second is the cultural initiative that clearly belonged to the upstart plebeians who struggled for fame and riches in a highly competitive, de facto meritocracy. The rivalry among bullfighters represents a model market economy, with the public as the ultimate judge of quality. The fact that both noble and plebeian initiatives combine in a spectacle of animal slaughter only increases the salutary social effect: watching the agony and death of a large bovid, says Gil, is such a dynamic and moving experience that it liberates you from the place you occupy in a contradictory society, providing a new perspective on the social order and a new consciousness of your own autonomy and independence. For this reason, Gil affirms, modern bullfighting can never be a mere question of *pan y toros*.[9]

And that is only the beginning. According to Gil, tauromachy is a uniquely Spanish form of pedagogy. Bullfighting teaches, educates, socializes, and provides valuable lessons in the art of politics. As the public looks on, the bullfighter channels the "antisocial and unsociable selfishness" of the bull into collective, publicly useful directions, thereby showing us that our own violent or antisocial tendencies are to be altruistically sacrificed to the common good.[10]

To fight a bull is to subdue and pacify the bull's antagonistic tendencies: catharsis is always a resolution of conflict. And this is the principal revelation of bullfights, their capacity for communicating the message of the Enlightenment. The information that the fiesta de los toros transmits is that of socialization: how to conquer the obstacles that threaten the construction of civic maturity. This implies, in essence, liberating oneself from subjection to the prejudices of obscurantism and emancipating oneself from the tyranny of birth, lineage, and caste to elude the dark powers of the bull. But it also implies . . . learning how to halt, moderate, and command life itself, taking charge of it like free and independent subjects, like adult individuals, civilized and fully capable of defending their rights. Thus, the bullfight shows how to overcome invincible adversities, how to oppose the coercion of physical violence, how to draw strength out of weakness and virtue out of necessity. And thus we learn, like enlightened and civilized democrats, that brain is always better than brawn.[11]

Gil is not, to be sure, the first Spanish intellectual to see bullfighting as didactic. In 1951 Enrique Tierno Galván penned an influential essay in which he argued that "the bullfight is the event that has most educated the Spanish people, socially and even politically."[12] The idea was also expressed by Ramón Pérez de Ayala, the author cited at the beginning of this chapter, who compiled two lengthy volumes of essays under the rubric of *Política y toros*.[13] What distinguishes Gil from earlier authors is his insistence that bullfights impart the most mature and politically enlightened ideas possible to their spectators. This approach is unquestionably in tune with the times: Spain's peaceful transition to democracy after Franco died in 1975 was a political miracle matched only by recent events in the Soviet Union and Eastern Europe. Gil can hardly be blamed for attempting to read democratic ideals into one of his country's chief symbols of identity. But has he really hit upon the positive social value of bullfighting? Does watching the agony and death of a large bovid really teach Spaniards to take charge of their lives as free, independent, civic-minded adults? Is a bullring really a school of democracy?

It would be grand indeed if we could unhesitatingly answer these questions in the affirmative, but our search for the truth cannot be oriented by wishful thinking. After all, a superficial glance at Spanish history of the past two centuries reveals that periods of genuine democracy have been few and far between; bullfighting grew up and thrived not in the context of political freedom but against a backdrop of coercion that was as subtle or gross as a given decade required. As we look more closely into how Spain actually functioned for much of the past two centuries, we discover that bullfighting and Spanish politics did indeed interrelate, shed mutual light on each other, and even mirror each other. For the sake of argument, and as a tribute to Gil's enthusiasm for democratic ideals, we can certainly entertain the hypothesis that somehow Spanish bullfighting secretly harbored or nurtured a bold new consciousness of autonomy and civic maturity. But we must also be prepared to admit something far less pleasant if the data so demand. Let us embark once again, therefore, on a tour of Spain, not to observe fiestas but to observe the powers that be or that have been.

Focusing on the nineteenth and twentieth centuries (the very period of bullfighting's maximum expansion and appeal), let us endeavor to discover what sort of men had the power, where they got it, and how they held on to it.

The Curse of Spain

In Chapter 2, we saw how a great traditionalist worldview known as casticismo came into its own in eighteenth-century Spain, quashing the petimetres, consecrating the majos, and rejuvenating old-fashioned concepts of honor, valor, and morality. These qualities were never so necessary as in the bloody but successful fight to expel Napoleonic armies from the peninsula in the first part of the nineteenth century. Unfortunately, the blind workings of history served to reinforce not only the positive aspects of casticismo but the negative ones as well, that is, obscurantist Catholicism, fatalism, monarchical messianism, and xenophobia. King Fernando VII, a wily reactionary if ever there was one, rode to power on a wave of purblind nationalism and stayed there for years, keeping the progressives in exile or in prison and doing his best to preserve the ancien régime status quo. When liberal-minded men finally did take over, Spain was bankrupt and the old umbilical cord of taxes and commissions from the New World colonies had been severed.

As with many other new governments in this century and the last, land reform was the first order of business. But the ruinous state of the economy forced Spain's first liberals to end aristocratic and ecclesiastical entail in a way that only worsened the perennially unjust agricultural system. Under the Spanish brand of disentailment known as *desamortización*, "serfs with land became free men without it."[14] Unlike anywhere else in Europe, the aristocracy willingly supported the end of archaic inheritance laws and feudal privileges to enter into a new bourgeois class of absentee landlords. What holds for Spain holds doubly for southern Spain, where the brave bull and the grape soon formed the basis of immense fortunes. Andalusia's middle-class landowners were practically liquidated by the new laws, and the landless day laborers who were already growing in number in the eighteenth century became the most numerous class in the nineteenth.[15]

Desamortización, in other words, had made losers out of those who should have been winners and vice versa. To make matters worse, the industrial revolution sweeping over Europe and America was stillborn in

Spain, confined to a few provinces in Catalunya and the Basque country. It was never to be enough to absorb the unlucky masses of landless ex-serfs. In Old Castile and Aragon, frustrated peasants poured into the ultra-Catholic and monarchist Carlist movement, keeping Spain in a constant state of civil war. In the south, peasants were forced into desperate pursuits like anarchism, smuggling, banditry, and, naturally, bullfighting. The much-feared Guardia Civil was created in 1844 to protect property rights and repress malcontents.[16] A few years later, the laws on foreign investment were liberalized and, in a pattern typical of underdeveloped nations, railroad concessions and mining interests fell quickly into British and French hands. Spain's subordinate role in the industrialized West and the international economic system was assured.[17]

By the middle of the nineteenth century, power was effectively in the hands of a plutocracy that was largely dominated by the Andalusian agrarian bourgeoisie, supported by the mercantile and financial community, tolerated by the military, and administered from Madrid by a legion of loyal bureaucrats and politicians. Officially Spain was a modern constitutional monarchy governed by a freely elected parliament. But in reality, as Kern points out, "liberalism never imparted the belief that fundamental liberties were of greater importance than the protection of established hierarchies."[18] Behind the elaborate new parliamentary facade, many vices of the old order lived on—paternalism, patronage, familialism. From the old vices sprang forth a new one, an informal but marvelously effective system of political control known as *caciquismo*. Let us focus in on these diverse vices now, for once we have grasped how they shaped (or misshaped) Spanish society and politics for generations, we will be in a position to gauge the true sociopolitical significance of bullfighting.

From the days of its inception and consolidation at the close of the ancien régime, the landholding plutocracy had realized that to maintain its power in Madrid it needed to control towns and villages throughout the countryside (where its lands were located). Thus, the cornerstone of the political architecture that evolved was the local boss, big shot, or power broker. Known as *caciques* (from the West Indies word for chieftain), these men maintained their power through their ability to supply votes to the right candidate. In a narrow sense, caciquismo was pure and simple election fraud, but in everyday practice it was much more. Caciquismo had its roots in the familial and social relations of a given community and was the automatic—and the only—resort for anyone who needed something from the powerful. Spanish politics was, as Tusell puts it, "the kingdom of the favor."[19] A cacique was nothing more nor less than a doer of favors (and a collector of them) at the local and provincial level. In all cases, achieving power went hand in hand with distributing spoils. As Cuenca has written:

> Once the ideal man was elected and sent to Madrid, the moment for rewards and compensations arrived. The triumphant government and candidate went to great pains to satisfy the demands, favors, and petitions solicited for himself and for his clients by the cacique, a man as indispensable to the central government as to his fellow citizens, who quite correctly saw in him the dispenser of aid and also of useful services for the entire community.[20]

As a pragmatic and adaptive institution, caciquismo remained relatively free of the sectarian conflicts that often beset nineteenth-century Spain; in addition, the role of favor-dispenser was open to both highborn and low-born individuals. Ambition and results, not ideology or class background, vindicated the relevance of a given influence peddler in a given community. There was, therefore, a sui generis kind of social mobility involved, a degree of elbow room for individual ambition or merit. Thus, many different kinds of people came to be caciques in Spain. According to Cuenca, a cacique could be a canon or priest, especially in those towns where the authority of the Church was intact; he could be a lawyer, notary, or scrivener in possession of skills much prized in a mostly illiterate country; he could be a large landowner, with all the power that belonged to his status as the very foundation of a local economy; he could be a retired military man, with his power based on the enormous prestige that the uniform has always had in Spain; he could be a mayor or a judge, a doctor or a customs inspector. What they all had in common was an ability to concentrate in their hands a degree of power uncontemplated by any law.[21] They shared, in addition, a certain ethos of power use in which arbitrariness and despotic caprice were major elements.

One of the most ominous aspects of caciquismo was the way in which it facilitated military interference in politics and political meddling with the military. As noted historian Raymond Carr has pointed out:

> When politicians could not spread limited supplies over the different operational armies, it became a necessity for commanders to have friends in the government in order to secure what supplies there were. . . . Military rule [in Spain] is incomprehensible unless we remember that the division between military and civilian society was indistinct. There was little social difference between an underpaid officer and an underpaid civil servant: both were members of the under-employed middle class which depended on political patronage for

promotion. . . . Thus military rule was a symbiotic growth where politicians leant on soldiers and soldiers appeared as working politicians.[22]

A clear connection can thus be established between caciquismo—the personalistic patronage system that held sway in Spanish political life—and caudillismo, the military version of the same, wherein local or national caudillos (chiefs or strong men) garnered and peddled influence and promotions and intrigued right along with the politicians. It could be said, without excessive risk of oversimplification, that the caudillo was a military cacique and the cacique was a political caudillo. Both caciques and caudillos were men of ambition, opportunistic, demagogic, unscrupulous, clever, and clannish. They were magnanimous with their protegés, niggardly with their foes, and arbitrary or despotic with everyone else.

The Spanish system of personalistic patronage with its civilian/military symbiosis was pervasive, all-powerful, and incredibly resilient over time. By the last quarter of the nineteenth century it had begun its golden age, with "Liberal" and "Conservative" parties in collusion to take turns in power (the so-called "peaceful rotation"). It is not that the system was corrupt, as numerous scholars have noted, but rather that *corruption was the system*. To be sure, Spain was one of the first European countries to enact universal male suffrage—on paper. The huge numbers of new voters ironically made caciques more powerful and more necessary than ever before. As Ward wrote in 1911:

> Government majorities are raised by rural returns obtained, not through the ballot-box, but by the vote-rigging of "bosses" and their satellites, who thwart the public will and dominate local life. The system perpetuates servility, stifles social ambitions, atrophies law, gives license to caprice and intolerance, opposes educational advance, and drives the man of enthusiastic and generous temperament into the ranks of red revolution. Caciquism is the brand of Spain's social and moral backwardness, and accounts for her impotence in the Councils of the Nations. . . . It is the curse of Spain.[23]

The connection between caciquismo and illiteracy cannot be emphasized too much. As Unamuno pointed out, it was ridiculous to talk about freedom of the press in towns and villages where no one was able to read.[24] According to Cuenca, oligarchs and politicians continually preached that education would do the underclass more harm than good.[25] It was no accident that caciquismo was most firmly entrenched in the most backward and socially stagnant regions of Spain, especially Galicia and Andalusia. A 1904 survey found that densely populated Andalusian provinces like Cádiz and Málaga had fewer schools and fewer students than any other part of Spain.[26] The fact that schools existed did not mean that they were actually open to the public: in 1918, for example, the schools of the Andalusian town of Belalcázar had been closed for four years.[27] The great irony, as Acosta puts it, was that the more Andalusian plutocrats dominated the central government, the weaker Andalusia became.[28] All over Spain, caciquismo was synonymous with the subversion of the educational system. At the university level, candidates who scored the worst on placement examinations would often win the post anyway, thanks to their connections.[29] Instead of a consistent system of rewards and punishments, Spaniards were conditioned to accept the arbitrary and unpredictable actions of the powerful.

According to Kern, the new leaders that emerged in the nineteenth century resembled the enlightened despots of the eighteenth in believing that economic modernization could be effected without social change. They continued to treasure "the values of hierarchy, patronage, and familialism in a period when achievement, not privilege, activated the positivistic liberal movements elsewhere in Europe."[30] Spain had a social and political system that reinforced opportunism, hollow rhetoric, and arbitrariness, instead of competence or principle. Nowhere is Pérez de Ayala's satire put to better use than in his description of the bungling, nepotistic Spanish parliament of 1917, a "house of cards" built up with one trick upon another:

One much-respected politician whom we will call Redomadillo has been a minister several times with "Liberal" governments. He has three sons and two sons-in-law; all five are legislators for life and occupy the highest governmental positions when the familial patriarch has his turn in the system of political rotation. The family is not known for wealth, nobility, culture, or intellectual capacity. All of the men who comprise the family are mediocre, ignorant, and incapable of efficient performance in public office. No one contradicts this opinion. Why then do they enjoy so much governmental power? Ah! the other oligarchic families respond, because Redomadillo is the master of an entire province and has enough clout there to elect ten legislators. What do you mean "the master"? Let's travel to the province in question. Here, as in Madrid, Redomadillo and his men are still foolish, ignorant, vain, and incompetent. And nevertheless, the people obey them. Why? we ask. Ah! the naive inhabitants of the province respond, because Redomadillo is the master in Madrid and has enough clout to get ten legislators from here. This means that Redomadillo has been able to appoint his own supporters as the provincial governor, the mayors and judges of the towns, even the mailmen, and thus has the whole province in his back pocket.[31]

In a later essay Pérez de Ayala sums up the curse of Spain in one sentence: "The Spanish political system of recent years has been the unjust empire of the official lawyerly lie."[32] For his part, Cuenca has affirmed that despite the good that some caciques had done in some towns,

> the only conclusion that can and must be extracted from its long and lamentable existence in Spanish life is that it was an authentic cancer. For as long as it lasted caciquismo was a continual source of civic degradation and a school of moral corruption, with absolute disregard for personal dignity. If our country was always lagging behind other more developed ones in the same geographic/cultural area, it is due in large part to caciquismo. . . . The great masses of the country remained absolutely at the margins of political life, without any active or responsible exercise of citizenship, functioning merely as an inert force of the system at the service of the interests of the governing oligarchies.[33]

In one form or another caciquismo, and the whole social and economic quagmire that it thrived in, continued far into the twentieth century. As Tusell flatly states, "no political force was capable of renovating the political system. Neither, as it was logical to expect, did the political system renovate itself."[34] In southern Spain, candidates opposed to the system were elected a mere thirteen times out of a thousand contested seats in the period from 1890 to 1931.[35] Contrary to the hopes of the reformers, Spain's short-lived Second Republic (1931–1936) did not eradicate the problem. "Although during the Second Republic the ruling elites of the country were renewed in a fundamental way," notes Tusell, "the same thing did not occur at the provincial or local level. . . . For a long time local Spanish life was destined to remain at this level of patronage."[36] Whatever renovation had taken place was wiped out by Franco's victory in the Spanish Civil War (1936–1939). Franco was the caudillo, the strong man, the chief of a conservative reaction that effectively restored the great social injustices of the land tenure system and the spoils system alike. The same oligarchy and the same civilian/military patronage symbiosis that had misgoverned Spain during the nineteenth century had returned to power. In Kern's view, in fact, the manipulation of parliamentary institutions in the previous century had anticipated, in a primitive way, Spain's later slide into authoritarian traditionalism.[37] From 1939 through 1977, say Carr and Fusi, the dominant class reproduced itself through "familial nepotism."[38] Naturally the Caudillo treated his people to the usual charade of a parliament and occasional plebiscites whose outcome was a foregone conclusion.

Fortunately, Spain's middle classes evolved rapidly in the 1960s and

1970s, and by 1977 the country was a constitutional monarchy once again, with institutions that were, and are, far more democratic than anything in Spanish experience. But old ways die hard—especially when they are based on the fabric of social life itself. Spanish life remained personalistic in many ways, and the specter of familialistic favoritism has once again reared its ugly head. As Santos Juliá wrote in 1989:

> It is in this area that the politicians of the new democracy have most deeply frustrated the hopes that society had deposited in them. Not that they are corrupt personally: the majority, it goes without saying, are not; it was only to be hoped that their presumed rationality as reformers of the State would have led them to break the knots of the "old corruption." They have not done so: it is impressive to see just how much friendship, to say nothing of kinship, retains its political value among us.[39]

Striking proof of the accuracy of this evaluation was forthcoming in the first weeks of January, 1990, when the brother of Vice-President Alfonso Guerra was connected to over 30 cases of influence peddling. Most of the influence was peddled right out of a government office in Seville: by cannily using his brother's name and camouflaging his shady deals behind dummy corporations, Juan Guerra managed to put together an immense financial empire in just three years. Only a few weeks later the main opposition party was rocked by a major financial scandal. With such evidence that Spain still suffers from cronyism and the abuse of patronage, many Spaniards have become deeply pessimistic about the future of their newly-won democratic institutions.[40]

Bullfighting and Politics

Having now completed our sketch of the uses and abuses of power in nineteenth- and twentieth-century Spain, we must ask what light they may shed on bullfighting, or vice versa, during approximately the same period. This is obviously the big question, one that is as complex as it is crucial. I am prepared to assert that bullfighting has been nothing less than a microcosm of the Spanish social order. I affirm that to an uncanny degree it has replicated almost every feature of the Spanish political system. By way of substantiating these assertions, I will focus in on the main points of connection or intersection: (1) corruption and fraud in bullfighting; (2) the internal patronage system of bullfighting; (3) the matador as padrino; (4) the mat-dor as demagogue; and (5) the distorted notions of power, authority, and democracy that were derived from or reinforced through public behavior at bullrings.

First, a quick review of what many have seen as "the curse" of bullfighting—fraud. There is almost no aspect of a bullfight that cannot be or has not been tampered with in some way over the years. Numerous procedures exist to make bulls less dangerous: their horns can be shaved, four-hundred-pound sandbags can be dropped on their shoulders, they can be injected with sedatives. They can also be overfed, or made to carry weight far beyond what would be right for their frames. This may be the major reason behind the phenomenon of the "falling bull" that has plagued tauromachy since the 1960s. As one critic asks, "If a three year old child were loaded with the armor of the Cid, do you think he would be able to play and run?"[41] Even if a fighting bull has not been "fixed," an unscrupulous picador can always take the fight out of him in a dozen illicit ways.

But this is only the beginning of the possibilities for fraud in bullfighting: as it turns out, critics are like bulls in that they can be disarmed, made less dangerous, or even converted into a bullfighter's secret ally.

> The taurine critics with clean souls can be reckoned on the fingers of one hand. Then comes the battalion of critics who tell half-truths. Then come the numberless "comprised" critics, well-known because of their literary insignificance and poor syntax: they are the critics who suffer from "the disease of the envelope." Woe to you, beginning bullfighter, if those critics do not receive your envelope on time! Many newspapers consider the room devoted to taurine criticism as paid publicity.[42]

The institution of the envelope dates from the beginnings of taurine journalism itself, around the middle of the nineteenth century, and was for many years an integral part of theatre criticism as well. At many newspapers, the critic who reviewed the opening night of a musical comedy and the critic who reported the day's events at the bullring were one and the same man. Singers and bullfighters alike had to make sure that the critic was, if not under control, at least not ill disposed toward them. There is a much-told anecdote about an up-and-coming bullfighter who sent an envelope to an important critic that contained not money but an IOU; in his review of the matador's performance the next day, the critic noted laconically that "so-and-so is *promising* but only time will tell if he can *deliver*."[43] The envelope remained a standard feature of bullfighting well into the twentieth century. It was often the matador's swordhandler who had the job of delivering envelopes to every critic in Madrid, the amount being determined by the importance of the newspaper. "The most honest and the best critics receive them," rationalized Hemingway, "and they are not expected to twist the matador's disasters into triumphs nor distort their accounts in his favor. It is simply a compliment that the matador pays them."[44]

This said, it must be pointed out that, at the level of overall fair play, bullfighting may well have been more honest than, say, the Spanish electoral system—thanks to the resolute desire on the part of all spectators and many critics to preserve the "truth" (read danger) of the Fiesta Nacional. One of the cruel ironies of Spanish bullfighting is that the most "honest" critics, the ones with the greatest reputations for integrity, are also the ones who are most determined to preserve the authentic risk of human life that the whole enterprise is founded upon. As one critic of unquestionable honesty wrote a few years back:

> Can you imagine a hunter who would cut the wings off partridges to down them more easily? What would hunting be then? Stupid slaughter deprived of all emotion. Emotion! Whether we want it or not, emotion is the essence of the fiesta. If the danger of the bull is curtailed, what is left of bullfighting? It is reduced to a stupid slaughter adorned with affected and ridiculous preciosity.[45]

More information could be given about the technical aspects of fixing bulls' horns or the various dishonest schemes designed by managers, impresarios, ticket-scalpers, and other denizens of the planet of the bulls. Yet we cannot give graft more attention than it deserves. Thanks in part to demanding critics like the above, bullfighting has been restored to health (as demonstrated by recent gorings and deaths of professional toreros). It is vital to bear in mind, furthermore, that taurine corruption was only the symptom anyway, not the disease. The abuses were just one aspect, one logical outcome, of an entire system that has proved basically resilient over time. Fixing bulls, in other words, is like fixing elections. Just as the nefarious Spanish system of personalistic patronage cannot be reduced to election fraud, bullfighting goes far beyond tricks and venality. In its own way it is an arbitrary "kingdom of the favor" whose operating principles have been exactly the same as those of the larger society. At least that is what I will seek to demonstrate in what follows.

In the beginning, of course, was the capea. If we were to "decode" the rural fiesta de toros, we would find that one of its principal messages was a sort of cautionary tale about what could happen to people without connections or friends. For in numberless places, at least traditionally, the star performer of the capea was the ragged young would-be torero, the male-tilla. According to Barea, Araúz de Robles, and other authors cited earlier, mayors preoccupied with giving their supporters a maximum of fun had no qualms about acquiring the largest and most fearsome bulls for the ma-letillas to struggle with and occasionally succumb to. In the interest of a balanced perspective, however, mention must be made of Ciudad Rodrigo (Salamanca) and its famous Bolsín Taurino. Founded in 1956, this organi-zation not only arranges a series of contests and prizes but also food and lodging for penniless apprentice toreros. It has helped thousands of male-tillas over the years, as many as five hundred in a given year. In keeping with Spain's predominating social patterns, the internal structure of the Bolsín Taurino is like a family: it consists of thirty cattle breeders and eigh-teen managers, whose membership is strictly hereditary; the oldest rancher is the patriarch of the group.[46] Formal bullfighting schools have also helped to ameliorate the age-old injustices of the maletilla system. The Es-cuela Nacional Taurina was founded in 1976, changed its name to the Es-cuela de Tauromaquia de Madrid in 1982, and in 1990 had some hundred students. Ten other taurine schools were founded in the decade of the 1980's, two of them in France.[47]

Even in areas and in epochs without charitable paternalistic institutions or schools, the capea did provide opportunities for toreros without con-nections to make a name for themselves. There was another—and faster—route to the top, but access to it was far more restricted. This route led through the miniature bullrings on the *fincas*, or ranches, of brave cattle breeders; the owners used these rings to test the qualities of their cows and calves. These testing sessions, called *tientas*, were important social occa-sions, especially in Andalusia, and breeders often invited impresarios, critics, famous matadors, and local power brokers to attend. The large landowners presided over a closed, personalistic system that was, like the Spanish system as a whole, a "kingdom of the favor." In their biography of El Cordobés, Collins and Lapierre provide a glimpse into the nature of this kingdom and the maletillas on the outside looking in:

> The world they were trying to enter was one of the most inbred, most closed societies in existence. Courage and ambition alone were not enough to buy ad-mission to its ranks. Friendship was needed, and the aid of someone already inside. Access to that world was natural to a Dominguín or an Antonio Ordó-ñez. Sons of matadors, they were born inside its perimeters. They had only to present themselves at the gates of a finca to be invited in to display their skills.

To Manolo Benítez and the hundreds of faceless young men like him, the gates of those fincas were firmly closed. . . . The ranchers extended such privileges to adolescents already known to them or those recommended by men whose judgment they trusted. Sometimes they included a boy who pressed a frayed and stained calling card into their hands. Those cards might come from another rancher, once mildly impressed by the bearer's skills, a retired manager or a second-class matador; they were passports into the world of the corrida issued by one of its citizens. The maletillas who had them cherished them more than a thousand-peseta note. Often they could not even read the few words scribbled on them. But they carried those dirty, thumb-worn scraps of paper with the same ardor they bore the medals of local Virgins around their necks.[48]

Bullfighting is a profession to which many are called but few are chosen. In our earlier discussion of the selection process that has blindly chosen the few and eliminated the multitude, we discussed the importance of *padrinos* or godfathers, men with connections who were in a position to facilitate or impede the career of a given young man. Sooner or later a would-be bullfighter is going to have to find such padrinos, the more the better, or he will get nowhere. El Cordobés wandered around for years without such connections, and when he finally did find them they were, appropriately enough, desperate gambling types much like himself who were willing to take a chance on a brash newcomer. In the case of Belmonte, several years of murderous capeas and covert nighttime excursions to private fincas earned him a local following in Seville; one friend led to another, and one padrino to still another, and he was eventually introduced to landowners and impresarios who exploited him until he was in a position to exploit them. His talent, temerity, masochism, and good luck sustained him throughout.

   In the case of many novice toreros, the chain of friends or padrinos will break at its weakest link. In an article entitled "Not Everyone Can Be El Cordobés," Lyon recounts the sad but all too typical trajectory of Pedro Giraldo, a native of Palencia who recalls his misspent youth with nostalgia: "Life as a maletilla was the harshest one could imagine, but the most beautiful one, too. We always dreamed about the glory of bullfighting, that one day a manager in a Mercedes would appear and make us famous." Serious gorings in the genitals and digestive tract did not deter him, but eventually he found out that manliness and professionalism were insufficient without a "strong house" to back him up.[49]

   On the planet of the bulls, of course, one never knows how much truth there is in a failure's story and how much he is shifting the blame for his own defects to others. Nor is it surprising that in a personalistic power structure, the actions of the powerful will be taken personally by the weak; rejection can easily breed hate. In June 1987, a matador named Pedro Castillo found out that he had been excluded from the annual Feria Taurina de Algeciras (Cádiz) by the organizer, an impresario named Carlos Corbacho. As Corbacho drove away from the bullring in his Mercedes, the frustrated matador attempted to drive his sword through the car window into the impresario. Castillo missed the mark and was later charged with attempted homicide.[50] One can only wonder if the matador's lack of ability with the sword could have been a factor in the impresario's decision to exclude him.

Or one can refer the case to others in which excellent bullfighters have been excluded because of the whim or the corruption of the powerful. In one critic's view, arbitrary exclusion is just another aspect of racket in the bullfighting world:

> The fact that a man or two or three have been permitted to block with impunity the careers of other men who wished to exercise their profession freely is intolerable. The fact that a poor bullfighter whose only property was his passion and clothes, has been forced to save, to go hungry, to incur debts, and everything in order to pay a trust of millionaires for his right to be in a bullfight is something beyond explanation. Tricks of merchants![51]

The other side of this coin of unfair exclusion, of course, is unfair inclusion. Sánchez Garrido cites the case of a Cordoban bullfighter called Parrita, who had the kind of connections that hungry maletillas only dream of: his father was a successful matador from Madrid and his mother was the niece of Manolete himself. As the boy grew tall and handsome, a host of cattle breeders, critics, and aficionados "intuited" that he would be the next Manolete; opportunities to fight easy bulls were showered upon him in the 1970s. Little by little, however, the spoiled Parrita's lack of ambition extinguished his career.[52]

Even more instructive is the case of a novillero of the 1930s named Alfredo Corrochano. As the son of Gregorio Corrochano, possibly the most influential taurine critic of the twentieth century, Alfredo was on a fast track from the start. In Hemingway's contemporary account:

> Alfredo is a dark, slight, contemptuous and arrogant boy with a rather Bourbonic face a little like that of Alfonso XIII as a child. He was educated in Switzerland and trained as a matador at the testings of the calves and brood stock of

the bull ranches around Madrid and Salamanca by Sánchez Mejías, his father and all those who toady to his father. . . . Due to his father's position, his presentation in Madrid aroused much feeling and he was made to feel all the bitterness of the enemies his father's often excellent and extremely well written sarcasms had made, as well as those who hated him as a son of the middle-class royalist and believed he was depriving boys who needed bread to eat of the chance to earn it in the ring. . . . He showed he was a good banderillero, an excellent dominator with the muleta, with much intelligence and vista in handling of the bull, but with a lamentably bad style with the cape and an utter inability to kill properly or even decently.[53]

Hemingway went on to predict that the young bullfighter's career would be washed up when the novelty of his surname wore off—a prediction that did not come true. Corrochano took several cornadas in stride, corrected his defects, went on to become a fairly successful matador, and even attained a delirious triumph at Belmonte's last corrida in 1935.[54]

Even though bullfighting is a true kingdom of the favor, therefore, whose only consistent principle is that of arbitrariness, a bullfighter will always need the right personal qualities to get ahead. Like modern Spain itself, bullfighting combines an element of individual merit or upward mobility with archaic patronage mechanisms. Furthermore, the careers of friendless maletillas and protected prodigies alike demonstrate that trajectory is everything. The prestige earned in any one corrida has to be reaffirmed again and again; the matador must build momentum. Eventually we will take a look at the corrida, the bullfight spectacle itself, in terms of the mass psychology that constitutes one of the causes and/or results of the whole patronage system. But let us focus for now on bullfighting as an institution and a profession, as well as a means of advancement that replicates the caudillo and cacique systems in propelling opportunistic men into power and making them defenders of the very status quo that forced them into bullfighting in the first place. As we will see, the whole point of a bullfighter's career is to go from being a dependent, a client, a receiver of favors in a more-or-less corrupt system of personalistic patronage, to being a dispenser of favors and patronage—the boss of his cuadrilla, a landowner, a "big man" in his community, and a promoter of personalistic corruption at one level or another.

The nineteenth century witnessed the consolidation of the movement toward professionalism that was already underway in the eighteenth. As Garcia-Baquero and his co-authors have argued, it was the then-dominant guild system that served as the model for turning the craft of public bull slaughter into a profession. This involved: (1) the drive to submit every one of the bullfight's suertes to strict regulation; (2) hierarchism, with a particular nomenclature for each of the successive ranks or specializations (picador, banderillero, novillero, etc.), as well as ritual observance of authority and seniority and a more or less defined period of apprenticeship for novice toreros; and (3) the drive to get governmental authorities to guarantee the exclusivism of the new profession and the strict imposition of the ordinances.[55] In a similar vein, Díaz Yanes affirms that few other groups in nineteenth-century Spain were as committed as bullfighters were to the ideal of professional perfection, pushed onwards by a ferocious degree of internal criticism and the will to submit every kind of bull to the intelligence of the matador.[56] From here, of course, it is just a step to Gil Calvo's notion that bullfighting rationalism was nothing less than the cutting edge of an underground or de facto Spanish Enlightenment that he alleges to have occurred. So it is important to remember two things. First, the most professional and technically advanced bullfighters (like Pedro Romero or José Redondo) were never as popular as the crowd-pleasing, suicidally valiant type (like Pepe-Illo or Curro Cúchares)—much to the chagrin of discriminating critics.[57] Second, the basic unit of professional organization in bullfighting was, and still is, the cuadrilla. In Spain the cuadrilla preceded the guild system and has outlived it; its principle of organization has not been rationality so much as dominance and submission. For centuries it has been Spain's archetypal format of all-male, small-group dynamics in many different settings, as well as a paradigm of personalistic power. In the words of Arévalo and Moral:

> The bullfighting cuadrilla is something more than a team. It is an archaic social cell of workers, rooted in the countryside, nomadic and close-knit, with its origins among warriors and hunters. Possibly, Spain is not a country of individualists but of cuadrilla members. Certainly in Spanish history there is no great individual without his cuadrilla. They exist for purposes of friendship, for carrying saints, for fighting, for taking power, for taking plunder. They seep into political parties, companies, the Church, and the Army. And all of them have their metaphor in the bullfighting cuadrilla. . . . The cuadrilla is an action-oriented family, strictly masculine: the other family. In this hidebound and insolidary country, anyone who doesn't belong to a cuadrilla is lost.[58]

As the Spanish saying has it, "el que se arrima a buen árbol, buena sombra le cobija" (roughly, he who gets close to a good tree will be sheltered by a good shade). The weak get by, in other words, by clinging to the strong, especially in a country like Spain, as Arévalo and Moral would remind us, a nation built not on individuals but on quasi-familial factions. A "strong man" ultimately derived his strength from the debility of his supporters; the weak got nowhere without patriarchs, padrinos, bosses, caciques, or caudillos, men who bestowed rewards and punishments in accordance with their mood swings.

From its earliest days, bullfighting on foot was always a group activity, each man with a role to play, clear-cut obligations and privileges, and an almost feudal loyalty to his chief. The chief of a bullfighting cuadrilla, like that of a band of warriors or a gang of bandoleros, legitimated his authority in his all-male group by being more male—more willing to kill or be killed in confrontations with rivals of one species or another. The loyalty of subordinates and the obsequiousness of parasites was bought and paid for by the chief as a further prerogative of his role. We saw all this in Chapter 2. Now it can be observed that the triumph of bullfighting on foot was in the last analysis a new road for poor but ambitious men with cuadrillas to rise in society while remaining within the boundaries of the law. (Outlaws could be popular heroes, of course, but they would never hope to hobnob with high society in the style of a successful matador.) Eugenio Noel was not misguided in seeing the popular matador as the dream come true of an impoverished people oppressed by caciques; their idolatry is a function of

> the dazzling sight of one of their own sons, only yesterday a ragamuffin, dust, nothing, who with only willpower and his own efforts rises with incredible rapidity to become nothing less than the equal of that cacique, marrying his daughter, riding around in his carriages, buying his lands.[59]

José Delgado Guerra, alias Pepe-Illo, was the eighteenth-century prototype of the process; historians tell us that he was generous to a fault, given to acts of philanthropy, and sought after as a godfather by everyone with a baby. He was the first matador to adorn his majo suit with gold and silver. He was strong, manly, proud, and impulsive; he benefited from the patronage of the aristocracy and arbitrarily bestowed his own patronage on selected lower-class fans and admirers in Seville.[60] We are also told that he had a great sense of humor, but it is hard to imagine a parasite not laughing at any joke Pepe-Illo might have told.

As bullfighters conquer ever greater levels of popularity, respectability, wealth, and social power, bullfighting as a whole merges with, or repli-

cates, the other mainstream methods by which ambitious men with supporters grow powerful. As Gil theorizes, the bullfighter's leadership is "unequivocally military"—since he is a warrior who wields the sword in a duel
to the death—and "unequivocally political"—since he possesses the knack
of using the power of another (the bull) for his own purposes.[61] Be that as
it may, it is a fact that, starting in the nineteenth century, matadors come
to have careers that parallel those of caudillos or political power brokers,
and some even become caciques. Here the most famous example is Mazzantini. In what was probably the most meteoric career in bullfighting history, Mazzantini went from being a railroad station manager to wealthy
bullfighter in two years. (His true desire had been to sing opera, but he
lacked the voice for it.) He fought bulls from 1884 to 1905 with enormous
success, magnetizing the masses with his brazen, superbly effective killing
style and winning the hearts of downtrodden people everywhere with spectacular displays of generosity. In 1891 he helped a candidate from Puerto de
Santa María (Cádiz) to win office by promising to hold a bullfight for the
voters.[62] Mazzantini's ambition was like one of the trains he used to direct.
He learned to speak several languages and went on to become a friend of
King Alfonso XII, an impresario, and a breeder of brave cattle, ending his
career, appropriately enough, as a civil governor.[63]

Other bullfighters were content to mingle with powerful caciques, equal
partners that they were in the maintenance of the status quo. Rafael
Guerra, Mazzantini's contemporary, was on intimate terms with the boss
of Seville, Rodríguez de la Borbolla. Following his retirement, Guerra dis-
pensed advice and favors from his own club in the center of Córdoba; people who passed by the patriarch's establishment would often curtsy or bow
and some even made the sign of the cross.[64] Such anecdotes tell us a great
deal about popular attitudes toward the powerful.

The political parallels of an up-and-coming bullfighter's charisma are
described with special lucidity by Belmonte in his autobiography:

Suddenly I realized that I was the axis of the group, the most important person-
age in our little gang. The things I said soon acquired a resonance that they
never had before. We were the same as always, we spoke of the same things, but
those people were listening to me now, and doing what I said. I started to over-
hear words like "Juan says that . . ." or "Juan doesn't like. . . " and so on. That
had a strange effect on me, and sometimes it made me blush. I began to notice,
besides, that I was making all kinds of new friends; around the valiant little
bullfighter was beginning to form that court that forms around political big
wheels when it is announced that there will be a change of situation that could

take their faction into power. My friends were always with me, they laughed at my jokes, and they never left me until dawn.[65]

Like Pepe-Illo, Belmonte was much sought after as a padrino. In an effort to get rid of one new friend who begged him to be his son's godfather, Belmonte claimed to be a jinx whose godsons always died in their infancy. The excited man shouted his reply: "It doesn't matter, it doesn't matter!"[66]

Like so many famous matadors before and since, Belmonte went on to become a wealthy Andalusian landowner and pillar of the same status quo that victimized him as a youth. People in need of evidence for the essentially conservative nature of bullfighting need look no further than the bullfighters themselves, the successful ones that literally go from rags to riches without questioning the system. Matadors are not social revolutionaries by any stretch of the imagination, and any redistribution of wealth that they undertake follows the traditional Spanish patterns of charity or capricious favoritism. To obtain a complete picture of the matador's place in Spanish society, therefore, we must not only look at his rise to power but his enjoyment of the same.

Almost any successful bullfighter who survived and retired young and wealthy may serve as an example of the general pattern. Let us focus in on El Cordobés, a matador about whom we already know a great deal. Now we can go beyond the ten biographies that describe his harsh years as a maletilla and his stunning rise to prominence and turn to accounts of how he lived after his retirement in 1971. Manuel Benítez found himself the owner of no fewer than eight vast fincas, some eleven thousand hectares altogether; one of his properties bordered the lands of Don Félix Moreno, the man who had exploited the Benítez family and almost everyone else in Palma del Rio. El Cordobés had given cars or houses to his friends and family; he had donated televisions to the old folks of Palma and built a trade school for the young. He had squandered vast sums in orgies at his own hotel in Córdoba, using his wealth to buy off enraged husbands or fathers and cover up the sort of activities for which poor men were sent to jail. His companions were other wastrel landowners like himself, ancestral exploiters of Andalusia's *jornaleros*, or landless day laborers. These same jornaleros had once cheered wildly in the bullrings, knowing that Manolo had been one of them; but they soon found out that El Cordobés as landowner was like all the others. One day Benítez found out that two of his workers were poaching rabbits on one of his fincas. He pursued them on horseback. The men reminded him that in his youth he had himself stolen rabbits, chickens, oranges, and everything he could lay his hands on. Benítez rode off to inform the Guardia Civil, the same Guardia Civil that had beaten him silly for his larceny years before.[67] It would be pointless, in my view, to hold Benítez personally responsible for his mentality or upbraid him for his hard-hearted actions. He was only behaving, after all, in accordance with what his country and its institutions had made him. While El Cordobés had gone from one end of the social spectrum to the other, the spectrum itself had remained much the same.

It is easy to see the parallels between matadors, politicians, and other men of ambition. Whatever means they had originally employed to obtain their power and charisma, they maintained it through largesse, influence peddling, *personalismo*, or simple coercion. It is not so easy, however, to see the actual formal similarities between matadors and politicians in the obtention of power itself. Herein lies a more subtle point of connection between bullfighting and the Spanish political system, one pointed out by Julio Caro Baroja, one of Spain's most eminent social historians. Caro is the author of a brief but suggestive meditation on the rhetorical nature of the matador's art, written in response to the question brusquely put to him one day by a taurophobic friend: "Do you really think it makes any sense to move one's buttocks with elegance before Death?"

> It does make some kind of sense, undoubtedly: and certainly it is necessary to consider bullfighting as a kind of dangerous rhetorical exercise. An exercise that in some cases consists of sober, pithy, concise forms and formulas, and in others, of flowery forms, and in still others, of grandiloquent forms. Every famous torero has had his own rhetoric, and the same holds true for the great Andalusian orators. In southern lands, the closest thing to an orator is a bullfighter. The effect that both seek to provoke is quite similar and in olden days the places they performed in were the same. In great bullrings an orator can fire up the multitude just like a matador, gesticulating. He can elicit similar critiques, solemn reviews that discuss "form" and "content." And the taurine journalist of a popular newspaper, in fact, is twin brother to the one who writes or wrote the review of parliamentary sessions.[68]

Bullfighting, then, like Andalusian political oratory, can be seen as a series of dramatic gestures made in public for the public. And there is another, more ominous implication, one not voiced by Caro: like political rhetoric, the sign language of bullfighting can easily slide into demagogy. In fact, a strong case can be made for seeing *every bullfighter* as a potential demagogue—a person who stirs up the emotions of a crowd to become a leader and achieve his own ends. A bullfighter achieves power and wealth when he learns how to sway the masses, to mesmerize and spellbind them, to harness their passion for his private profit. The matador rides to the top of society on the backs of mass enthusiasm. Virtually any famous faena of the past two centuries, therefore, could be reinterpreted as an exercise in populist demagogy. Consider, for example, the eloquent discourse that Belmonte made with his body language in the "forum" of Madrid in 1913. Before the unbelieving eyes of thousands, he gave the bull five Veronica passes without shifting terrain.[69] This was a first in the history of bullfighting, and even though Belmonte was trampled by the next bull, he had won over the masses and the critics alike. After years of trials, he had needed only an instant to become the supreme leader of Spanish bullfighting. The demogogic nature of bullfighting was never more in evidence than in the 1960s, when Manolo Benítez confounded the patriciate of elitist critics and rode to power on the acclamations of the millions of plebeians who glorified his graceless but electrifying achievements in the bullring.

Like caciquismo, taurine demagogy begins at home—that is, in small towns and villages across Spain. As the reader will recall, the small-town fiesta de toros has been an important means for local leaders to gain or maintain popularity. Nothing can be more demagogic than a capea, it would seem, for here local authorities have traditionally given the people exactly what they wanted to see. Like unscrupulous traders who supplied the Indian tribes of the American plains with alcohol, opportunistic local strong men supplied villagers with another sort of addictive pastime—riotous yearly bull-baiting. This is a charge that can be made even today: as discussed earlier, animal-rights groups in Spain have sharply criticized the many post-Franco mayors who had never attended a capea or encierro in their lives but who became bull enthusiasts overnight when they saw the political value of the fiestas.

And that is not all. The sacred dimension of the fiesta de toros can be seen as a replication or projection of the secular dimension. Rural festivities are always held in honor of a patron saint, a kind of supernatural cacique in touch with the Central Authority and in a position to do favors for his or her local "clients." If people regale their patron with fiestas it is because they are grateful for favors rendered in the past and hopeful about future ones. Such beliefs have been reinforced by generations of ecclesiastical orators. Thus, the web of complicities that makes bull-baiting possible is inseparable from the local belief system and the local power structure—each component enhancing the other.

In the final analysis, demogogy—including the taurine variety—depends for its success on a peculiar kind of "democracy," one in which emotional factors play a predominant role. No bullfighter could sway the masses, after all, if they were not disposed to be swayed. And, as we shall see, this mobile disposition is intimately related to popular concepts of power, authority, and justice. Let us turn our attention away from the bull and the bullfighter to become spectators of the spectators. In the bullring's bleachers we may well discover the most important links between bullfighting and political culture in Spain.

Taurine Democracy

As the reader will recall from our earlier study, power was attained and maintained in nineteenth- and twentieth-century Spain in rather retrograde ways. Even though the system made room for numerous men of ambition to acquire power, it preserved the plutocracy, sustained the bloated bureaucracy, impeded educational reform, corrupted the military, sanctioned autocratic leadership styles, and set the stage for dictatorship. Most ironic and damning of all, perhaps, the Spanish political system served to keep most Spaniards out of politics altogether, instilling in them a fatalistic attitude vis-á-vis the whims of authority. As Carr has written, "There can be no doubt that caciquismo prolonged and intensified the conditions which made it necessary and possible—the political ignorance and apathy of the Spanish electorate."[70] Now, throughout the two-century period that concerns us, the bullfight was far and away the most popular pastime of Spain; it brought together enormous numbers of people, men and women of all social classes. Surely an examination of the behavior of these teeming taurine masses ought to tell us, once and for all, whether bullfighting is truly a microcosm of the Spanish social order.

The uproarious mob atmosphere of eighteenth-century bullfighting on foot reflected its structural and psychological proximity to the capea; by comparison, the urban bullfight spectacle as we know it today is, relatively speaking, an orderly and well-choreographed affair. This remarkable transformation involved three distinct varieties of domestication, two of which we have already examined. First to be tamed were the antisocial guapos and majos, who learned to use their swords on bovids instead of each other. Then the wild *bos taurus* underwent a de facto domestication on the lands of cattle-breeding aristocrats who successfully projected their own blood mythology onto an animal species. The third entity to be tamed was the bullfight public itself: slowly, and with great difficulty, people were persuaded or coerced into staying out of the bullring while the new taurine professionals fought the newly bred brave bulls. In each of these three instances, of course, the domestication carried out was only relative; even today, matadors, bulls, and spectators can be unpredictable, wild, and obstreperous. It was enough, however, to transform the Goyesque chaos of the fiesta de toros into the ritual art of the so-called Fiesta Nacional.

The capea-like crowds of the eighteenth century were so boisterous and anarchic on bullfighting days that troops were needed to clear the plaza to make way for the parade of cuadrillas. In Seville, for example, the clearing of the plaza (*el despejo*) was entrusted to a detachment composed of a captain, two lieutenants, twenty corporals, thirty-seven grenadiers, and numerous drummers. The plebeians were never easily cowed: at one bullfight in 1748, several knaves jumped down into the plaza and began to strike at the bull with their own swords. When a soldier tried to beat them off with his cartridge belt, the crowd roared its disapproval, then chased the soldier all the way to his garrison screaming for "justice."[71] Numbers of troops were steadily increased as the eighteenth century wore on, but there were never enough to please José Daza, the varilarguero we met earlier, who complained bitterly that the bullring of Seville was no more respected than a bordello.[72] Gradually a complete body of taurine rules and regulations was drawn up in which the rights and responsibilities of the public were clearly defined and enforced by the presence of soldiers and the police-like authority of the *presidente*.

Popular attitudes about the military changed from hostility to hero-worship in the early nineteenth century as a result of the war with Napoleon, the struggle against Absolutism, and the Carlist conflicts. Bullfighting in the nineteenth century faithfully reflects the interpenetration of military and civilian society in Spain. It was not uncommon for matadors to receive their swords from military officers, such as General Espartero, and bulls were sometimes fought by men in uniform.[73] As places where people of all social classes and professions congregated, bullrings became de facto forums for the expression of political passions; there were Conservative or Absolutist bullfighters and there were Liberal ones, and spectators cheered them on or reviled them not in terms of taurine merit but in accordance with their own factionalist persuasions. Throughout the nineteenth century, the popular concept of bullfighting will be not that of a fine art so much as that of a martial art; matadors come to be identified as warriors or caudillos and their performances as so many episodes of a grandiose national saga—with musical accompaniment.

The military origins of bullfighting music have been firmly established by Delgado-Iribarren. For one thing, every change of suerte in a bullfight was, and is, signaled by a bugle call; the melodies employed are much the same as those used in infantry and cavalry barracks. In addition, the *pasodoble*—the stirring music played even today by bullring bands—is a direct descendant of the military march. During the war with France it became the emblem of patriotic guerrillas, incorporating diverse elements from the jota, the bolero, and other kinds of folk music. The military past of the over five hundred pasodobles now in existence is seen in their binary marching rhythm, their allegro movement, their simple melodies, and their facile execution by bands of wind and percussion instruments.[74]

Unlike other European nations during this period, Spain saw its colonial possessions shrinking instead of expanding. It could well be argued that bullfighting provided an important psychological compensation for many Spaniards, a gratifying fantasy of national potency to make up for the less than glorious reality. In attempting to account for the veritable explosion of taurine novels in the nineteenth century, one literary historian reasons that

> behind this proliferation there lies a sort of Spanish reply to what in those same years the adventure novel represents in foreign literatures, that emerges in the exotic settings revealed by the new European colonialism, in expansion precisely during the same decades. In Spain, victim of such an inverse historical process, that source of thematic possibilities is curtailed and the imaginative gaze of the Spanish writer tends more and more towards endogamy.[75]

There were definite nationalistic overtones to special corridas that pitted the brave bull against animals that supposedly represented other nations or their colonies. When the good Spanish bull bested the elephant, the lion, or the Bengal tiger, crowds would shout ¡*Viva España*! and sing patriotic hymns. The band was always on hand to set the right tone of militance. Following the loss of Spain's last colonies to the United States in 1898, numerous bullfights were organized in which people wore the national colors and bullfighters made inflamatory speeches.[76] During the Spanish Civil War (1936–1939), both sides sponsored corridas: bullfighters would appear with clenched fists or fascist salutes, whichever was appropriate. And in the darkest days of their country's isolation under Franco, Spaniards flocked to bullrings to reaffirm their identity with something they knew was their own and which they took to represent their finest qualities. However barbarous its beginnings, therefore, however sordid some of its practices, the fiesta de toros had truly become Spain's Fiesta Nacional.

In return for their renunciation of certain behaviors and attitudes, conclude García-Baquero and his fellow authors, taurine spectators were compensated with a new and enormously gratifying role: they were to be the honorary judges and critics of every aspect of the taurine performance. This is even the explicit message of several *tauromaquias* ghostwritten for famous matadors to explain the art and science of bullfighting.[77] Even after taurine criticism had become a dependable source of income for professional journalists, the people themselves retained their judgmental prerogatives, expressed not in prose but in cheers, curses, handkerchief-waving, shouted witticisms, and so forth. Spectators have also felt themselves empowered to second-guess the maximum authority at the bullring, the "president," when he witholds trophy ears or refuses to withdraw defective bulls. If bullfighting is indeed one of the world's fine arts (the jury is still out), then it would seem to possess a unique accessibility: whereas devotees of other arts meekly defer to experts, bullfight spectators evaluate artistic merit for themselves and express their views instantly and unselfconsciously. The downside of this refreshing spontaneity, however, is that popular value judgments tend to be arbitrary and emotionalistic. A bullring is undisputably a "pit of passion." In every epoch and in every plaza, vast numbers of spectators have rushed in to judge where the equanimous feared to tread. Historically speaking, finesse or level-headedness have never been characteristics of such mass evaluations. True justice cannot be administered spontaneously, without reflection, on the spur of the moment. In the words of Pérez de Ayala:

> Impulsive justice is practiced at bullfights. And justice should be reflexive. Impulsive justice starts out by being too severe in its decisions; then shortly afterward it relents, feels regret, and errs in the direction of leniency. It never maintains its sanctions. The bullfight spectator applies momentaneous, impulsive sanctions to bullfighters: he rains vile insults upon them, he denigrates them, he mentions their mothers, he throws cushions, oranges, and other throwable items at them. But when the next bull comes out and the matador executes his cape pass with a flashy whirl, the spectator has already forgotten everything.[78]

There are, to be sure, a small number of aficionados who might evaluate what they see in a dispassionate way. But if there is one thing about which taurine and anti-taurine writers have been in complete agreement over the years, it is their disgust for the arbitrary and unreasoning majority. In addition, nearly every famous matador has said at one time or another that he feared the public more than the bulls. Small wonder: idolatry can easily become iconoclasm on the planet of the bulls. In atmospheres of passion and mass excitement, the first thing to be lost is the ability to distinguish properly between justice and injustice. In its worst form, the impulsive justice of bullfight crowds has unnerved and rattled bullfighters and led them to commit acts that have resulted in serious injury and even death. At the Feria de Almeria in 1981, for example, Curro Romero was gored in an attempt to appease a hastily judgmental crowd. As he later explained, "The public was very hotheaded and I had to work miracles to calm it down. In other circumstances that bull would never have wounded me. But the public was furious and I had to do it. A useless cornada for nothing!"[79] Afterwards the public was very sorry, of course—as sorry as it had been in 1920 after it hounded Joselito into fatal temerity at Talavera or in 1947 when it drove Manolete to impale himself on the horns of Islero. As a noted critic has written, Joselito and Manolete were not killed by the cornadas of bulls but by "the monster that fills the bleachers and demands, with absolute ignorance and cruelty, something that is beyond human power."[80] As readers of Blasco Ibáñez's *Blood and Sand* will recall, the novel ends with a description of the public: "The beast roared: the real one, the only one."[81]

For some critics, ironically, the crowd is not monstrous enough. In 1913, Felix Borrell, writing under the pseudonym F. Bleu, blamed the decline of bullfighting on the effeminate masses who preferred a gay, decaffeinated form of bullfighting to the grandiose and cruel drama he had grown up with.[82] In 1970, another eminent critic decried the excessive "benevolence" that had become a characteristic of the public of the Franco years.[83] It might well be asked who is crueler or more sadistic: the emotionalistic spectator who goes from rage to joy in the space of a few moments, or the serene critic who consciously and consistently demands that bullfighting remain as authentically dangerous as possible?

It should be clear from the above that, at the very least, the public generally judges the taurine performance in an arbitrary, capricious, and personalistic manner. Since the decisions of the bullring presidente form part of the entire affair, they too fall under the scrutiny—and often the vociferous condemnation—of the public. Like Spain itself, perhaps, the bullfight is a mise en scène of an authoritarian power in uneasy relationship with a blasphemous and rebellious public. For Pérez de Ayala, the crowd's impulsive style of reacting to duly constituted authority was the worst evil of bullfighting, one that reconfirmed Spaniards in their submission to the despotic whims of the powerful.

> In order to be well-governed, a nation requires a people that knows how to adopt one of two attitudes with regard to authority, whichever is appropriate: either voluntary submission, as long as authority does not exceed its own juris-diction, or unshakeable resistence, if authority were arbitrary or abusive. In bull-fights the people learn and habituate themselves to acting in exactly the two opposite ways: with mockery and contempt for just or inoffensive authority, with weakness vis-à-vis arbitrary or abusive authority. . . . In public life the Spanish citizen behaves like a bullfight spectator. . . . Taurine psychology spreads itself throughout Spanish life.[84]

In many ways, the figure of the presidente is a reflection not only of the Absolutist age in which his functions were first spelled out but of the au-tocratic forms of power that Spanish society has harbored ever since. For one thing, no special competence in matters taurine is required; the presi-dente can be a police sergeant, a governor, an alderman, or, in the old days, a cacique. As the maximum authority at the bullfight, he may take into consideration the desires of the public but he is in no way obliged to. As the very embodiment of arbitrary power, he possesses total immunity and his decisions cannot be appealed. The public's only recourse is to whistle, hoot, or insult—a momentarily gratifying but ultimately sterile activity. In much the same manner as the old African monarchies described by anthro-pologists, the bullfight arranges for, and even encourages, a ritualistic contestation of power that is emotionally satisfying but essentially incon-sequential.

In his own way, of course, the matador polarizes the spectators' criteria of dominance and submission: whatever power he possesses must be seen in terms of popular concepts of power—who deserves to have it and who does not. The bullfight public bestows power in accordance with criteria worked out long ago during Spain's traumatic history of war and civil con-flict. In the popular mind, power belongs in the hands of a strong man. Let us momentarily yield the floor to sociologist Tierno Galván:

> In my judgment, bullfights are a collective act of faith. Faith in what?—in the male of the species. The bullfight spectator believes in certain qualities inherent in a man that constitute manliness, and precisely because he believes in them he goes to see bullfights. The bullfighter presents himself as the standard-bearer of manliness, and ratifies in each moment of the bullfight that the faith in a certain

kind of man, in which the public believes, makes complete and continuing sense. . . . For this reason the bullfighter is a symbol.[85]

According to Araúz de Robles, the bullfight

is built on "machismo," that is, on the primacy and I would almost say the social apotheosis of masculinity. . . . In a country characterized by a lifestyle clearly marked by machismo, the taurine rituals and games constitute a pragmatic theory of said machismo, a clearly comprehensible dramatization of it available to all.[86]

We must be careful not to conclude that bullfighting can be reduced to machismo or to male domination and so on. This is only one part of the picture: whatever element of the male mystique might be involved cannot be considered apart from the patterns of power that have conditioned Spaniards to expect certain things from bullfighters, or from caudillos, or from caciques, or other authority figures. As anthropologists like Brandes and Gilmore have established, machismo in a Spanish/Andalusian context can never be simply a question of males over females but of consciousness of domination as well—*male* consciousness of domination by other males.[87] Tierno's "faith in manhood," therefore, has important political overtones, and it cannot be considered apart from the political domination that Spaniards have been subjected to for all these years. What Brandes calls "testicular willpower"—the popular notion that the male genitals are or should be the locus of authority—is intimately related to Spaniards' restless subordination to despotic caprice and their reproduction of the same power pattern in the domestic sphere. And vice versa: in the political sphere, willful caudillos envisioned the army as the nation's virile member. In the 1920s, the Bourbon dynasty made a last-ditch attempt to salvage the status quo with an old-fashioned authoritarian dictator who ruled by decree. Primo de Rivera sprinkled his speeches with constant references to manliness; it was even said that all the bull testicles he had eaten had gone to his brain.[88] If a specialist in political pathology were to examine the Spanish case, wrote Pérez de Ayala, his diagnosis would have been

orquitis, that is, inflammation or hypertrophy of the male organs. (I allude to the symbolic organography of the state and to the part of it that supposedly embodies politically the masculine organ.) Prognosis: sterility. In a paradoxical way, it is evident that the apparent hyperbole of maleness, called orquitis, produces incurable sterility. It is surprising that among us it is still considered dogma that virile energy and its most rudimentary manifestation, the military temperament, depend on the cubic content of semen.[89]

We have already explored the chief characteristics of the type of male that bullfight fans have faith in—his insouciant body language, his atavistic warrior ethos, his impulsiveness, his masochism, his casual readiness to triumph or die, his deep-rooted conservatism. If the bullfighter is indeed a symbol, as Tierno affirms, then perhaps he is a symbol that mediates between two varieties of fantasy fulfillment, the personal and the national. My reasoning is as follows: Properly defined, machismo is a psychological mechanism of compensation that provides a fantasy image of superiority in the absence of real maturity or sociopolitical power. Mutatis mutandis, bullfighting might have served a similar function in certain decades, a psychological compensation for a national inferiority complex that sought to fill the power gap with manly hyperbole. It is not, in the last analysis, an enviable concept of manhood nor of nationhood. In one of his best essays, Eugenio Noel contrasts the death of a bullfighter named Dominguín with that of antarctic explorer Robert Scott, two men who died bravely but in the service of wholly antithetical notions of valor:

> Dominguín gored, tossed, frightfully wounded in the entrails, horribly contracted on the sand—does this not give you the image of a sad kind of valor that is not glorious at all but sterile and antiesthetic? . . . Is it a socially useful sort of valor, a healthy valor, a manly valor, to let oneself be pulled in by the vertigo of the abyss, of the hurricane of the impossible, of the vanity of an afternoon of sun, shouts, and thrills? . . . Why does our race create Dominguíns and not a Scott? His valor was serene, conscious, grave, silent, without arrogance or brazen acts; this scientific valor is humanitarian, the greatest and most heroic trait that a man could ask of another man. This valor has a good end, it involves a positive utility. . . . The young men of Spain are able to spear a charging bull; but the polar circles, the machines, the explorations that give a Congo to Belgium, the railroad from the Cape to El Cairo, Panama, Aswan—that is the work of the young men of other countries, of their moral valor that obliges the body to make overwhelming efforts.[90]

My prolonged discussion of bullfighting and politics has now come to an end. As the reader will recall, it was begun in response to Gil Calvo's assertion that the corrida de toros inculcates civic maturity and Enlightenment-style democratic ideals in Spaniards. I hope to have demonstrated that such thinking is not warranted by the evidence. Gil seems to have carried out a Polyanna-like projection of his own fine democratic ideals onto the historical reality of the fiesta de toros. To term a passionate blood sport enlightening, or to portray it as a kind of unofficial Spanish Enlightenment, is an ingenious but ultimately untenable stance. The evidence would appear to be on the side of those who argue that bullfighting is the legacy of obscurantism, that it is emblematic of the manipulability of the people, their gullibility, their irrational hero-worship, their subjection to social and political corruption, their immaturity and incivility (not their civic maturity as Gil would have it). It would surely be absurd to see bullfighting as the "cause" of Spain's former political backwardness, but it was certainly no cure.

5. Psychosexual Aspects of the Bullfight

OF ALL THE QUESTIONS that have been asked about bullfighting in the twentieth century, one in particular has generated much curiosity and provoked the broadest variety of answers: What does bullfighting have to do with sex? Although in terms of credibility the answers have ranged from dubious to unhinged, they have at least served to stimulate debate and further inquiry. At the present time, for better or worse, no serious student of bullfighting can avoid coming to terms with the sex question. I will therefore attempt to grasp it by the horns in this concluding chapter of my study.

Men, Women, and Bulls

To begin, let us gently remind ourselves that a bullfight is not a live sex act. If we were to restrict our purview to the empirical, only one answer could be made to the question "What does bullfighting have to do with sex?"—nothing. The bullfight is a sport, an art, a pseudo-hunt, or a slaughter; and any acrobatics engaged in by a matador are sporting, creative, venatical, or sanguinary, not sexual. Even if an occasional matador compares his best performances to coitus (see Chapter 2), he is in no danger of being arrested for bestiality. If bullfighting has something to do with sex, therefore (and as unregenerate creatures we are ill-disposed to think otherwise), then the connections will have to be located below the surface, or behind the "manifest content," of the phenomenon. Once we jettison empiricism, our answers to the question "What does bullfighting have to do with sex?" will be limited only by our imagination or our shame. In consequence, sexual readings of the bullfight have multiplied incessantly, to the point that any attempt to systematize them would seem doomed to failure. Nevertheless, I think one can say that sex has been imputed to bullfighting in only three ways: extrinsically, metaphorically, and intrinsically. With this convenient framework in mind, let us endeavor to discover whether there is any real fire beneath all the smoke.

The extrinsic category includes all of the opinions and observations that locate sex not in the nature of bullfighting itself but in the circumstances of its public exhibition. This perspective was exemplified by eighteenth-century moralists preoccupied with the promiscuous mixing of the sexes in crowded bullrings. As the reader will recall from Chapter 3, the self-appointed "Thinker of Madrid" was particularly aroused (into indignation) by the provocative movements of the majas as they seated themselves and by the wine-induced pressing of one body against another. Such commentators tended to view bullfighting as an excuse or pretext for people anxious to get on with more exciting endeavors. And in fact, almost any crowded public spectacle could, and did, fulfill a similar function in eighteenth-century Spain. Sex was therefore no more inherent to bullfighting than it was to a Holy Week procession or to an opera performance—other favorite places for bodies to rub together in "suspicious" ways.

Historically speaking, the most common way to relate sex to bullfighting has been through the medium of metaphor. Here the comparisons have been authored or enthusiastically repeated by the Spanish people themselves for centuries. In contrast to the extrinsic mode of relationship, the metaphorical mode finds something in bullfighting itself, with its close encounters of man and beast, that suggests or recalls or is applicable to sexual behavior. Unlike the intrinsic mode, however, the figurative one does not claim that dangerous taurine liaisons are erotic in themselves, ipso facto. Most of the taurine metaphors to be found in Spanish folklore are connected to courting behaviors, and most of these limit themselves to a projection of male and female behaviors onto toreros and toros, irrespectively. In other words, both men and women have pictured themselves as the bullfighter and the opposite sex as the bull. The tendency, in fact, if one can be identified, would seem to be toward the "feminization" of the matador. In evidence, a few songs from the taurine *cancionero*:

Ven aquí, torico,	Come here, little bull,
ven aquí, galán,	come here, gallant one,
que soy la torera [fem.]	for I am the bullfighter
que te va a matar.	who is going to kill you.
Cuando me citas,	When you "cite" me,
me siento toro bravo	I feel like a brave bull
niña bonita.	pretty girl.

Con la capa el torero	With his cape the bullfighter
maneja al bicho,	handles the beast,
y la mujer al hombre	and the woman handles the man
con su abanico.	with her fan.
Si me ves con otro hablando,	If you see me with another man
no dudes de mi querer,	do not doubt my love,
el hombre es siempre un toro	man is always a bull
y un torero la mujer.	and woman the bullfighter.[1]

To be sure, woman is not always the bullfighter in sexually oriented taurine metaphors. Specialized terms that allude to a bull's imposing and fully matured appearance (*trapio*, *buena lámina*) have sometimes been used to refer to a woman of striking appearance or well-developed proportions.

The metaphorical connection between bullfighting and sex was carried to new heights of humorous double-entendre by clever taurine journalists of the nineteenth century. Noted reviewers would often spice up their accounts of humdrum bullfights with bawdy verses like the following, penned in 1887:

Dije al ver que un toro huido	On seeing a bull shy away and
cejaba al sentirse herido:	desist when wounded, I said:
—Llega bien, mas no remata,	"He approaches well but doesn't finish up,"
y por lo bajo una chata	and in a low voice a belle
añadió: —¡Así es mi marido!	added: "Just like my husband!"

Even more risqué are these verses published in 1902, which ostensibly refer to the final act of the bullfight, known variously as the *suerte de matar*, the *suerte suprema*, "the moment of truth," and so on:

Yo comprendo muy bien	"I understand very well,"
—me dijo Asunta—	Asunta told me,
que cuando el bicho	"that when the creature
las dos piernas junta,	brings both legs together,
si el espada no da	if the swordsman does not
el golpe certero,	deliver the right thrust,
y carece de práctica	and is lacking in practice
y salero,	and grace,
no le puede meter	he cannot introduce
más que la punta.	more than the point."

A great deal of ribald humor revolves around the fact that a bull has horns, thus making him the ready symbol of "horned" or cuckolded men everywhere.

En nuestra plaza de toros	In our plaza de toros, and
y desde el palco cuarenta,	from the fortieth box,
admiró la cornamenta	Juan Amores was admiring
de un Miura Juan Amores;	the horns of a Miura;
y su esposa (esto es notorio)	and his wife (this is famous)
le dijo con mucho mimo:	sweetly said to him:
—Cuernos como ésos mi primo	"Horns like that my cousin has
te ha puesto en el dormitorio.	given you in our bedroom."[2]

Beginning in the 1920s, writers whose imaginations had been fertilized by the seminal theories of Freud engendered scores of essays and articles that carried the old metaphorical folklore to new lengths. Wenceslao Fernández-Flórez was among the first to make literary capital out of the symbolic masculinity of the bull and the symbolic femininity of his human opponent.[3] But what this author meant to be ironic or tongue in cheek was taken seriously by contemporaries like Henri de Montherlant or Waldo Frank,[4] or later writers like Carlos Luis Alvarez:

> The bull is a propitiatory victim. Is the bullfighter, therefore, the priest of its sacrifice? No. The bullfighter is the priestess. It is necessary to reveal, even at the risk of being immediately stoned to death, the essential womanliness of the bull-fighter. . . . There was nothing so impudent, if we disregard the immense beauty of the performance, as Belmonte's pompous hip ("take it, little bull; come here, little bull") that the bullfighter offered to placate the desire of the horned beast. This hip, besides, looked like a bosom and a womb by its concave shape ready for the fatal surrender. Hence, nobody ever gave bullfighting the anguish and tragic beauty that Juan did. Nobody developed as he did that feminine strategy to dazzle the male as central in the art of bullfighting.[5]

Lest we lose our bearings in this realm of taurine fantasy, it might be well to remember what happened to Juanita Cruz, Conchita Cintrón, Angela Hernández, and other bullfighters who were real, not symbolic, females; they found that bullfighting was very much an activity reserved for men. Such *señoritas toreras*, as they were called, may well have been representatives of a brash, sui generis Spanish feminism. In her memoirs, Conchita Cintrón writes that her rise to prominence in Spain's plazas was strongly resisted by male bullfighters and often misunderstood by the public at large.⁶ Bullring impresarios were quick enough to respond to and exploit the novelty of señoritas toreras, but the long-term result was to group them with midgets, clowns, and other performers who were, in Cossio's categorization, "at the margins of bullfighting."⁷ Taurine fantasy is one thing, therefore, and taurine reality another. The presence of the feminine in taurine metaphors far exceeds their actual presence in the arena. (At any rate, many feminists would argue today that the cause of women's rights is not necessarily advanced by having women imitate any and every benighted masculine behavior.)

From the diverse samples of popular writing or folklore that we reviewed above, it should be clear that for every metaphor that pictures the woman as a wild creature that must be dominated and penetrated with a long instrument, there is another that pictures the man as a gullible patsy whose blind charges are easily governed by a woman. There is by no means universal agreement among Spaniards as to which metaphor is more appropriate; to the contrary, Spaniards of both sexes employ both varieties as their fancy dictates. Unfortunately, this healthy tolerance of ambiguity has been woefully lacking in certain intellectuals. Carried away with one version or another of the metaphor, a theorist will conveniently ignore the other possibility; he or she will then go on to claim that his or her one-sided distortion of the evidence is nothing less than the true nature of bullfighting. What we have here is an illegitimate crossing of the border between sex as taurine metaphor and sex as taurine essence. Such trespassing is easy enough to forgive in a journalist hurrying to meet a deadline or amuse readers. It is less forgivable in social scientists and alleged experts on Spanish life.

We now have scholarly readings of the bullfight that see it as the triumph of women over men, and other equally erudite interpretations that come to the opposite conclusion.⁸ These readings must be rejected for one or both of the following reasons: First, for their misunderstanding of taurine metaphors, a misunderstanding that can lead to a) intolerance and subsequent suppression of the metaphorical ambiguities that ordinary Spaniards enjoy, and/or b) taking them literally. Second, for their explicit or implicit assumption that male-female relations constitute the main sphere of taurine metaphorical action in the first place. This is by no means the case. Cossio, for example, lists some 220 different sayings and metaphors derived from bullfighting, and no more than ten apply to female appearance or sex relations.⁹ Abundant as the taurine sex metaphors may be, it is nevertheless far more common—in Cossio and in everyday Spanish conversation—to employ taurine phrases to refer to deception, difficult or dangerous situations in general, skill, finesse, and anger.

Let us make a simple analogy with American football. As everybody knows, this sport can lend itself rather readily to sexual metaphors—scoring, tight ends, and so on. Does this authorize us to turn around and say that therefore football is "about" sex? Any social scientist who leaped to such a conclusion would immediately merit the scorn of her or his colleagues. It would be much less risky, however, to say that football is about "maleness," because maleness—in football or bullfighting or any other cultural drama—involves a great deal more than sexual commerce. Thus, there is no contradiction here with what was stated in the last chapter with regard to the cult of manliness that bullfighting seems to have fomented during the past two centuries. Tierno's "faith in manhood" might well be a major feature of spectator behavior, as long as we remember that such a faith has numerous links to Spanish society, politics, and military history. It cannot be reduced to the sexual sphere alone. Something that is "about" manhood, in other words, does not necessarily have to be "about" sex. And if the evidence adduced for such a claim consists of metaphors taken out of context, the methodological error is compounded.

We have yet to deal seriously with the final possible category for relating sex to bullfighting—intrinsically. We have simply shown that intrinsic connections ought not to be arrived at through the metaphorical back door, so to speak. If it is going to be worth anything, an "inherent" relationship between the bullfight spectacle and sex must begin not with what bullfight spectators *say* but with what they *do*. Let us turn away, therefore, from the ribald metaphors and their tone-deaf exegetes, and consider the one element of the bullfight that clearly has a structural (not a metaphorical) similarity with sex—physiological arousal. No one who visits a bullring can fail to observe the special brand of mass excitement, the element of emotion that bullfighting on foot inherited from capeas, the passion that can raise up or crush a matador in a matter of seconds. What, if any, is the erotic component or cause of this mass arousal? In the final analysis, the observable reactions of spectators must be the ultimate referent, the fundamental ground, for any theory that sees bullfighting as inherently erotic.

Instead of rushing headlong into a psychosexual approach to this question (for which there is always time), let us momentarily bracket the bullfight and bring another data base into play. In the history of the Western world, there has been only one other culture in which blood sport played as central a role as it has in Spain—ancient Rome. Can the *hysteria libidinosa* that often accompanied Rome's extinct spectacles provide us with new insight into the mass psychology of taurine spectacles of today?

Blood Sport in Ancient Rome

The "sinister" legacy of Rome, to be sure, was cited centuries ago by medieval churchmen in their impassioned but ineffective diatribes against bullfighting. In modern times, the association of Spanish bullfighting with the gladiatorial or bestiarial combats of Rome has been made by foreign writers like Montherlant and Frank or by native authors like Araquistáin and Ortega y Gasset. According to the former, "It is not the spirit of Greece but that of Rome—with its echoes of blood sacrifice—that presides over our bullfights."[10] In the much-quoted view of Ortega,

> The Romans went to the circus as if it were a tavern and the bullfighting public is the same: the blood of gladiators, wild beasts, or of bulls operates like a stupefacient drug. Likewise, war is always simultaneously an orgy. Blood has an incomparable orgiastic power.[11]

Among the sociologists of bullfighting, Pérez Delgado is the one who has most emphasized what we might call "the Roman connection." Unfortunately, the comparisons he makes are superficial and beset with factual errors.[12] But this need not deter us. If we carry out a condensed but conscientious exploration of Roman blood sport, focusing in on spectator arousal and eroticism, we should be able to return to modern Spain with a wider, more authoritative perspective. Naturally it is not a question of positing any sort of causal or genetic relationship between Roman and Spanish spectacles; such a link would be exceedingly difficult to substantiate. It is enough for our purposes to make a straightforward, transhistorical, cross-cultural comparison between two peoples and two emotional climates.

As we go into the numerous similarities between Roman and Spanish blood sports, it will be well to recognize that, beyond a certain point, all similarities evaporate. Nothing has ever happened in a bullring that could possibly match the sheer savagery of the amphitheatre, where human and many other species were slaughtered in unbelievable quantities. Whereas bullfighting is a self-regulating ecological preserve, Roman *venationes*— best thought of as sportive holocausts—completely and permanently transformed the animal kingdom. As early as 169 B.C., sixty-three lions, forty bears, and several elephants were slaughtered in a single spectacle. As the centuries went by, the most exotic animals were hunted into near extinction to satisfy Roman demand.[13] Human lives were treated with a similar contempt. As Hopkins puts it:

> The welter of blood in gladiatorial and wild-beast shows, the squeals of the victims and of slaughtered animals are completely alien to us and almost unimaginable. For some Romans, there must have been associations with battlefields, and more immediately for everyone, associations with religious sacrifice—except that after gladiatorial shows the victims were not eaten. In gladiatorial contests and in wild beast shows, the Romans came very close, even at the height of their civilization, to performing human sacrifice.[14]

Such passages should be required reading for starry-eyed enthusiasts of "the Roman way." I am not attempting to redeem or justify bullfighting, but it is clear that, historically speaking, the Spanish blood sport is a relatively benign affair. If Spaniards have enjoyed an occasional comic bullfight with midget performers, Romans could laugh at the midgets hacking each other to pieces.[15] So even as we proceed to make "mutatis mutandis" comparisons, let us assure their validity by making all of the necessary historical adjustments.

Such a caveat is necessary, for the more one delves into the social history of Roman blood sports, the more one is struck by the resemblances to the Spanish variety. One of the more amazing coincidences comes right at the beginning. Public, official gladiatorial games were begun in 105 B.C. in an effort to counteract the reputedly effeminate influences of Greek culture.[16] What began as a reaffirmation of traditional bellicose virtues vis-à-vis a more enlightened neighboring culture grew into a great institution, thanks in large part to the support of the Roman upper classes. Originally, the performers at gladiatorial shows (*munera*) were all slaves; as time went by, they were joined by ne'er-do-wells, outcasts, or brave and desperate men looking for a chance to rise in the world or die trying. Let us yield the floor to one of the great historians of this period, Ludwig Friedländer:

> The profession of a gladiator must have really attracted men of rude courage; it had its advantages, rewards, and fame. The victors were generally rewarded: the provider of the festival sent them, whilst in the arena, bowls of goldpieces, the number of which the spectators shouted out loud or signified with the fingers of the left hand. Tried fighters commanded high prices: Tiberius paid some veteran gladiators for one appearance 100,000 sesterces. . . . The heroes of the

arena were as popular in Rome as those of the racecourse, not only with the lower classes; in the upper, also, they had pupils, admirers and imitators. Several emperors sought proficiency in the gladiator's art. . . . The gladiators were sung by poets, saw their portraits on vases, dishes, lamps, glasses and seal-rings, and their exploits scratched by idlers on walls with coal and nails. In Rome and the provinces artists were incessantly occupied in decorating theatres, tombstones, palaces and temples with sculptures, mosaics and pictures, designed to immortalize, as they actually have, the fame of the combatants. Hence it is easy to understand that the taste for this bloody pastime was not only widespread, but became a passion. The bold found its very danger an incentive; and they might hope to emerge from a series of combats rich and free. . . . Gladiators might easily pass into more honourable employs; even the Emperor Macrinus was rumoured to have been a gladiator. Thus their legal 'infamy' to a certain degree became meaningless; and the association of the upper classes with them helped to diminish the idea of disgrace in their work, thus continuously lowering the barriers between these pariahs and respectable society. In modern Spain bullfighting exercises a similar magnetism, and for the same reasons; it is not labelled infamous and is less dangerous on the whole.[17]

Like famous Spanish matadors of the nineteenth and twentieth centuries, many veteran gladiators went on fighting even though they were no longer obliged to do so by servitude or poverty. Shows with men fighting of their own "free will" were deemed to be of greater quality. Similarly, and despite their lowly status, gladiators cultivated a sense of their own honor that verged on the punctilious.[18] Despite their brief lifespans, notes Hopkins, gladiators were often glamour figures with careers that recall the ephemeral but intense notoriety that our own age bestows upon celebrities:

Modern pop-stars and athletes (tennis-players, gymnasts and footballers) have only a short exposure to full-glare publicity. Most then fade rapidly from being household names into obscurity, fossilised in the memory of each generation of adolescent enthusiasts. The transience of the fame of each does not diminish their collective importance. So too with Roman gladiators.[19]

So too, we might add, with Spanish bullfighters.

We can also find remarkable similarities in the overall organization of the games and their sociopolitical aspects. Status-seeking aristocrats competed for reputation and career advancement through sponsorship of public spectacles. In this they were only taking their cue from the emperor himself, always the center of attention at the games in Rome. Roman historians record that Claudius was the emperor who most closely identified with the masses in his enthusiasm for the combats and wild beast shows.

Roman blood sports were nothing less than "political theatre," as well as a means of social control that Juvenal referred to as *panem et circenses*.[20] Although it was especially important for the powers-that-were to divert the mob of the capital, the games enjoyed a genuine grass-roots enthusiasm. All over the Latin-speaking world, local big shots stayed popular with the locals by organizing lavish spectacles—"the more murderous, the more splendid they were deemed."[21] For every show the services of a *lanista* were indispensable. The lanistas were slave-traders, managers, and impresarios all rolled into one. First they bought, rented, or contracted gladiators for the combats and then they set the prices for different seats, arranged for publicity posters, and hired musicians (amphitheatrical performances were typically accompanied by strident martial music). Since they were not above any kind of chicanery to fatten their profits, their profession was held in disrepute.[22]

It was not uncommon for fathers to pass on the profession of *bestiarius*, or wild beast slayer, to their sons, and there were even families of gladiators. Women occasionally ventured into the arena: the British Museum preserves a stone relief of two bare-breasted female gladiators. "In some instances," notes Hopkins, "women gladiators were classed as oddities with dwarfs."[23] (We could hardly find a more striking parallel with the señoritas toreras of modern Spain.) For its part, the Roman public was thoroughly familiar with the technical aspects of parrying and thrusting; crowds despised cowardice and hailed a cheerful willingness to bear pain and death. The authorities were as vigilant of the health and muscle tone of the combatants as they were of the authenticity of the combats. Schools were set up all over Italy to train troops of gladiators. There were even distinguished surgeons who specialized in the treatment of sword and trident wounds.[24]

Let us now focus in on the erotic aspects of Roman blood sports in the hope that we may find something useful to take back to modern Spain. History records that the appeal of the *munera* was well-nigh polymorphic in its perversity. For one thing, it seems that the successful gladiator had every bit of the sex appeal and prowess attributed to the matador.

> The victorious gladiator, or at least his image, was sexually attractive. The word *gladius*—sword—was vulgarly used to mean penis. Even the defeated and dead gladiator had something sexually portentous about him. It was customary for a new bride to have her hair parted with a spear, at best one which had been dipped 'in the body of a defeated and killed gladiator.' . . . This evidence suggests that there was a close link, in some Roman minds, between gladiatorial

fighting and sexuality. Other evidence corroborates this association: for example, a terracotta gladiatorial helmet shaped suggestively like a penis, and a small
bronze figurine, from Pompeii, of a cruel-looking gladiator, fighting off with
his sword a dog-like wild-beast which grows out of his erect and elongated
penis. . . . Gladiators' strength and bravery, their risk of death, attracted some
Roman women. Yet to pursue and love slave gladiators was socially dangerous,
even disastrous. Even if they were free men by birth or socially distinguished by
origin, as gladiators they were déclassé, outcasts. Indeed, because they were in
such close contact with death, they were polluted and sometimes therefore, like
suicides, excluded from normal burial. In spite of these social dangers, or perhaps because of them, even aristocratic women fell for gladiators.[25]

A number of erotic elements or levels of lasciviousness can be located in
the above. The association of the blood of a dead gladiator with weddings,
for example, is reminiscent of the long extinct Spanish custom of the nuptial bull. As the reader may recall from Chapter 1, the bride was expected
to stain her clothing with bull's blood in order magically to tap his sexual
potency for purposes of human fertility. Alongside what might be called
the "sexual magic" of the gladiator, we find a phallic dimension that can
take the form of simple references to his *gladius* or far more cryptic works
of art that may also have, as Hopkins notes, a magical or talismanic character.[26] At yet another level we encounter a sort of Roman-style "fatal attraction," an erotic *frisson* that was built into Rome's rigidly stratified class
structure. Human desire being what it is, the degree of attraction felt by
some female aristocrats may well have been a function of social distance
itself. We saw something of this nature in eighteenth-century Spain, when
members of the titled nobility became enamoured of the plebeian stars of
the music hall and the bullring; for the past two hundred years, taurine
literature has ceaselessly elaborated the motif of the well-bred, upper-class,
cosmopolitan woman who either casts her spell over or succumbs to the
spell of the virile proletarian animal killer.[27] In Rome, nobleborn ladies
who fell for gladiators seem to have been responding as much to the at-
tractiveness of the forbidden, as Hopkins adroitly insinuates, as to the
magical or phallic dimensions of the gladiatorial image—bearing in mind
that these dimensions themselves possess an aura of taboo. In primitive
cultures the world round, blood's ability to work wonders is inseparable
from its ability to defile. Men charged with spilling blood—warriors, for
example—have always had a "special" status and have always been subject
to rituals of atonement or purification.

This brings us closer to understanding something that perplexed Tertullian. This well-known Christian iconoclast of the second century pointed out that actors, charioteers, and gladiators—"to whom men surrender their souls and women their bodies as well"—were held in dishonor by the very classes that organized the spectacles:

> On one and the same account they glorify them and they degrade and diminish them; they keep them religiously excluded from council chamber, rostrum, senate, knighthood, and every other kind of office and a good many distinctions. The perversity of it! They love whom they lower; they despise whom they approve. . . . What sort of judgment is this—that a man should be blackened for what he shines in? Yes, and what a confession that things are evil, when their authors at the top of their popularity are in disgrace![28]

Tertullian's well-wrought rhetorical antitheses closely reflected reality. It was indeed a perverse situation, more so when we consider that the popularity of a performer was a *function* of his disgrace, and vice versa. The gladiator's hold on the Roman imagination was inseparable from his marginal social status and his proximity to blood, death, and pollution. Thus, he was the perfect symbol of the fascinating but threatening power of the prohibited. As Georges Bataille has discussed, eroticism, sacrifice, and even religious ecstasy revolve around this paradoxical power, born in the anguish that founds the interdict and the desire that drives us to infringe it.[29]

In undertaking to fathom the erotic aspects of violent Roman spectacles, we come face to face with the violent structure of eroticism itself. It would be beyond the scope of this essay to engage in a prolonged discussion of this great enigma, but let us at least extract a few relevant ideas from Bataille's masterful treatment of it. For Bataille, the "logical" outcome of every sex act would be death, inasmuch as sex seeks to break down the physical barriers between two normally discontinuous beings and fuse them into one continuous being. Continuity of being is to be understood as the essence of Nature itself, characterized as it is by the exorbitant and often wasteful expenditure of individual beings. Sexuality and death are two high points of the same fiesta—Nature's orgy of creation and annihilation. Union with Nature is to be understood as the ultimate goal of erotic desire. Death is to be understood as the one sure way to overcome individual self-interest and re-establish an animalistic continuity with Nature. Thus, the desire to kill, the deliberate and premeditated intention to rupture the normal bounds of discontinuity, is analogous to erotic desire: both tend toward the disruption, dissolution, and destruction first of social norms, then of religious taboos, and finally of the self-enclosed beings themselves. By their very nature, then, eroticism is violent and violence is erotic; society must contain and control both by interdicts. Taboos are based on the fear of degradation, that is, dissolution, that desire propitiates. Taboos ensure that a person who degrades another through murder will in some way be ostracized, or that murderous violence will be reserved for people already on the fringes of society. But in the meantime, desire may secretly caress the notion of murder, or lead a few well-bred women to degrade themselves by drawing closer to the "heroic" degraders. For example;

> Modern excavators working in the armoury of the gladiatorial barracks in Pompeii, found eighteen skeletons in two rooms, presumably of people caught there in the ash storm; they included one woman who was wearing rich gold jewellery and a necklace set with emeralds.[30]

As Bataille would point out, the excesses of a few wealthy hedonists reveal the degrading and violent direction of all desire. As it is, most people do not transgress one taboo after another and set off on the primrose path to ruin. For most people, degradation never goes beyond the level of fantasy—if it even gets to that point. In the meantime, culture is there to provide official fantasy gratification as a safe substitute for the real thing. Order must be preserved, after all, even as desire requires some sort of release. One of the fundamental adaptive traits of human culture lies in its paradoxical ability to strengthen taboos by providing for their transgression in carefully designed collective formats of one kind or another. In Rome, a city without a regular police force, the solution lay in socially sanctioned mass arousal and the vicarious enjoyment of human degradation at the amphitheatre. The patently erotic nature of this enjoyment can be seen in its intoxicating quality, its addictive nature, and, above all, in its voyeurism.

Of the numerous sources that describe how many Romans, especially adolescents, were "hooked" on blood sports, none is as famous as the testimony of Augustine. In his *Confessions*, Augustine recounts what happened to a student of his named Alypius, a young man of high rank and good breeding who detested gladiator shows. While at Rome, however, a gang of fellow students urged him to do as the Romans did. When his pals dragged him into the Coliseum, Alypius adopted a strategy of passive resistance, promising simply to close his eyes and see no evil.

And would he had stopped his ears also! For in the fight, when one fell, a mighty cry of the whole people striking him strongly, overcome by curiosity, and as if prepared to despise and be superior to it whatsoever it were, even when seen, he opened his eyes, and was stricken with a deeper wound in his soul than the other, whom he desired to behold, was in his body. . . . For so soon as he saw that blood, he therewith drunk down savageness; nor turned away, but fixed his eye, drinking in frenzy, unawares, and was delighted with that guilty fight, and intoxicated with the bloody pastime. Nor was he the man he came, but one of the throng he came unto, yea, a true associate of theirs that brought him thither. Why say more?[31]

For Alypius, intoxication and subsequent addiction to blood sports came to him through his visual sense. It could hardly be otherwise: the whole point of a show or a spectacle is to watch it. But it is one thing to watch, say, the annual Tournament of Roses Parade and quite another to watch spectacular bloodshed and death. In any performance that involves taboo violation, the aura of the taboo extends to the act of witnessing the performance itself. *Looking*, in fact, can be seen as the first taboo to be transgressed in a potential process of erotico-violent degradation, a process that is paradoxically restrained through the creation of an authorized arena for the indulging of transgressive looking. Looking can still whet one's appetite nonetheless; it can still be deeply arousing and habit-forming. Greek intellectuals who opposed gladiatorial games argued that "the degeneration of taste infected the other senses, and the eye no longer took pleasure in dances, pictures and statues, but in death and wounds and fights as the most precious spectacle."[32] Even though there may be nothing explicitly sexual in the scenes viewed, it would be appropriate to refer to their viewing as voyeuristic, in light of the twin dynamics of eroticism and violence outlined above. Perhaps the old phrase "blood lust" bespeaks a vague intuition of these interrelated drives.

For additional confirmation of the relationship between ecstasy and the viewing of horrible violence, we need look no further than Augustine's predecessor, Tertullian. The better to censure the pagans' enthusiasm for blood sports, Tertullian devotes the final section of *De Spectaculis* to visualizing the bloodshed of Judgment Day. "How vast the spectacle that day," he begins, "and how wide! What sight shall wake my wonder, what my laughter, my joy and exultation?" He then goes on to exult in the fantasy of kings groaning, poets trembling, philosophers blazing, actors declaiming in anguish, magistrates liquefying, and circus performers "hurled in the fire—unless it be that not even then would I wish to see them, in my desire rather to turn an insatiable gaze on them who vented their rage and fury on the Lord."[33] In this passage, Tertullian reveals himself to be the true spiritual kin of the pagans or, to paraphrase Augustine, one of the throng he believed himself superior to. Whatever the rationalization, the "desire to turn an insatiable gaze" on violence will always be a way to participate vicariously in transgression.

The Nature of Taurine Titillation

In view of the above, the soundest "Roman connection" that can be made with modern bullfighting may well lie in the element of ocular transgression. Mutatis mutandis, it is the intoxicating and addictive nature of voyeurism that constitutes the closest link between the mass psychology of the extinct blood sports of Rome and the thriving one of modern Spain. There is, to be sure, a world of difference between the sportive slaughter of men and that of bulls. This is because the march of civilization has altered the makeup of the spectacles that people can be safely titillated by. It would be foolhardy to think that blood lust is now confined to the plazas of Spain, however. In recent motion pictures, American society has found an authorized outlet for the sort of sadistic fantasies that even Tertullian would have blushed at. As we complete our study of Spain's relatively old-fashioned modes of institutionalized fantasy gratification, we come all the closer to understanding the more "advanced" ones of our own culture.

What led us into a consideration of Roman blood sport to begin with, as the reader will recall, was a desire to discover whether or not there could be something intrinsically erotic in bullfighting. The idea was to go beyond the merely metaphorical and beyond scholarly approaches that abuse the metaphorical. In the light of Bataille's exploration of the profound structural link between violence and eroticism, it appears that our quest is on the verge of fulfillment. Interestingly, Bataille stated that his study had found its starting point in an essay on bullfighting published by Michel Leiris.[34] In *Miroir de la tauromachie* (1937), this French enthnologist and man of letters used the bullfight to anchor a brilliant series of meditations concerning the role of transgression in the erotic and the sacred. Leiris argued that the bullfight was the only spectacle of the modern world that gave us everything that a spectacle should, that is, "the very image of our emotion."[35] He appropriated Baudelaire's concept of *malheur* to explain why the bullfight is not simply a sport or an art but a "violent game of contrasts" that courts a paroxysmal denouement in the manner of tragedy, sacrifice, and sex.[36] Although he penned a stimulating evocation of bull-fighting's sexual analogies, Leiris concluded that coitus was too primitive and unpredictable to allow for the bullfight's "majestic governance" and "optimistic conclusion," that is, the manner in which it satisfactorily resolves the very transgressive ambiguities that it provokes.[37] As an ethnologist, Leiris was aware of ritual's paradoxical ability to confirm taboos through their authorized public violation. Since the sex act is not a public ritual (at least not until recently), it cannot possess culture's canny capacity to control potential disorder or reaffirm norms. By contrast, the bullfight spectacle is never carried out in private, but in the open glare of the sun and the consensus of the taurine community.

Even as we take due notice of the bullfight's ritualistic aspects, however, we must guard against calling it a ritual. In a true ritual, like the Catholic Mass, the officiant and the communicants are engaged in deliberately symbolic activity; their every word and action has an agreed-upon spiritual referent; moreover, everything is rigidly predetermined, nothing is left to chance. None of these qualities can be found in a bullfight. There is no deliberately symbolic activity, only simple signals like handkerchief-waving and clarion calls. The bullfighter's actions do not "stand for" anything beyond themselves, and the people are always entitled to disagree about the actions. Instead of communicants and officiants, therefore, we have performers and spectators. Finally, a great deal is left to chance. It is impossible to predict a bull's, or a crowd's, or a matador's behavior beforehand. There is always a fair chance that things will turn sour and anti-climactic, or tragic and ugly, instead of majestic and optimistic. Thus, the bullfight is no more a ritual than a boxing match or a gladiatorial combat. This does not mean, however, that it cannot reinforce group norms. As sociologists have shown, any large gathering that arouses excitement and focuses attention can contribute to social cohesion.[38] The mechanics of the process are easily observed in the bullfight. First, everyone's attention is focused on what is happening in the arena below. As physiological arousal grows among spectators, so does their reliance on group definitions in order to feel this arousal as appropriate. Awareness that others share the same state of arousal contributes to its intensification, and from there to an "awareness of supra-individual power," and from there to an attribution of this pleasing sense of power to one's commitment to the group's norms.[39] The bullfight need not be a ritual, therefore, to achieve a sui generis sort of *communitas*.

There is certainly one way in which bullfighting can lose its air of majesty and optimism—a goring. Leiris did not dwell on the occasional deaths that are meted out to humans in bullrings, nor did he focus on the crucial elements of risk and spectacle. But it is here, to follow through on the logical consequences of the ideas of Leiris and Bataille, that we recover the full gamut of transgressive or erotico-violent possibilities inherent to bullfighting. After all, spectators gather not only to savor the sight of large bulls being dispatched but also to watch young men taking totally unnecessary risks with their lives. The Romans, to be sure, were addicted to stronger stuff; they flocked to amphitheatres knowing full well that they were going to see human blood spilled. The "blood lust" of the Spanish crowds is much milder, but perfectly capable of pushing bullfighters into brinkmanship and precipitating horn wounds. The following anecdotes can be added to the ones already cited in Chapter 4. As one famous matador was rushed to the bullring infirmary in Valencia, he flung the blood gushing out of his thigh at the spectators who had been cursing him only a few moments before, shouting, "Here! Take it! The blood of El Chato!"[40] In *Death in the Afternoon*, Hemingway recounts a similar incident involving a matador named Varelito who was eviscerated by a bull in 1922:

> As they were carrying him down the passageway around the ring to the infirmary, . . . Varelito kept saying, looking up at [the crowd], "Now you've given it to me. Now I've got it. Now you've given it to me. Now you've got what you wanted. Now I've got it. Now you've given it to me. Now I've got it. Now I've got it. I've got it." He had it although it took nearly four weeks for it to kill him.[41]

It was Eugenio Noel's opinion that people came to bullfights out of a desire to see human blood.[42] In addition, there is a consensus among taurine historians that overly demanding spectators led directly or indirectly to the deaths of Joselito and Manolete. In the twentieth century, however, a growing awareness of the importance of "art" has led spectators to be more tolerant with certain faint-hearted but graceful bullfighters, like Joselito's brother Rafael Gómez (alias El Gallo) and the famous Curro Romero. And even in the nineteenth century, crowds tried to restrain—in vain—one suicidally valiant matador by chanting "No te tires, Reverte!"[43] So again, the cruelty of bullfighting publics is relative, and certainly pales in comparison to that of the Roman "mob."

Let us now focus in on the element of transgressive seeing that necessarily accompanies any spectacle of killing and gratuitous risk of life. It is extremely difficult for human beings to gaze upon transgression without being aroused in some way. Ironically, even reactions of horror and nausea confirm that violent spectacle is inherently erotic. Properly defined, disgust is nothing but negative arousal, caused by the fear of degradation that accompanies the desire to give way to the instincts and surpass all taboos.[44] Physiological arousal, whether of a gratifying or guilty variety, is an automatic result of viewing bullfights, since they are transgressive by definition and fully participate in the erotic dynamics of violence. We have already seen enough, therefore, to justify calling the bullfight pornography—in a purely empirical, not judgmental, sense.

Bullfighting could also be seen as pornographic under the expanded definition that Leslie Fiedler adopts in his studies of popular culture. In Fiedler's view, books, plays, and movies that enjoy mass popularity can be seen as belonging to one of three genres—Sentimental Literature, Classic Pornography, or Horror Literature:

> There is a real sense in which all three of these forms can be regarded as varieties of pornography or titillation-literature: handkerchiefly or female-oriented porn, erotic or male-oriented porn, and sado-masochistic, or universally appealing porn. . . . Terror, indeed, seems sometimes the only form capable of crossing all conventional role boundaries: not only generational and sexual, but ethnic as well. . . . In any case, the pornographic classification seems appropriate in light of the fact that all three sub-genres aim at "watering the emotions," rather than purifying or purging them by way of the famous Aristotelian process of "catharsis." Indeed, the whole baffling and unsatisfactory theory of catharsis seems to me at this point a pious fraud perpetrated by the dutiful son of a doctor; drawing on the terminology of his father's socially-acceptable craft, in order to justify his own shameful taste for what seemed to more serious thinkers of his time exactly what pop literature seems to their opposite numbers in ours. Greek Tragedy, as a matter of fact, aimed at evoking precisely the responses stirred by Sentimental and Horror porn in all ages, responses which Aristotle called honorifically "pity and terror.". . . We need, therefore, another term than catharsis to say how we are moved, a term less anal and more erotic.[45]

Fiedler takes a perverse delight in showing how plays by Sophocles and Euripides can be seen as pornographic, buttressing thereby his stinging refutation of the elitist critics who in every age have attempted to rationalize or sanitize the ecstatic moments of "privileged insanity" that the three subgenres of popular culture provide.

Defined in this way, "pornography" becomes a convenient term for all kinds of expressive culture whose objective is physiological arousal rather than edification. Bullfighting would surely belong to the category that Fiedler calls "sado-masochistic or universally-appealing porn," the kind that bridges the generation gap and the gender gap alike. The mortal thrills of bullfighting have been enjoyed by the widest spectrum of spectators since the very beginning. Few of them, presumably, would be willing to describe their pleasure as pornographic in nature, but an elitist critic like Bergamín had no qualms about spelling it out. A text I cited in the Introduction bears repeating here:

> Since the true emotion of bullfighting is the emotion of art, the spectator who gets emotional for another reason destroys it by replacing it with a kind of mortal pornography that converts him into a suicidal masochist and a sadistic assassin all at once: both things are only imagined, of course, and unknown to himself, as he feels pleasure and pain in the frustrated manner of an unconscious phantasmagorial onanism.[46]

It would be hard to find a more explicit description of the way in which bullfighting "waters the emotions." But unlike conscious consumers of obscene literature or film, Spaniards have consumed bullfights without looking over their shoulders. In general, they have enjoyed the titillating spectacle without guilt or moral qualms of any kind. The group norms that hold sway at a bullfight permit each spectator to accept his or her physiological arousal as entirely appropriate. Intense stimulation actually increases commitment to the group's rationalization of it. This is the sociopsychological mechanism that has permitted Spaniards to experience titillation at bullfights and associate it, at a conscious level, with patriotism, manly ideals, integrity, art, and so forth. Bergamín's taurine onanists only experience their unspeakable pornographic emotions at an unconscious level, as he clearly states.

What happens to this happy group consensus when a goring occurs and the transgressive nature of bullfighting is fully achieved and brought out into the open? As Gubern points out in his study of pornography, the simulation of death by the world's best movie actor will never equal the cruel dramatism of any human's real death in public.[47] Bullfighting is hardly a stranger to mortal "accidents." Community norms are already in place that will provide the appropriate cognition to accompany the intense physiological arousal that spectators experience when a matador is gored. These stand-by norms quickly forge a new group consensus whose conscious elements are pity, grief, forbearance, resignation, and, ultimately, a reaffirmation of all the fine qualities that led the matador to risk his life in the first place. The normative emotionality that takes shape around the fallen matador goes far beyond the bullring in its sociocultural implications and lasts for many years after the tragedy. There is still plenty of folkloristic and literary debris left over from the emotional explosions that accompanied the deaths of star matadors. The shock waves from Paquirri's death in 1984 have been felt for several years now. Images of his widow and children and stories of how they are coping constantly appear in Spanish mass-circulation magazines (what Fiedler would call female-oriented sentimental porn).

The innocent enjoyment of the national pornography, and its subsidiary pornographic productions, may well be related to a culture-wide predilection for strong sensations in general. As we saw in the first two chapters of this book, urban bullfighting prospered because it represented a recovery and a reaffirmation of the emotional intensity that rural Spaniards had always found in their capeas. According to Fernández Suárez, in fact, the national enthusiasm for such spectacles provides evidence that Spain, unique among the nations of Europe, has preserved an archaic "cult of emotion." In this cult we re-encounter the same elements of intoxication, addiction, and voyeurism that accompanied blood sport in ancient Rome:

> Emotion is the most important thing for a Spaniard because, in the last analysis, it represents life itself. For this reason he has such a great avidity for spectacles, and particularly religious spectacles, as was the case with people in Antiquity. To enjoy an emotion the Spaniard will travel, spend a fortune, do anything risky and senseless, and end up exhausted, with nothing left to store up. The Spaniard is a devourer of, and devoured by, emotions—unlike the typical European, who is a devourer of, and devoured by, things. The Spaniard is content with passing emotion: everything begins and ends therein, save the memory of "that great afternoon," retained without even a minimum degree of objectivity.[48]

Were we to accept this characterization at face value, we would have no choice but to classify Spaniards as hysterical.[49] But Fernández Suárez's diagnosis was already something of an exaggeration when he made it in 1961, and subsequent decades have further eroded its validity. In the past thirty years, Spaniards have made enormous strides in the "Europeanization" of their country; nowadays the consumption of things must surely take pride of place over the consumption of emotions. Generally speaking, today's Spaniard is not a sensation-junkie. Nevertheless, bullfighting can only be understood in terms of a renewable Spanish legacy of emotional volatility.

As the greatest spectacle of them all, the bullfight remains in place, ready to serve even the most Europeanized Spaniards—and innumerable European visitors—as a conduit to "privileged insanity" and archaic *ekstasis*.

Having discussed the spectators who can enjoy the emotion-watering thrills of bullfighting in good conscience, let us briefly discuss those few who have somehow fallen from innocence, those who have trouble experiencing their bullfight-induced physiological arousal as appropriate. They normally fall into one of two general categories: (1) those who reject the whole spectacle with attitudes that range from simple distaste to crusading obsession, and (2) those who accept it but with reservations that can verge on the puritanical. If Eugenio Noel exemplified the first category, the prime example of the second would be an aestheticist like Bergamín.

Bergamín actually had all of the purgative zeal of a Noel. He thought he could cleanse bullfighting of its erotico-violent aspects and elaborate an elevated, ethical, and pollution-free way to watch the blood sport. It is incumbent upon us to gently point out the self-deception in the Spanish poet's strategy, and indeed in any elitist critic's attempt to project all of the "bad" emotions onto the masses and reserve the "sublime" ones for himself. In my view, the ecstatic pleasures experienced by the critical elite are not structurally different from the ecstatic or emotionalistic attitude of the crowd: in both cases, emotions are being watered through transgressive observation of killing and gratuitous risk of life. The whole psychological dynamics of transgression is what makes taurine aesthetics possible in the first place. It is highly significant that taurine critics never fail to locate the maximum possibility for taurine beauty at the "moment of truth"—the climactic instant when the matador plunges his sword into the bull. A matador of integrity must kill honestly and be ready to receive a cornada if the bull so desires. Without this element of deliberate mortal risk, there can be no beauty. In other words, Beauty is Truth, Truth Beauty, and both combine at the climax of Spanish roulette's degrading thrills.[50]

Is there no difference, then, between sophisticated or sophistical critics and spectators at large? Yes, but the variation occurs at a conscious, rationalizing, ex post facto level, when the aestheticist replaces the norms of one group with those of another (much smaller) one. An increase in cruelty may even accompany this intellectual ploy. For example, Bergamín argued that matadors who attempt to curry favor with the base multitudes by melodramatically underlining the risk element "do not even deserve a clean mortal wound," and if they do get one, "sentimental spectators tremble with pleasure while the intelligent ones turn their faces away as they would before a disembowelled horse."[51] The Spanish poet was something of a modern-day Tertullian—able to enjoy his transgressive fantasy only through the outward condemnation of another. Significantly, Bergamín was totally attuned to the visual ecstasy of bullfighting, even as he was determined to take it out of its orgiastic context and elevate it to the stain-free realm of Timeless Art. In reality he was as titillated as the next person, but imaginative enough to sublimate his emotion and fashion his own system of rationalizations far from the madding crowd.

Bullfighting's emotion-watering nature is what unites the aestheticists with the unconscious onanists, the eighteenth-century knaves with the aristocrats, and the rustics of the capeas with today's middle-class housewives. In this book we have explored the often unpleasant social realities that bullfight-induced emotion has paradoxically reinforced by attempting to disguise. More than a little of bullfighting's success can be attributed to its counter-historical inclination, its implicit drive to transcend the reality principle and return to some heroic realm out of time. If myth is the end, emotion is the means. Even if we do not enter into the spirit of this emotion, we have learned much from observing it in action. All spectacles, to paraphrase Leiris, ought to give us the very image of human emotion. We gather together, focus our attention on performers who situate themselves between life and death, and, deep inside us, desire enters into a secret complicity with the performance. Spectacles seem to take us away from civilization's restraints and back not just to our childhood but to the cave dweller lurking in all of us, or still further, to the old animal continuity with Nature that Bataille spoke of. In the last analysis, our personal reactions to bullfighting may depend on our willingness to indulge the child, or the troglodyte, or the animal, in ourselves.

Notes

Introduction

1. For an interesting critique of the mythico-religious view of tauromachy and its artistic consequences, see Angel González Garcia, "Pintura y toros," in *Arte y tauromaquia*, ed. Universidad Internacional Menéndez Pelayo (UIMP) (Madrid: Turner, 1983), pp. 187–223.

2. José Ortega y Gasset, *La caza y los toros* (Madrid: Espasa-Calpe, 1962), p. 148 (my translation).

3. Ortega affirmed that, besides himself, no Spaniard knew anything worthwhile about bullfighting (p. 141 of *La caza y los toros*). As Rosario Cambria has pointed out, Ortega's actual contribution to our understanding of bullfighting always lagged behind his braggadocio. See Rosario Cambria, "La tauromaquia hecha verdadero problema intelectual: Ortega y Gasset," in his *Los toros: tema polémico en el ensayo español del siglo XX* (Madrid: Gredos, 1974), pp. 118–144. See also José Carlos Arévalo, "Ortega y los toros," *Revista de Occidente* 36 (1984): 49–59.

4. Monroe C. Beardsley, "History of Aesthetics," in *The Encyclopedia of Philosophy*, ed. Paul Edwards (New York: Macmillan, 1967), vol. 1, p. 27. Burke's *A Philosophical Enquiry into the Origin of Our Ideas of the Sublime and Beautiful* was first published in 1756.

5. John Hospers, "Problems of Aesthetics," in *Encyclopedia of Philosophy*, ed. Edwards, vol. 1, pp. 36–37.

6. Fernando Claramunt, "Los toros desde la psicología," in *Los toros: Tratado técnico e histórico*, vol. 7 (Madrid: Espasa-Calpe, 1982), p. 160 (my translation).

7. Ernest Hemingway, *Death in the Afternoon* (New York: Charles Scribner's Sons, 1932), p. 163.

8. Angeles García, "Evocación de un verano sangriento: Amigos y estudiosos de Hemingway ven su pasión por el toreo como plasmación de su temor al sexo y la muerte; Seminario en la Universidad Internacional Menéndez Pelayo [Santander] en el 25 aniversario del suicidio del escritor," *El País*, 25 July 1986, p. 22.

9. See Lawrence R. Broer, *Hemingway's Spanish Tragedy* (University: University of Alabama Press, 1973).

10. Enrique Tierno Galván, *Desde el espectáculo a la trivialización* (Madrid: Taurus, 1961), p. 75 (my translation).

11. I do not mean to imply that Hemingway was incapable of aesthetic emotion. Nevertheless, his psychological proximity to the typical bullfight spectator earned him the scorn of certain elitist critics. See Chapter 3, note 60.

12. Fernando Savater, "Caracterización del espectador taurino," in *Arte y tauromaquia*, ed. UIMP p. 122 (my translation).

13. In his best-sellling book of taurine biographies, for example, Rafael Ríos

Mozo frequently refers to the *faenas*, or muleta performances, that he has experienced "spiritually." At one point he confesses: "I did not actually see Joselito and Belmonte perform because of my age, but I feel in my spirit all that they were and represented, and that in my secret and deep self I saw and lived those glorious years." Rafeal Ríos Mozo, *Tauromaquia fundamental* (2d ed.; Granada: Editoriales Andaluzas Unidas, 1985), p. 38 (my translation).

14. José Bergamín, *El arte de birlibirloque* (orig. pub. 1930; Madrid: Turner, 1985), p. 31 (my translation).

15. Ibid., p. 39.

16. José Bergamín, *La música callada del toreo* (Madrid: Turner, 1981), p. 50 (my translation).

17. José Bergamín, *La claridad del toreo* (Madrid: Turner, 1985), p. 107.

18. Ibid., pp. 33–34.

19. Bergamín, *La música callada del toreo*, pp. 39–41.

20. In fact, Bergamín's first book was one long attack on Belmonte's crowd-pleasing temerity, unfavorably contrasted with Joselito's light and athletic style. Eventually, however, Bergamín's own nostalgia for bullfighting's "Golden Age" moved him to reverse his opinion. See *La claridad del toreo*, p. 115–118, for Bergamín's re-elaboration of the myth of Belmonte.

21. Bergamín, *La claridad del toreo*, p. 38 (my translation; italics in original).

22. Eugenio Noel, *España nervio a nervio* (Madrid: Calpe, 1924), pp. 97–98 (my translation).

Chapter 1: Fiesta de Toros

1. The preceding itinerary of Spanish fiestas has been assembled from my own experiences and from a number of published accounts. I am especially indebted to Maria Ángeles Sánchez, *Guia de fiestas populares de España* (Madrid: Tania, 1983) and Carlos Blanco, *Las fiestas de aquí* (Valladolid: Ambito, 1983). I have also made use of two works by Spain's leading anthropologist, Julio Caro Beroja: *El Carnaval: Análisis histórico-cultural* (1965) and *El estío festivo: Fiestas populares de verano* (1984), both published in Madrid by Taurus. Other sources include J. M. Gómez-Tabanera, "Fiestas populares y festejos tradicionales," in *El folklore español*, ed. J. M. Gómez-Tabanera (Madrid: Instituto Español de Antropología Aplicada 1968), pp. 149–216; Consolación González Casarrubios, *Fiestas populares en Castilla–La Mancha* (Ciudad Real: Junta de Comunidades de Castilla–La Mancha, 1985); and a collection of essays edited by Honorio Velasco, *Tiempo de fiesta* (Madrid: Alatar, 1982).

2. Cited by Inmaculada Gómez Mardones in "La crueldad como fiesta," *El País*, 23 June 1985, p. 32.

3. Ibid., p. 33.

4. Announcements like this began to appear in Spanish newspapers in 1985. The animal-rights organization has since changed its name to the Asociación Nacional para la Defensa de los Animales (ANDA). For readers desiring more information about the treatment of animals in festal Spain, its address is Gran Via, 31 / 28013 Madrid / Spain. The gracious president of ANDA, M. Sanz de Galdeano, told me in a letter (20 Oct. 1989) that some cattle breeders are now making more money with local fiestas than with formal urban bullfights, since the bulls or bullocks used

in the fiestas do not need to meet the same standards of health and presentation required by bullring veterinarians.

5. Alfredo Valenzuela, "El inglés, contra el toro," *El País*, 26 June 1987, p. 24.

6. *El País*, 13 Sept. 1989, p. 29.

7. Arturo Barea, *The Forging of a Rebel*, trans. Ilsa Barea (New York: Reynal & Hitchcock, 1946), p. 40.

8. Eugenio Noel, *Nervios de la raza* (Madrid: Sáez Hermanos, 1915), p. 132 (my translation).

9. Vicente de la Fuente, "Costumbres provinciales: La novillada," *Semanario Pintoresco Español*, 1838), p. 221. Cited by Alberto González Troyano, *El torero, héroe literario* (Madrid: Espasa-Calpe, 1988), p. 169 (my translation).

10. Eugenio Noel, *Escritos antitaurinos* (orig. pub. 1914; Madrid: Taurus, 1967), p. 123 (my translation).

11. Ibid., p. 121 (my translation).

12. Barea, *Forging of a Rebel*, pp. 40–41. The translator of this work, Ilsa Barea, renders *toro del aguardiente* as "Bull of the First Drop."

13. Eugenio Noel, *Las capeas* (Madrid: Imprenta Helénica, 1915), p. 92 (my translation).

14. Ernest Hemingway, *Death in the Afternoon* (New York: Charles Scribner's Sons, 1932), p. 23.

15. *El País*, 15 August 1989, p. 13.

16. Antonio Blázquez, "Miguel Angel Garzón murió instantáneamente," *Aplausos: Seminario taurino*, 24 February 1986, p. 26. The photo that accompanies this article shows a hospital team trying in vain to revive the hapless Garzón, his face a mask of caked blood.

17. Bernardino Dominguez Sánchez, *Fiesta y sangre* (Madrid: M. Nuñez Samper, 1914), p. 64.

18. Noel, *Escritos antitaurinos*, p. 125.

19. José Delfín Val, "Donde en la vieja casa de la Sra. Flavia se cuenta la triste historia de la muerte de Mariano Mera," *Revista de Folklore* 2, 6 (1981): 31–32 (my translation).

20. Vicente Blasco Ibáñez, *Blood and Sand*, trans. Frances Partridge (orig. pub. 1908; New York: Frederick Ungar, 1958), p. 52.

21. Ibid., p. 53.

22. Barea, *Forging of a Rebel*, p. 41.

23. Ramón Carande, "Chronological Statistics of Victims of Bullfighting," in *Los toros / Bullfighting*, ed. J. Fernández Figueroa (Madrid: Indice, 1964), p. 195.

24. Santiago Araúz de Robles, *Sociologia del toreo* (Madrid: Prensa Española, 1978), p. 144 (my translation).

25. William S. Laughlin, "Hunting: Its Evolutionary Importance," in *Physical Anthropology and Archaeology: Introductory Readings*, ed. P. B. Hammond (New York: Macmillan, 1976), pp. 42–58.

26. Antonio García Baquero González, Pedro Romero de Solís, and Ignacio Vázquez Parladé, *Sevilla y la fiesta de toros* (Sevilla: Servicio de Publicaciones del Ayuntamiento de Sevilla, 1980), pp. 24–25 (my translation).

27. Hemingway, *Death in the Afternoon*, p. 24.

28. For general overviews of the evolution of ritual killing, see Walter Burkert, *Homo Necans* (Berkeley: University of California Press, 1983 [1972]); René Girard, *Violence and the Sacred* (Baltimore: Johns Hopkins University Press, 1978 [1972]); or M. F. C. Bourdillon, ed., *Sacrifice* (London: Academic Press, 1980).

29. For a more detailed look at any or all of these ancient ideas of the bull, see Jack Randolph Conrad, *The Horn and the Sword: The History of the Bull as a Symbol of Power and Fertility* (New York: E. P. Dutton, 1957); Angel Alvarez de Miranda, *Ritos y juegos del toro* (Madrid: Taurus, 1962); J. M. Gómez-Tabanera, "Origen de las fiestas taurinas," in *El folklore español*, ed. J. M. Gómez-Tabanera (Madrid: IEAA, 1968), pp. 269–295; Joseph Campbell, *Creative Mythology* (vol. 4 of *The Masks of God*; New York: Penguin Books, 1968).

30. Gómez-Tabanera, "Origen de las fiestas taurinas," pp. 272–287.

31. Ibid., pp. 292–293.

32. The scholar in question was L. Siret, and his farfetched theory was based on a bizarre combination of linguistics and choreography. See Alvarez de Miranda, *Ritos y juegos del toro*, pp. 45–46.

33. Fernando Claramunt, *Historia ilustrada de la tauromaquia* (Madrid: Espasa-Calpe, 1989), vol. 1, pp. 21–54.

34. Ibid., p. 62.

35. Gómez-Tabanera, "Origen de las fiestas taurinas," pp. 274–275.

36. Julio Caro Baroja, *Ritos y mitos equívocos* (Madrid: Istmo, 1974), pp. 77–110. The fiesta in question was apparently celebrated for centuries in many towns of Cáceres and Badajoz, the two provinces of Extremadura. Every April 25, villagers sought out the fiercest bull available and beckoned him forth in the name of San Marcos, whereupon the bull meekly joined in the procession, suffered himself to be adorned with garlands by the women and girls, entered the church to attend Mass, and so forth. On the following day, the bull recovered his natural ferocity. The yearly "miracle" might have been assisted by having the chosen bovid lap up enormous amounts of wine on the night of April 24. Caro considers *The Bacchae* of Euripides to be the fundamental text for associating Dionysus with the bull, the procession, the temple, the enthusiastic women, and the inebriation that characterized this extinct Spanish fiesta.

37. See, for example, B. Aitken, "Las fiestas de Viloria, pueblo natal de San Domingo," *Revista de Dialectología y Tradiciones Populares* 9 (1953): 499–503, and Antonio Herrera Casado, "San Agustín y el culto totémico," *Revista de Dialectología y Tradiciones Populares* 29 (1973): 427–433.

38. Ludwig Friedländer, *Roman Life and Manners Under the Early Empire*, trans. J. H. Frelse and L. A. Magnus (4 vols; London: Routledge & Kegan Paul, 1908), vol. 2, pp. 62–74.

39. Claramunt, *Historia ilustrada de la tauromaquia*, vol. 1, p. 69.

40. Enrique Casas Gaspar, *Ritos agrarios: Folklore campesino español* (Madrid: Escelicer, 1950); Alvarez de Miranda, *Ritos y juegos del toro*; Manuel Delgado Ruiz, *De la muerte de un dios: La fiesta de los toros en el universo simbólico de la cultura popular* (Barcelona: Nexos, 1986).

41. Alvarez de Miranda, *Ritos y juegos del toro*, pp. 93–96.

42. Ibid., pp. 99–100 (my translation).

43. Ibid., pp. 210–211 (my translation).

44. Delgado Ruiz, *De la muerte de un dios*, pp. 146–147, 190–191 (my translation).

45. Ibid., pp. 204–210.

46. Ibid., pp. 242–250.

47. Ibid., pp. 247–259.

48. For a formal rebuttal of Delgado's matriarchal paranoia, see Timothy Mitchell, *Violence and Piety in Spanish Folklore* (Philadelphia and London: University of Pennsylvania Press, 1988), pp. 167–168.

49. V. Pérez Díaz, *Pueblos y clases sociales en el campo español* (Madrid: Siglo XXI, 1974), pp. 165–166. Cited in Delgado Ruiz, *De la muerte de un dios*, pp. 162–163.

50. Julio Caro Baroja, "Toros y hombres . . . sin toreros," *Revista de Occidente* 36 (1984): 24 (my translation).

51. J. M. Gómez-Tabanera, "Fiestas populares y festejos tradicionales," in *El folklore español*, ed. J. M. Gómez-Tabanera (Madrid: Instituto Español de Antropología Aplicada, 1968), p. 156 (my translation). This folklorist ably synthesizes the ideas of Kerenyi, Eliade, Cassirer, and other well-known students of religion and mythic thought.

52. "277 heridos en Elche por el uso imprudente de productos de pirotecnia." *El País*, 15 August 1990, p. 15.

53. Mikel Muez, "42 heridos en el último encierro," *El País*, 15 July 1990, p. 26.

Chapter 2: The Rise of Modern Bullfighting

1. José Ortega y Gasset, *La caza y los toros* (Madrid: Espasa-Calpe, 1962, p. 141 (my translation).

2. J. H. Elliott, "The Decline of Spain," in *Rensaissance, Reformation, and Absolutism*, ed. N. F. Cantor and M. S. Werthman (2d ed.; New York: Thomas Y. Crowell, 1972), pp. 202–252.

3. Based on investigations carried out by the historian López Izquierdo and cited by Fernando Claramunt, *Historia ilustrada de la tauromaquia* (Madrid: Espasa-Calpe, 1989), vol. 1, p. 164.

4. Cited by Antonio García-Baquero González et al., *Sevilla y la fiesta de toros* (Sevilla: Servicio de Publicaciones del Ayuntamiento de Sevilla, 1980), p. 60.

5. This anonymous account was first printed in Amsterdam in 1700. Cited by Santiago Araúz de Robles, *Sociología del toreo*, (Madrid: Prensa Española, 1978), p. 74 (my translation).

6. Angel Alvarez de Miranda, *Ritos y juegos del toro* (Madrid: Taurus, 1962), p. 121 (my translation).

7. Cited by Rafael Pérez Delgado, "Sobre las corridas de toros: Notas sociológicas," in *Homenaje a Julio Caro Baroja*, ed. Antonio Carreira et al. (Madrid: Centro de Investigaciones Sociológicas, 1978), p. 865.

8. Cited by Araúz de Robles, *Sociología del toreo*, p. 75 (my translation).

9. Among the authors who mention this practice are the Jesuit priest referred to above and Claramunt, *Historia ilustrada de la tauromaquia*, vol. 1, p. 166.

10. José María de Cossío, *Los toros: Tratado técnico e histórico*, vol. 4 (Madrid:

Espasa-Calpe, 1961), pp. 850–854; Claramunt, *Historia ilustrada de la tauromaquia*, vol I, pp. 166–176.

11. Joaquin de la Puente, *Los toros en el arte* (Granada: Fundación Rodriguez Acosta, 1964), p. 24 (my translation). Although the etchings in question were not printed until 1815, they were made to accompany Moratín's famous *Carta histórica sobre el origen y progresos de las fiestas de toros en España* (1777) and thus they feature bullfighting behaviors observable in the last quarter of the eighteenth century.

12. García-Baquero et al., *Sevilla y la fiesta de toros*, p. 59.

13. José Daza, *Precisos manejos y progresos condonados en dos tomos: Del forzoso peculiar Arte de la Agricultura que lo es del toreo (manuscrito inédito de 1778)*, ed. José Maria Gutiérrez Ballesteros, Conde de Colombi (2 vols.; Madrid: Unión de Bibliófilos Taurinos, 1959).

14. García-Baquero et al., *Sevilla y la fiesta de toros*, p. 66.

15. Ibid., pp. 67–68 (my translation).

16. Gabriel H. Lovett, *Napoleon and the Birth of Modern Spain* (New York: New York University Press, 1965), vol. 1, p. 3.

17. Carmen Martín Gaite, *Usos amorosos del dieciocho en España* (Barcelona: Lumen, 1981), pp. 76–77 (my translation).

18. José Ortega y Gasset, *Goya* (Madrid: Revista de Occidente, 1966 [1963]), p. 39 (my translation).

19. Martín Gaite, *Usos amorosos del dieciocho en España*, pp. 40–41.

20. Ibid., pp. 54–73.

21. Charles E. Kany, *Life and Manners in Madrid, 1750–1800* (Berkeley: University of California Press, 1932), p. 189. Cited by Martín Gaite, *Usos amorosos del dieciocho en España*, p. 90.

22. Lovett, *Napoleon and the Birth of Modern Spain*, vol. 1, pp. 18–19.

23. Theodore Ropp, *War in the Modern World* (New York: Collier, 1962), pp. 126–127.

24. Ibid., p. 127.

25. Lovett, *Napoleon and the Birth of Modern Spain*, vol. 1, p. 24.

26. Federico Bravo Morata, *El sainete madrileño y la España de sainete* (Madrid: Fenicia, 1973), p. 221.

27. Ortega y Gasset, *Goya*, p. 31 (my translation).

28. Martín Gaite, *Usos amorosos del dieciocho en España*, p. 305 (my translation).

29. Ibid., p. 99.

30. Ibid., p. 106 (my translation).

31. Julio Caro Baroja, *Ensayo sobre la literatura de cordel* (Madrid: Revista de Occidente, 1969), pp. 215–216.

32. Martín Gaite, *Usos amorosos del dieciocho en España*, pp. 101–104.

33. These verses form part of a *tonadilla*, or light tune, from *The Torero, the Maja, and the Petimetre*, a sainete by Esteve. Cited by Caro Baroja, *Ensayo sobre la literatura de cordel*, p. 216 (my translation). See also José Subirá, *Tonadillas teatrales inéditas* (Madrid: Calpe, 1932), p. 142.

34. Ibid., pp. 107–108.

35. Alberto González Troyano, *El torero, héroe literario*, (Madrid: Espasa-Calpe, 1988), pp. 125–133.

36. Garcia-Baquero et al., *Sevilla y la fiesta de toros*, pp. 87–90.

37. Claramunt, *Historia ilustrada de la tauromaquia*, p. 202.

38. Julio Caro Baroja, "Honor y vergüenza," *Revista de Dialectología y Tradiciones Populares* 20 (1964): 444–445 (my translation).

39. Julio Caro Baroja, *Las formas complejas de la vida religiosa: Religión, sociedad y carácter en la España de los siglos XVI y XVII* (Madrid: Sarpe, 1985), pp. 455–456.

40. Bartolomé Bennassar, *Los españoles: Actitudes y mentalidad desde el s. XVI al s. XIX* (San Lorenzo del Escorial, Madrid: Swan, 1985), pp. 196–206, 218–219.

41. Francisco M. Garcia Ferrero, "Valor etnográfico de las 'Guías de Forasteros': El caso de Sevilla," in *Antropología cultural de Andalucía*, ed. S. Rodriguez Becerra (Sevilla: Consejeria de Cultura de la Junta de Andalucia, 1984), p. 276.

42. Taken from the *Relación de los arrojos y valentías de Don Miguel de Arenales, y el fin dichoso que tuvo*, cited by Caro Baroja, *Ensayo sobre la literatura de cordel*, p. 110 (my translation).

43. Ibid., p. 107.

44. Fernando Savater, "El torero como héroe," in *Las Ventas: Cincuenta años de corridas*, ed. M. Kramer et al. (Madrid: Diputación Provincial de Madrid, 1981), pp. 410–414.

45. Ernest Hemingway, *Death in the Afternoon* (New York: Charles Scribner's Sons, 1932), pp. 64–65.

46. Manuel Chaves Nogales and Juan Belmonte, *Juan Belmonte, matador de toros* (orig. pub. 1935; Madrid: Alianza, 1969), p. 142.

47. Cossío, *Los toros*, vol. 4, p. 881 (my translation).

48. Manuel Fernández y González, *Las glorias del toreo* (Madrid, 1879); cited without page number by Manuel Chaves Nogales, "Rasgos históricos de Pepe-Illo," in *La tauromaquia de Pepe-Illo*, ed. Bruno del Amo (Granada: Editoriales Andaluzas Unidas, 1984), pp. 13–14. See also, Claramunt, *Historia ilustrada de la tauromaquia*, pp. 196–210; and José María de Cossío, *Los toros: Tratado técnico e histórico*, vol. 3 (6th ed.; Madrid: Espasa-Calpe, 1969), pp. 221–231.

49. The case of Tragabuches is cited by Fernando Quiñones and José Blas Vega, "Toros y arte flamenco," Jose María de Cossío, *Los toros: Tratado técnico e histórico*, vol. 7 (Madrid: Espasa-Calpe, 1982), p. 711. The story of the violent Gypsy matador and smuggler gave rise to a well-known flamenco *copla*:

Una mujer fue la causa	A woman was the first
de mi perdición primera,	cause of my perdition,
que no hay ruina del hombre	for there is no man's ruin
que por la mujer no venga.	that doesn't come from woman.

50. Manuel Serrano Romá, "Diestros que actuaron como matadores de toros en los siglos XVIII y XIX, y alternativas que se concedieron en España, Francia y plazas no americanas al reglamentarse la fiesta," *Aplausos: Semanario taurino*, 17 February 1986, pp. 20–21. See also Hemingway, *Death in the Afternoon*, p. 77.

51. Hemingway, *Death in the Afternoon*, pp. 100–103.

52. Antonio de Hoyos y Vinent, *Oro, seda, sangre y sol* (Madrid: Renacimiento, 1914), p. 223 (my translation).

53. Enrique Gil Calvo, *Función de toros: Una interpretación funcionalista de las corridas* (Madrid: Espasa-Calpe, 1989), pp. 91–101.

54. Araúz de Robles, *Sociología del toreo*, p. 90.

55. F. Bleu (pseudonym of Félix Borrell), *Antes y después del Guerra: Medio siglo de toreo* (orig. publ. 1913; Madrid: Espasa-Calpe, 1983), p. 248 (my translation).

56. Ibid., pp. 246–247.

57. Larry Collins and Dominique Lapierre, *Or I'll Dress You in Mourning* (orig. pub. 1968; London: Granada, 1969), p. 305.

58. Fernando Claramunt López, *Los toros desde la psicología*, vol. 7 of Cossío, *Los toros* (Madrid: Espasa-Calpe, 1982), p. 165.

59. The bullfighter in question was Nicanor Villalta (Hemingway, *Death in the Afternoon*, pp. 221–222).

60. As quoted by Rosanna Torres, "El síndrome del gladiador," *El País*, 27 July 1986, p. 10 (my translation).

61. As quoted by Torres, ibid. (my translation).

62. In the words of Juan Mora, "Those are things that should not be spoken of: it is something that must remain among ourselves [bullfighters]." As quoted by Torres, ibid. (my translation).

63. Georges Bataille, *L'érotisme* (Paris: Editions de Minuit, 1957).

64. C. Scott Littleton, *The New Comparative Mythology: An Anthropological Assessment of the Theories of Georges Dumézil* (3d ed.; Berkeley: University of California Press, 1982), pp. 80–81.

65. Francisco de Cossío, *Los toros: Tratado técnico e histórico*, Vol. 8 of the encyclopedia founded by his uncle José María de Cossío (Madrid: Espasa-Calpe, 1986), pp. 35–36 (my translation).

66. José Luis Sánchez Garrido, *Córdoba en la historia del toreo* (Córdoba: Publicaciones del Monte de Piedad y Caja de Ahorros de Córdoba, 1985), p. 48.

Chapter 3: Brave Cattle, Brave Men

1. Julián Pereda, S. J., *Los toros ante la iglesia y la moral* (2d ed.; Bilbao: Editorial El Mensajero del Corazón de Jesús, 1965), p. 139 (my translation).

2. Ibid., pp. 24–32, 135–165, 167–201.

3. As is well known, the Jesuit order itself exemplified the fruitful symbiosis between religious idealism and military organization that characterized the Spanish Church as a whole for a thousand years. Regarding Spanish priests' enthusiasm for soldiers and military exploits, see Julio Caro Baroja, *Las formas complejas de la vida religiosa. Religión, sociedad y charácter en la España de los siglos XVI y XVII* (Madrid: Sarpe, 1985), pp. 437–446.

4. See especially José Maria de Cossío, *Los toros. Tratado técnico e histórico*, vol. 2 (Madrid: Espasa-Calpe, 1947), pp. 83–204; and Rosario Cambria, *Los toros. tema polémico en el ensayo español del siglo XX* (Madrid: Gredos, 1974).

5. See José Ortega y Gasset, *La caza y los toros* (Madrid: Espasa-Calpe, 1962), pp. 125–156; and *Una interpretación de la historia universal: En torno a Toynbee,* (Madrid: Alianza, 1984). Ortega's view is admirably summarized by Enrique Gil Calvo, *Función de toros: Una interpretación functionalista de las corridas* (Madrid: Espasa-Calpe, 1989), pp. 143–144.

6. Rafael Pérez Delgado, "Sobre las corridas de toros. Notas sociológicas," in *Homenaje a Julio Caro Baroja*, ed. Antonio Carreira et al. (Madrid: Centro de Investigaciones Sociológicas, 1978), p. 864.

7. Santiago Araúz de Robles, *Sociologia del toero* (Madrid: Prensa Española, 1978), pp. 70–78.

8. Cited by Ramón Perez de Ayala, *Politica y toros*, vol. 3 of his *Obras completas* (Madrid: Aguilar, 1963), pp. 790–791.

9. Gil Calvo, *Función de toros*, p. 144 (my translation).

10. Statistics compiled by the historian Vicens Vives and cited by Araúz de Robles, *Sociología del toreo*, p. 57.

11. Statistics compiled by the historian Jover and cited by Araúz, p. 55.

12. Fernando Claramunt, *Historia ilustrada de la tauromaquia* (Madrid: Espasa-Calpe, 1989), vol., p. 171.

13. Pedro Romero de Solís, "El papel de la nobleza en la invención de las ganaderías de reses bravas," in *Arte y tauromaquia*, ed. Universidad Internacional Menéndez Pelayo. (Madrid: Turner, 1983), pp. 49–52.

14. Ibid., pp. 37–38. See also Cossío, *Los toros: Tratado técnico e histórico*, vol. 1 (5th ed.; Madrid: Espasa-Calpe, 1964), 788–800 on the subject of dogs and *desjarretadores*.

15. Romero de Solís, "El papel de la nobleza," pp. 53–57.

16. Ibid., pp. 57–59.

17. Gil Calvo, *Función de toros*, p. 152.

18. Ortega y Gasset, *La caza y los toros*, p. 143.

19. Romero de Solís, "El papel de la nobleza," pp. 62–63.

20. Ibid., pp. 40–41.

21. Claramunt, *Historia ilustrada de la tauromaquia*, vol. 1, pp. 172–174. See also Cossío, *Los toros*, vol. 1, pp. 129–456 and vol. 4 (Madrid: Espasa-Calpe, 1961), pp. 203–292; and Alvaro Domecq y Díez, *El toro bravo* (Madrid: Espasa-Calpe, 1986).

22. Juan Fernández Figueroa, "Bulls on the Honor Roll," in *Los toros/Bullfighting*, ed. J. Fernández Figueroa (Madrid: Indice, 1964), pp. 197–198.

23. Cossío, *Los toros*, vol. 1, pp. 323–406.

24. Ernest Hemingway, *Death in the Afternoon* (New York: Charles Scribner's Sons, 1932), pp. 110–114.

25. Ibid., p. 7.

26. Ibid., pp. 8–10. For another angle of this aspect of bullfighting, see Larry Collins and Dominique Lapierre, *Or I'll Dress You in Mourning* (London: Granada, 1969), pp. 179–182, wherein the authors supply a mini-biography of Antonio Cruz, a failed bullfighter who became the biggest horse contractor in Spain. Cruz "sent 13,000 horses out to die in bullrings—more than Napoleon had lost marching to Moscow" (p. 182). "Success, for Cruz, rested on his ability not to lose more than one horse per bull. . . . Achieving that was his primary occupation during the corrida. His first-aid treatment to keep his gored animals alive for a second appearance in the ring was brief and rudimentary. He 'stuffed their guts back into their bellies with a fist', then 'sewed them up with a needle and twine'. If any lingering piece of anatomy pushed its way through his hurried stitches, Cruz snipped it off with a pair of scissors. He took a very special pride in his skills in impromptu horse

surgery. 'No vet ever touched my horses,' he could later boast. 'I did it all myself. I really understood horses.' " (pp. 180–181)

27. Francisco de Cossío y Corral, *Los toros. Tratado técnico e histórico*, vol. (Madrid: Espasa-Calpe, 1986), p. 33 (my translation). The bullfighting biographies are to be found in vol. 3 (6th ed., 1969), pp. 5–1008; vol. 5 (1980), pp. 569–1172; and vol. 6 (1981), pp. 7–598.

28. Ramón Carande, "Chronological Statistics of Victims of Bullfighting," in *Los toros/Bullfighting*, ed. Fernández Figueroa, p. 195.

29. For an ample discussion of horn wound surgery complete with operating room photographs, see Cossío, *Los toros*, vol. 6, pp. 1039–1090.

30. Hemingway, *Death in the Afternoon*, p. 255.

31. Gonzalo Argote, "Cogida muy grave de Pepe Luis Vázquez. La cornada más grave en los últimos años," *El País*, 26 May 1989, p. 53.

32. "Curro Romero evoluciona bien dentro de la gravedad," *El País*, 11 June 1989, p. 54.

33. Angel Cebrián, "Cogida grave de José Luis Parada en Barcelona," *El Pais*, 12 June 1989, p. 37.

34. Gonzalo Argote, "Finite de Córdoba, Cogido muy grave," *El país*, 15 August, 1989, p. 17.

35. Ibid.

36. Gonzalo Argote, "Importante faena de Joselito, que sufrió una cornada grave," *El País*, 18 August 1989, p. 23.

37. *El País*, 12 September 1989, p. 32.

38. Dr. Bartolomé Beltrán, "Paquirri pudo haber salvado la vida," *La Revista del Mundo*, 8 October 1984, p. 104.

39. Eugenio Noel, *Nervios de la raza* (Madrid: Sáez Hermanos, 1915), pp. 75–77.

40. Collins and Lapierre, *Or I'll Dress You in Mourning*, pp. 32–34.

41. Raúl del Pozo and Diego Bardón, *El ataúd de astracan: El regreso de El Cordobés* (Barcelona: Zeta, 1980), p. 37.

42. Cited by Collins and Lapierre, *Or I'll Dress You in Mourning*, p. 272.

43. For an interesting glimpse into the intense family politics that forged a vengeful and dominating bullfighter like Paquirri, see José Carlos Arévalo and José Antonio del Moral, *Nacido para morir* (2d ed.; Madrid: Espasa-Calpe, 1985), pp. 49ff. For Riverita's comeback attempts and interviews, see *Diez Minutos*, 27 April 1985, 1 July 1985, or 1 October 1985.

44. José Luis Sánchez Garrido, *Córdoba en la historia del torero* (Córdoba: Publicaciones del Monte de Piedad y Caja de Ahorros de Córdoba, 1985), pp. 48–114. (I have translated the chapter titles referred to.)

45. Ibid., p. 69.

46. Ibid., p. 100.

47. Ibid., pp. 104–105.

48. Ibid., p. 108 (my translation).

49. Ibid., pp. 114–115.

50. Other useful sources include José Aguilar Beltrán, *Cien años de historia del toreo de Castellón* (Castellón, 1987); Segundo Ayllón Rubio, *Tauromaquia en Soria* (Soria, 1987); Juan Barceló Jiménez, *Los toros, el periodismo y la literatura en Murcia* (Murcia, 1982); Juan Barranco Posada, *De Paquiro a Paula. En el rincón del sur* (Ma-

drid, 1987); Alejandro Ramos Folques, *La tauromaquia en Elche. Seis siglos de la fiesta de toros* (Elche, 1980); Carmelo Ruiz and Mario Moya, *Matadores de novillos. Notas biográficas* (Madrid, 1916); Antonio Solera Gastaminza, *Los toros en Guipúzcoa* (San Sebastián, 1983); and William Lyon, *La pierna del Tato. Historias de toros* (Madrid, 1987).

51. Cossío, *Los toros*, vol. 7, p. 33 (my translation).

52. Stanley Brandes, *Metaphors of Masculinity: Sex and Status in Andalusian Folklore* (Philadelphia and London: University of Pennsylvania Press, 1980), p. 92 et passim.

53. Jorge Cela Trulock, *Blanquito, peón de brega* (Valladolid: Gerper, 1958), p. 40; also cited by Linda Gail Lasker, *El tema de los toros en la novelística española contemporánea* (New York: Abra, 1976), p. 53. For other novels that deal in depth with the theme of failed bullfighters, see José López Pinillos, *Las águilas: De la vida del torero* (Madrid: Renacimiento, 1911); Ramón Gómez de la Serna, *El torero Caracho* (Madrid: Agencia Mundial de Librería, 1926; Pedro Antonio Tasso, *Pases de castigo* (Madrid: J. L. Cosano, 1954); Angel Maria de Lera, *Los clarines del miedo* (Barcelona: Destino, 1958); and Elena Quiroga, *La última corrida* (Barcelona: Noguer, 1958). In contrast to such works, the vast majority of taurine novels belong to the genre of "novel of historical adventures" that gives short shrift to psychological subtleties in order to follow the struggles, glorious ascent, and love affairs of some real or fictional matador. See Alberto González Troyano, *El torero, héroe literario* (Madrid: Espasa-Calpe, 1988), pp. 191–192.

54. Carande, "Chronological Statistics," p. 195.

55. For an overview of the origins and evolution of taurine journalism in Spain, see José Altabella, "Notas para una historia de la crítica taurina," in *Crónicas taurinas*, comp. and ed. J. Altabella (Madrid: Taurus, 1965), pp. 7–47; Néstor Luján, "Los toros y el periodismo," in Cossío, *Los toros*, vol. 7, pp. 301–333; and above all Francisco de Cossío y Corral, "La fiesta de toros a través de las crónicas periodísticas," in Cossío, vol. 8 (1793–1883), vol. 9 (1883–1920), and vol. 10 (1920–present; in preparation).

56. Hemingway, *Death in the Afternoon*, p. 164.

57. Ibid., p. 227.

58. Ibid., pp. 17–18, 223–225.

59. Ibid., pp. 226–227.

60. Gregorio Corrochano, the dean of Spanish taurine critics, compares Hemingway to a vulture in *Cuando suena el clarín* (Madrid: Alianza, 1961), pp. 9–32. Fernando Claramunt goes farther in the introduction to his *Historia ilustrada de la tauromaquia* pp. 16–17: he strips Hemingway of the title of true aficionado because he drank in the stands, bellowed insults, and felt occasional urges to throw cushions at disappointing toreros—all very common behaviors in Spain, it must be noted, but considered brutish by Claramunt.

61. Popular pronunciation in Andalusia tends to eliminate the [d] sound in words ending in *-ado* or *-ada*, hence *cornadas* becomes the barbarism "*cornás.*"

62. Pérez Delgado, "Sobre las Corridas de toros," p. 862.

63. Pérez de Ayala, *Política y toros*, p. 1241.

64. See A. Fernández and F. Martínez, "Análisis psicopatológico de la figura del torero," in vol. 3 of *Los toros en España*, ed. C. Orellana (Madrid: Orel, 1969), pp.

79–95; and Fernando Claramunt, "Los toros desde la psicologia," in Cossío, *Los toros*, vol. 7, pp. 40–41. Claramunt contrasts the masochistic matador with the sadistic *matarife* or butcher.

65. Manuel Delgado Ruiz, *De la muerte de un dios: La fiesta de los toros en el universo simbólico de la cultura popular* (Barcelona: Nexos, 1986), pp. 169–170. Delgado combines this study with a number of symbolic ones in order to argue that death instincts are inseparable from sexual instincts in bullfighters, and that the bullfight as a whole symbolizes the castration of men by the marriage-minded matriarchal communities of Spain (pp. 172–177).

66. Manuel Chaves Nogales and Juan Belmonte, *Juan Belmonte, Matador de toros* (orig. pub. 1935; Madrid: Alianza, 1969), p. 196 (my translation).

67. Collins and Lapierre, *Or I'll Dress you in Mourning*, pp. 96, 130, 142, 151.

68. Ibid., p. 152.

69. Ibid., pp. 193–194.

70. See Enrique Vila, *Historia de la rivalidad taurina (1777–1947)* (Madrid: Gráficas Tejario, 1947), or Cossío, *Los toros*, vol. 8, pp. 40–60.

71. Claramunt, "Los toros desde la psicología," p. 78.

72. The expert was Julián Zugasti and his observations are cited by Joaquín Marco in *Literatura popular en España en los siglos XVIII y XIX* (Madrid: Taurus, 1977), vol. 2, p. 435.

73. Julio Caro Baroja, *Ensayo sobre la literatura de cordel* (Madrid: Revista de Occidente, 1969), pp. 387–388.

74. Cf. René Girard, "Psychologie interdividuelle," part three of *Des choses cachées depuis la fondation du monde* (Paris: Grasset, 1978), pp. 401–592. The interpretation I present here is based on the findings of Girard, of gambling psychologists like Edmund Bergler, of taurine psychologists like Claramunt and of keen-eyed analysts of the Spanish psyche like Unamuno.

75. Claramunt, *Los toros desde la psicología*, p. 47.

76. Ibid., p. 47 (my translation).

77. Cited by Francisco de Cossío, pp. 16–17.

78. Arévalo and Moral, *Nacido para morir*, p. 149 (my translation).

79. Marcial Lalanda, "Marcial: Eres el más grande" [interview by José Luis Pecker], *La Caja* 8 (May 1989): 45 (my translation). Obviously an evil tongue could insinuate that Lalanda kept his sons away from the bullrings so that no one would contest his supremacy.

80. J. V. Puente, *Arcángel: Novela del torero "Manolete"* (Madrid: Rivadeneyra, 1960), pp. 260–265. This novel is discussed by Lasker, *El tema de los toros*, pp. 67–69.

81. Alejandro Pérez Lugin, *Currito de la Cruz* (Madrid: Hernando, 1921). This work is discussed at length by González Troyano in *El torero, héroe literario*, pp. 293–302. Interestingly, this scholar concludes that many of the taurine narrations he reviews could be assimilated to an interpretative model devised by René Girard whereby the hero's career is always a function of imitative rivalry with an explicit or implicit "Other" (p. 295). See René Girard, *Mensonge romantique et vérité romanesque* (Paris: Grasset, 1961). For a thorough examination of the relevance of Girardian theory to broad areas of Spanish culture, see Timothy Mitchell, *Violence and Piety in Spanish Folklore* (Philadelphia and London: University of Pennsylvania Press, 1988).

82. William Lyon, "Mayo del 68," *El País*, 18 May 1985, p. 35. Lasker also refers to this incident in her discussion of rivalry in the taurine world, *El tema de los toros*, p. 67.

83. Miguel de Unamuno, "La envidia hispánica" (orig. pub. 1909), in his *Obras completas* (Madrid: Escelicer, 1967), vol. 3, p. 284.

84. Miguel de Unamuno, *Abel Sánchez* (orig. pub. 1917), ed. and intro. José Luis Abellán (Madrid: Editorial Castalia, 1985).

85. Girard, "Psychologie interdividuelle," pp. 458–463. See also Jean-Michel Oughourlian, "Mimetic Desire as a Key to Psychotic and Neurotic Structure," in *Disorder and Order*, ed. P. Livingston (Stanford: Anma Libri, 1984), pp. 72–79.

86. Sánchez Garrido, *Córdoba en la historia del toreo*, p. 63.

87. Ibid., pp. 420–421 (my translation).

88. Arévalo and Moral, *Nacido para morir*, p. 164.

89. See, for example, his treatment of the bullfighter Maera in *Death in the Afternoon*, pp. 77–83, or his story "The Undefeated," in *The Short Stories of Ernest Hemingway* (New York: Modern Library, 1938), pp. 333–364.

90. Edmund Bergler, "Living Dangerously: Artificially-Created Neurotic Tensions, Such as Gambling," in his *Tensions Can Be Reduced to Nuisances* (New York: Liveright Publishing, 1960), pp. 184–186.

91. Pozo and Bardón, *El ataúd de astracán*, pp. 55–56.

92. Girard, "Psychologie interdividuelle," p. 435.

93. Cháves/Belmonte, *Juan Belmonte, matador de toros*, pp. 184–198.

Chapter 4: The Fiesta Nacional

1. Pérez de Ayala, *Política y toros*, book 1 (orig. pub. 1920), in *Obras completas*, vol. 3 (Madrid: Aguilar, 1963), p. 775 (my translation).

2. *Pan y toros* was the title given to a rabidly anti-Absolutist pamphlet of 1812 penned by León y Arroyal; it was also the title of a delightful and enormously popular zarzuela (Spanish light opera) composed in 1864 by Francisco Asenjo Barbieri.

3. Cf. José María de Cossío, *Los toros: Tratado técnico e histórico*, vol. 4 (Madrid: Espasa-Calpe, 1961), pp. 877–878; and Claramunt, *Historia ilustrada de la tauromaquia* (Madrid: Espasa-Calpe, 1989), vol. 1, pp. 227–230.

4. Jack Randolph Conrad, *The Horn and the Sword. The History of the Bull as a Symbol of Power and Fertility* (New York: E. P. Dutton, 1957), p. 185.

5. Ibid., pp. 190–191.

6. The idea that bulls were safe stand-ins for the nobility seemed to be borne out during the peasant revolt that took place in Spain during the first weeks of the Civil War. Traditional methods for letting off steam had failed, obviously, and people rose up thinking they could alter the economic status quo once and for all. As a number of historians have noted, the great landowners of Andalusia saw their prized bulls slaughtered and eaten by hungry peasants. What happened in the summer of 1936 in a small town of Córdoba was typical:

> Unable to avenge themselves on Don Félix Moreno himself, the men of Palma del Río fell instead upon his most treasured possession, his Saltillo bulls. . . . These townspeople who had spent a lifetime in ignorance of the taste of beef

could now digest only the choicest steaks and chops of the carcasses of Don Félix's treasured animals. The rest they tossed uneaten into the Guadalquivir. Each dead animal represented to Don Félix more money than the workers so happily consuming it could earn in years of punishing labor on his lands. Small wonder, then, that so many Palmeños savored in each morsel they tasted not just a new eating experience but a little personal vengeance on the man who represented so much of the misery in their lives. Larry Collins and Dominique Lapierre, *Or I'll Dress You in Mourning* (London: Granada, 1969), pp. 72–73.

Psycholanalytically minded interpreters of Spanish bullfighting could certainly find food for thought in such incidents, evidence for their talk of primal hordes, ritual parricide, totemic feasts, and other familiar Freudian themes. In any case, the eventual victory of the Nationalists, and the horrible revenge wreaked on the peasants by Don Félix and other landowners, gave a new lease on life to a state of affairs that had existed for centuries. In the process of crushing a freely elected, reform-minded government, it would seem that Franco made Spain safe for taurine "democracy."

7. Julián Pereda, *Los toros ante la iglesia y la moral* (2d ed.; Bilbao: Mensajero del Corazón de Jesús, 1965), pp. 216–217 (my translation).

8. Enrique Gil Calvo, *Función de toros: Una Interpretación funcionalista de las corridas* (Madrid: Espasa-Calpe, 1989), pp. 180–183 (my translation).

9. Ibid., p. 191.

10. Ibid., p. 207.

11. Ibid., p. 255 (my translation).

12. Enrique Tierno Galván, "Los toros, acontecimiento nacional" (orig. 1951) in his *Desde el espectáculo a la trivialización* (Madrid: Taurus, 1961), p. 65.

13. Book 1 of *Politica y toros* was first published in 1920, Book 2 in 1943. The essays were originally published in Spanish or Argentine newspapers, and the great majority of them deal with contemporary Spanish politics. Only three of the essays actually deal with the way in which the psychology of bullfighting pervades Spanish public life: "Politica y toros," "La muerte de Joselito," and "El público," pp. 810–831 of Book 1, *Obras Completas*, vol. 3.

14. Jordi Nadal, *El fracaso de la revolución industrial en España, 1814–1913* (Barcelona: Ariel, 1975), pp. 62–64.

15. Ibid., p. 83.

16. Antonio Miguel Bernal, "La disolución del régimen señorial, la propiedad de la tierra y la conformación del actual sistema agrario andaluz," *Crisis del Antiguo Régimen e industrialización en la España del siglo XIX* (Madrid: Editorial Cuadernos para el Diálogo, 1977), pp. 86–88.

17. José Acosta Sánchez, *Historia y cultura del pueblo andaluz. Algunos elementos metadológicos y politicos* (Barcelona: Editorial Anagrama, 1979), pp. 55–58.

18. Robert W. Kern, *Liberals, Reformers, and Caciques in Restoration Spain, 1875–1909* (Albuquerque: University of New Mexico Press, 1974), p. 120.

19. Xavier Tusell Gómez, "The Functioning of the Cacique System in Andalusia, 1890–1931," trans. A. K. Fleming and S. E. Fleming, in *Politics and Society in Twentieth-Century Spain*, ed. Stanley G. Payne (New York: New Viewpoints, 1976), p. 14.

20. José Manuel Cuenca Toribio, *El caciquismo en España*, Cuadernos "Historia 16" no. 188 (Barcelona: Grupo 16, 1989), p. 13 (my translation).

21. Ibid., pp. 4–8.

22. Raymond Carr, *Spain, 1808–1939* (London: Oxford University Press, 1966), pp. 216–217.

23. G. H. B. Ward, *The Truth About Spain* (London: Cassell, 1911), pp. 26–27.

24. Cited by Cuenca Toribio, *El caciquismo en Espana*, p. 11.

25. Ibid., pp. 10–11.

26. Statistics compiled by the Consejo de Instrucción Pública and published in 1904 by the Madrid magazine *Alrededor del Mundo*; cited by Federico Bravo Morata, *El sainete madrileño y la España de sainete* (Madrid: Fenicia, 1973), pp. 35–37.

27. Alfredo Pineda in the May 1918 issue of *Andalucía*; cited by Acosta Sánchez, *Historia y cultura del pueblo andaluz*, p. 63.

28. Ibid., p. 66.

29. From a report compiled in 1910 by three professors at the University of Oviedo (Asturias) and reproduced in Ward, *The Truth About Spain*, pp. 30–33.

30. Kern, *Liberals, Reformers, and Caciques in Restoration Spain*, p. 120.

31. Pérez de Ayala, *Política toros*, book 1, p. 703 (my translation).

32. Ibid., book 2, p. 849 (my translation).

33. Cuenca, *El caciquismo en España*, pp. 15–18 (my translation).

34. Tusell Gómez, "The Functioning of the Cacique System in Andalusia, 1890–1931," p. 19.

35. Ibid., p. 10

36. Ibid., p. 27. A new study by Francisco Comin, *Hacienda y economía en la España contemporánea, 1800–1936* (Madrid: Instituto de Estudios Fiscales, 1989), provides a superb description of the way caciquismo was intimately entwined with Spain's tax system.

37. Kern, *Liberals, Reformers, and Caciques in Restoration Spain*, p. 120.

38. Raymond Carr and Juan Pablo Fusi, *Spain: Dictatorship to Democracy* (2d ed.; London: George Allen & Unwin, 1981), p. 80.

39. Santos Juliá, "Vieja corrupción," *El País*, 14 June 1989, p. 15 (my translation).

40. Fernando Nadal, "Juan Guerra ha tejido una compleja red de empresas con importantes activos inmobiliarios," *El Pais*, 1 February 1990, p. 16; Juan Luis Cebrián, "Una cuestión estética," *El Pais*, 4 February 1990, p. 11.

41. Luis Fernández Salcedo, as quoted by Delicadezas, "Racket in the Bullfighting World," in *Los toros/Bullfighting*, ed. Juan Fernández Figueróa (Madrid: Indice, 1964), p. 182.

42. Ibid., pp. 182–183. As with any other problem or abuse in bullfighting, the problem of corruption has always been worse in the rural regions of Spain, where veterinarians have allegedly been more susceptible to bribes and some critics have ruthlessly extorted novice bullfighters.

43. It is entirely possible that this story was originally told not about a bullfighter but about an Italian tenor. See Pérez de Ayala, *Política y toros*, book 2, p. 1237.

44. Ernest Hemingway, *Death in the Afternoon* (New York: Charles Scribner's Sons, 1932), pp. 163–164.

45. Antonio Díaz-Cañabate, "Bullfighting Today," in *Los toros/Bullfighting*, ed. Fernández Figueróa, p. 148.

46. Joaquin Vidal, "El Bolsin Taurino de Ciudad Rodrigo empieza la selección de novilleros," *El Pais*, 25 January 1990, p. 50.

47. William Lyon, "Intuitivos, espontáneos y vivaces," *El País*, 8 September 1985, p. 39.

48. Collins and Lapierre, *Or I'll Dress You in Mourning*, pp. 156–157.

49. William Lyon, "No todos pueden ser El Cordobés," *El País*, 17 May 1986, p. 33.

50. "El fiscal pide seis años para el torero que hirió a un empresario por excluirle del cartel," *El País*, 27 May 1989, p. 21.

51. Delicadezas, "Racket in the Bullfighting World," p. 182.

52. Sánchez Garrido, *Córdoba en la historia del toreo*, p. 106.

53. Hemingway, *Death in the Afternoon*, pp. 229–230.

54. Claramunt, *Historia ilustrada de la tauromaquia*, vol. 2, pp. 162–163.

55. García-Baquero, Romero de Solis, and Vázquez Parladé, *Sevilla y la fiesta de toros*, pp. 99–109.

56. Agustín Díaz Yanes, "Joselito el Gallo: El último torero clásico," in *Arte y tauromaquia*, ed. Universidad Internacional Menéndez Pelayo (Madrid: Turner, 1983), pp. 234–239.

57. Bruno del Amo, "José Delgado (Illo): Apuntes biográficos por 'Recortes'," in *La tauromaquia de Pepe-Illo*, ed. Bruno del Amo (Granada: Editoriales Andaluzas Unidas, 1984), pp. 169–170.

58. José Carlos Arévalo and José Antonio de Moral, *Nacido para morir* (2d ed.; Madrid: Espasa-Calpe, 1985), p. 172 (my translation).

59. Eugenio Noel, *Señoritos chulos, fenómenos, gitanos y flamencos* (Madrid: Renacimiento, 1916), p. 20; cited by Rosario Cambria, *Los toros: tema polémico en el ensayo español del siglo XX* (Madrid: Gredos, 1974), p. 204 (my translation).

60. Manuel Fernández y González, *Las glorias del toreo* (Madrid, 1879); cited without page number by Manuel Chaves, "Rasgos históricos de Pepe-Illo," in *La tauromaquia de Pepe-Illo*, ed. p. 14.

61. Gil Calvo, *Función de toros*, pp. 203–204. Gil goes on to affirm that the matador's power is altruistic, whereas that of the bull is egotistical, and therefore the bullfight teaches spectators to sacrifice their personal interests to those of the social contract (p. 207).

62. Tusell Gómez, "The Functioning of the Cacique System in Andalusia," p. 17. Tusell cites Mazzantini's collaboration as a prime example of the ideological vacuum of caciquismo.

63. F. Bleu (pseudonym of Félix Borrell), *Antes y después del Guerra: Medio siglo de toro* (orig. pub. 1913; Madrid: Espasa-Calpe, 1983), pp. 224–242.

64. Pérez de Ayala, *Política y toros*, book 2, pp. 1242–1245.

65. Manuel Chaves Nogales and Juan Belmonte, *Juan Belmonte, matador de toros* (orig. pub. 1935; Madrid: Alianza, 1969), p. 112 (my translation).

66. Fernando Claramunt, "Los toros desde la psicología," in Cossío, *Los toros*, vol. 7, p. 158.

67. Raúl del Pozo and Diego Bardón, *El ataúd de astracán*. *El regreso de El Cordobés* (Barcelona: Zeta, 1980), pp. 27–36.

68. Julio Caro Baroja, "Toros y hombres . . . sin toreros," *Revista de Occidente* 36 (May 1984):10 (my translation).

69. José de la Loma (Don Modesto), "Desde la barrera. Belmonte, ¡Cinco verónicas sin enmendarse!" (orig. 1913) in *Crónicas taurinas*, ed. J. Altabella (Madrid: Taurus, 1965), pp. 132–137. The writer goes on to recommend two months of steak and potatoes for Belmonte, emaciated from his years as a maletilla.

70. Carr, *Spain, 1808–1939*, p. 217.

71. Garcia-Baquero et al., *Sevilla y la fiesta de toros*, p. 79–80.

72. As quoted by Santiago Araúz de Robles, *Sociología del toreo* (Madrid: Prensa Española, 1978), pp. 77–78.

73. Fernando Claramunt, *Historia ilustrada de la tauromaquia*, vol. 1, pp. 246–251.

74. Manuel Delgado-Iribarren Negrao, "Los toros en la música," Cossío, *Los toros*, vol. 7, pp. 580–598.

75. Alberto González Troyano, *El torero, héroe literario* (Madrid: Espasa-Calpe, 1988), p. 202 (my translation). Much the same point could be made about the Spanish lyrical theatre of the nineteenth and early twentieth centuries, with its numerous zarzuelas and revistas that consistently link bullfighting emotion to patriotic emotion.

76. William Lyon, "Otras razones para ir a la plaza," *El País*, 19 May 1985, p. 35.

77. Garcia-Baquero et al., *Sevilla y la fiesta de toros*, p. 108.

78. Pérez de Ayala, *Política y toros*, book 1, p. 812 (my translation).

79. As quoted by Claramunt, "Los toros desde la psicología," p. 159 (my translation).

80. Rafael Ríos Mozo, *Tauromaquia fundamental* (2d ed.; Granada: Editoriales Andaluzas Unidas, 1985), pp. 52–53 (my translation).

81. Vicente Blasco Ibáñez, *Sangre y arena*, in *Las novelas del toreo* (Barcelona: Luis de Caralt, 1962), p. 827 (my transiation).

82. F. Bleu, *Antes y después del Guerra*, pp. 318–320.

83. Antonio Diaz-Cañabate, *Paseíllo por el planeta de los toros* (Madrid: Salvat-Alianza, 1970), pp. 105–106. In another part of his book this critic speaks with nostalgia of the old capeas, which despite their barbarous cruelty were the best way for youngsters to learn the taurine profession (pp. 45–46).

84. Pérez de Ayala, *Política y toros*, book 1, pp. 811–813 (my translation).

85. Enrique Tierno Galván, *Desde el espectáculo a la trivialización* (Madrid: Taurus, 1961), pp. 74–75 (my translation).

86. Araúz de Robles, *Sociología del toreo*, p. 177 (my translation).

87. See Stanley Brandes, *Metaphors of Masculinity: Sex and Status in Andalusian Folklore* (Philadelphia and London: University of Pennsylvania Press, 1980) and David Gilmore, *Aggression and Community: Paradoxes of Andalusian Culture* (New Haven, Conn.: Yale University Press, 1987).

88. Hemingway, *Death in the Afternoon*, p. 396. Called *criadillas*, bull testicles have been considered a delicacy in Spain.

89. Pérez de Ayala, *Política y toros*, book 1, p. 665 (my translation).

90. Eugenio Noel, *Escritos antitaurinos*, (orig. pub. 1914; Madrid: Taurus, 1967), pp. 133–138 (my translation). Noel's description of a bust of Lagartijo—one of tauromachy's manliest heroes—offers additional insight into the bullfighter's symbolic function:

> Julio Antonio has studied the head of Lagartijo and has found in it the head of our nation. That Celtiberian face has the jaw of energy, the nose of audacity, the lips of willpower, the eyes of nobility, the forehead of force, the neck of subjugation, the chin of resistance, the cheekbones of sobriety: there is no intelligence under that skull, but it is nevertheless dolichocephalic, perfect. . . . That man is our people, our symbol, our representative personage. He has an iron will, but uneducated it yields, breaks, and turns to vice. He kills a bull because he cannot conquer an obstacle. He employs energy to fight bulls because he knows no other way to employ it. . . . He could have been brilliant, but he is only hysterical. He should have been creative, but he has exhausted himself. He is impulsive because he reacts to danger with a "So what?" *Escritos antitaurinos*, pp. 76–78 (my translation).

Chapter 5: Psychosexual Aspects of the Bullfight

1. Collected by Manuel Martínez Remis in his *Cancionero popular taurino* (Madrid: Taurus, 1963), pp. 70, 111, 176 (my translation).

2. Compiled by Luis Nieto, "El epigrama pícaro en la crónica taurina," *El País*, 21 May 1989, p. 35 (my translation). The very best of these licentious verses cannot be translated into English at all, since they make ingenious use of specialized taurine colloquialisms.

3. Wenceslao Fernández-Flórez, *Relato inmoral* (Madrid: Atlántida, 1927), pp. 240–241.

4. Henri de Montherlant, *Les bestiares* (Paris: Grasset, 1926); Waldo Frank, *Virgin Spain: Scenes from the Spiritual Drama of a Great People* (New York: Boni & Liveright, 1926). Hemingway devotes two pages of his own book on bullfighting to an amusing critique of such works, characterizing them as "overwritten journalism made literature by the injection of a false epic quality." Waldo Frank's "bedside mysticism" and "erectile writing" come in for particular censure. Hemingway insinuates that if Frank had had adequate sexual outlets in his life he might not have written the book at all. *Death in the Afternoon* (New York: Charles Scribner's Sons, 1932), pp. 53–54.

5. Carlos Luis Alvarez, "The Public Square and the Bullring," in *Los toros / Bullfighting*, ed. Juan Fernández Figueroa (Madrid: Indice, 1964), p. 42.

6. See Conchita Cintrón, *Recuerdos* (Madrid: Espasa-Calpe, 1962). For an overview of the entire phenomenon of female bullfighters, as well as an intriguing analysis of its political and erotic aspects, see Emilia Boado and Fermín Cebolla, *Las señoritas toreras: Historia, erótica y politica del toreo femenino* (Madrid: Felmar, 1976). These and other hard-to-find volumes can be obtained from Egartorre, Apartado 5073, 28024 Madrid (Campamento), Spain.

7. See Cossío, *Los toros*, vol. 1, pp. 747–758.

8. See Cambria's essay, in this volume, for a full discussion of the offending parties.

9. See Cossío, *Los toros*, vol. 2, pp. 232–242. To Cossio's list can be added the use that Catholic priests have made of taurine terms to portray the truths of the faith, a custom that goes back several centuries according to Father Pereda (Julián Pereda, S.J., *Los toros ante la iglesia y la moral* [2d ed.; Mensajero del Corazón de Jesús, 1965], pp. 24–32). The bullfight, for its part, has borrowed a number of ecclesiastical terms to refer to different aspects of the performance. As we saw in Chapter 4, Pérez de Ayala described the Spanish political scene in taurine terms and vice versa.

10. Luis Araquistáin, *El arca de Noé* (Valencia: Sempere, 1926), p. 257; as quoted by Rosario Cambria, *Los toros: tema polémico en el ensayo español del siglo xx* (Madrid: Gredos, 1974), p. 174 (my translation).

11. José Ortega y Gasset, *La caza y los toros* (Madrid: Espasa-Calpe, 1962), p. 75 (my translation).

12. Rafael Pérez Delgado, "Sobre las corridas de toros: Notas sociológicas," in *Homenaje a Julio Caro Baroja*, ed. Antonio Carreira et al. (Madrid: Centro de Investigaciones Sociológicas, 1978), pp. 844–849, 866–871. Examples of his errors: Pérez refers several times to the Roman circus as the site of gladiatorial combats, when in fact they were held in amphitheaters. He also refers to such combats as *ludi circenses* when in fact this term refers to races. He also refers to the "polemical literature" that the spectacles provoked, when in fact almost no classical Roman author spoke out against the games. Worst of all, Pérez unnecessarily limits his focus to the Roman *taurocenta* and thereby overlooks the genuine equivalent (in popularity and emotivity) of Spanish matadors—the gladiators. Incidentally, Spain's top matador of today, Juan Ruiz, uses the stage name of Espartaco, or Spartacus—the name of the gladiator who led a major slave rebellion in 70 B.C.

13. See Ludwig Friedländer, *Roman Life and Manners Under the Early Empire*, trans. J. H. Freese and L. A. Magnus (4 vols.; London: Routledge & Kegan Paul, 1908), vol. 2, pp. 62–74 ("Animal-Baiting"), and Keith Hopkins, *Death and Renewal* (*Sociological Studies in Roman History*, vol. 2; Cambridge, Eng.: Cambridge University Press, 1983), pp. 11–12.

14. Hopkins, *Death and Renewal*, p. 5.

15. Friedländer, *Roman Life and Manners*, vol. 2, p. 76.

16. Ibid., p. 41.

17. Ibid., pp. 49–52.

18. Ibid., p. 57.

19. Hopkins, *Death and Renewal*, p. 21.

20. Cf. ibid., p. 17:

Gladiatorial shows were political theatre. The dramatic performance took place not only in the arena, but also between different sections of the audience. Their interaction was part of Roman politics, and should be included in any thorough account of the Roman constitution. They are usually omitted, simply because in our own society, mass spectator sports count as leisure. The politics of metropolitan control included "bread and circuses" (Juvenal). "The Roman people," wrote Fronto, "is held together by two things: wheat doles and public shows. Control is secured as much by amusements as by serious things" (2. 216—Loeb edition).

21. Friedländer, *Roman Life and Manners*, vol. 2, p. 83.

22. Ibid., pp. 52–53.

23. Hopkins, *Death and Renewal*, p. 23.

24. Friedländer, *Roman Life and Manners*, vol. 2, pp. 56–61.

25. Hopkins, *Death and Renewal*, pp. 22–23.

26. Ibid., p. 22 and n. 32.

27. See Alberto González Troyano, *El torero, héroe literario* (Madrid: Espasa-Calpe, 1988), pp. 121–131.

28. Tertullian, *De Spectaculis*, trans. T. R. Glover (London: William Heinemann, 1931), p. 285.

29. Georges Bataille, *El erotismo*, trans. Toni Vicens (orig. pub. 1957; 3d ed.; Barcelona: Tusquets, 1982), p. 56 et passim.

30. Hopkins, *Death and Renewal*, p. 23.

31. Augustine, *The Confessions of Saint Augustine*, trans. E. B. Pusey (New York: Random House, 1949), bk. 6, pp. 107–108.

32. Friedländer, *Roman Life and Manners*, vol. 2, p. 85.

33. Tertullian, *De Spectaculis*, pp. 297–299.

34. Bataille, *El erotismo*, p. 18. For decades the bullfight theme had been treated by numerous French writers of a Symbolist or Decadent persuasion. In his youthful Surrealist phase, Bataille had even penned a libertine novelette with numerous taurine references. See Georges Bataille, *Histoire d'oeil* (Paris: Hachette, 1928). There is also a Spanish edition, *Historia del ojo*, trans. Antonio Escohotado (Barcelona: Tusquets, 1982).

35. Michel Leiris, *Miroir de la tauromachie* (orig. pub. 1937; Paris: G.L.M., 1964), p. 24 (my translation).

36. Ibid., pp. 31–38.

37. Ibid., pp. 54–55.

38. Susan Shott, "The Sociology of Emotion: Some Starting Points," in *Theoretical Perspectives in Sociology*, ed. S. McNall (New York: St. Martin's Press, 1979), pp. 455–456. Shott adopts a "symbolic interactionist" perspective on the diffusion and intensification of collective sentiments.

39. Ibid., p. 457.

40. This anecdote is told by the matador's nephew, as cited by Fernando Claramunt, "Los toros desde la psicología," in *Los toros: Tratado técnico e histórico*, vol. 7 (Madrid: Espasa-Calpe, 1982), p. 50 (my translation).

41. Ernest Hemingway, *Death in the Afternoon* (New York: Charles Scribner's Sons, 1932), pp. 253–254.

42. For a full account of the different writings in which Noel expressed this view, see Rosario Cambria, *Los toros: Tema polémico en el ensayo español del siglo XX* (Madrid: Gredos, 1974), pp. 209–212.

43. F. Bleu (pseudonym of Félix Borrell), *Antes y después del Guerra: Medio siglo de toreo* (Madrid: Espasa-Calpe, 1983), pp. 250–254.

44. On the erotic aspects of disgust, see Bataille, *El erotismo*, pp. 80–84.

45. Leslie A. Fiedler, "Towards a Definition of Popular Literature," in *Superculture: American Popular Culture and Europe*, ed. C. W. E. Bigsby (Bowling Green, Oh.: Bowling Green University Popular Press, 1975), pp. 40–41.

46. José Bergamín, *La música callada del toreo* (Madrid: Turner, 1981), p. 50 (my translation).

47. Román Gubern, *La imagen pornográfica y otras perversiones ópticas* (Madrid: Akal, 1989), p. 129.

48. Alvaro Fernández Suárez, *España, árbol vivo* (Madrid: Aguilar, 1961), p. 323 (my translation).

49. Cf. David Shapiro, "Hysterical Style," the fourth chapter of his *Neurotic Styles* (New York: Basic Books, 1965), pp. 108–133:

> In contrast to the compulsive's active and prolonged searching for detail, the hysterical person tends cognitively to respond quickly and is highly susceptible to what is immediately impressive, striking, or merely obvious. [p. 112] . . . One would think that vivid emotional life, strong feelings, would above all guarantee an equally vivid, sharp sense of oneself, but, in this case, it certainly does not have that result. [p. 125] . . . Emotion, particularly emotion of this labile sort, is, by its nature, a relatively immediate type of experience and does not necessarily require for its basic existence a great degree of psychological integrative activity. . . . It is apparent that the sort of emotional experience described—explosive and vivid but ephemeral and not "deeply" experienced—is consistent with the romantic and insubstantial experience these people seem to have of the world and of themselves. [p. 132]

50. Since Baudelaire, French theorists of the erotic have repeatedly argued that the mystical search for beauty is de facto transgression. The idea is ably summarized by Leiris: "Toute l'émotion esthétique—ou approximation de la beauté—se greffe finalement sur cette lacune qui représente l'élément sinistre sous sa forme la plus haute: inachèvement obligatoire, gouffre que nous cherchons vainement à combler, brèche ouverte à notre perdition" (*Miroir de la tauromachie*, p. 31). See also chap. 14 of Bataille's *El erotismo*.

51. José Bergamín, *El arte de birlibirloque* (orig. pub. 1930; Madrid: Turner, 1985), p. 32 (my translation).

Bullfighting and the Intellectuals

Rosario Cambria

IT WAS INEVITABLE, I suppose, that the bullfight should provoke varied comments and widely divergent analyses, from the most emotionally charged praise, to the most acerbic criticism, to calmly reasoned and dispassionate observations. Interestingly, despite the fact that we are dealing with such a quintessentially Spanish phenomenon, we can observe this divergence of interpretations and attitudes among both Spanish- and English-speaking writers. Although in the last ten years there has been a minor resurgence in the literature published on the subject in Spain, even today Hispanists in general do not consider the bullfight an acceptable topic for "serious" study. This attitude is unjustified and, in a sense, contradicted by the fact that important Spanish writers over the decades have dedicated their efforts to commenting on this unique spectacle, as I attempted to show in 1974 (see Bibliography).

English-Language Commentary

Since the present work is in English, let us begin by discussing a handful of articles that have appeared over the last thirty-five years in English in various professional journals, usually having to do with psychoanalysis. These psychoanalytic interpretations are usually thought-provoking, but they are at times contradictory and quite often contain factual errors concerning what goes on in a bullfight.

The first article is "The Bull-Fight as a Religious Ritual" by William H. Desmonde. Desmonde's basic thesis is that the bullfight goes back to the original parricide (the son kills and then eats his father): "The modern bullfight is a survival of the totem-feast in which primitive man commemorated the primal crime by killing and eating the total animal. . . . The bull was very frequently a totem animal in antiquity."[1] Following a historical and anthropological journey through various religions of antiquity and underscoring the important role that the figure of the bull played in them, Desmonde concludes that there is a strong possibility that the Spanish-style bullfight is, at least in part, a survival of the ancient pagan religion of Persia, Mithraism. His reasons are twofold. First, the sacrifice of the bull was the central rite of this religion; second, it has been established that this cult to Mithra made its way to the Iberian peninsula, brought by Roman legionnaires.[2]

Despite his reliance on an extensive bibliography, the authority of Desmonde's judgments is, to put it politely, somewhat undermined by numerous factual errors concerning the president-day corrida. For example, he states that the matador's cuadrilla consists of "two picadors, three or four banderillas [sic] and the puntillero; when throwing their pikes into the bull, the picadores must approach him closely, and at this moment horses are frequently severely gored. . . . The condition of the wounded horses is appalling; before collapsing, they may run about for a while with their entrails spilling out over the ground."[3] The inaccuracy of this description is not surprising, since Desmonde acknowledges that his description of the corrida, although written in 1952, is drawn mainly from two magazine articles published in English in 1902 and 1910, both well before the implementation of the *peto* (protective padding for the horse) in 1930.

Desmonde also remarks: "He [the matador] runs a considerable personal risk, and it is common for him to be killed or badly wounded. The matador enrages the bull by waving a red cloth in front of the animal; when it charges, the killer steps aside adroitly, letting the bull strike the cape." (This last statement completely contradicts the principle of modern bullfighting, established by Belmonte, that the feet are to be kept absolutely still during the pass, with the animal's charge being directed around—but close to—the man's body by his arm movements.) "The matador must observe the code in the smallest details. He must kneel to ask permission to kill the bull. When he throws his hat, he must toss it, not from in front, but from behind himself, under his left arm. . . . The matador accepts applause with his two swords crossed before him, lifting and lowering them as though in salute. . . . Even the most skillful swordsman will occasionally miss his stroke, and it would be beneath his dignity to repeat it." There are other examples, some equally strange, but these should adequately illustrate the point.[4]

"On Bullfighting," written in 1955 by Winslow Hunt, relies heavily on personal observation and analysis of various corridas, instead of turning to a great number of bibliographic sources. In spite of a different research methodology, Hunt reaches the same basic conclusion as Desmonde, through "looking at the bullfight as one might look at any work of art, noting its symbolism and the emotions it arouses."[5] From this personal and historical approach, he concludes that the principal unconscious significance of the bullfight is that it is an oedipal drama. The central "plot" of the corrida is "the story of a battle between a father and a son. At first the son flaunts his courage and manliness, then he is attacked by the larger and initially more powerful father, and finally, after a series of encounters, he dominates and defeats the father."[6]

Hunt explains the psychological process by which both the matador and the public avoid guilt feelings caused by these parricidal impulses that are present in the bullfight. He points out that the superego (that part of the human psyche known as the conscience) criticizes the matador for publicly torturing and killing the father (the bull). According to the superego, the matador is a nefarious person. To answer this, the ego (that part of the psyche that strives to be rational, is the source of repression, and censors the primitive drives of the id) replies that there has been no gratuitous torture or death; it was a fair fight between equals. The bull (the father) was strong and dangerous and tried to kill the bullfighter (the son). The latter could have acted like a coward, but didn't; he faced the danger squarely and, therefore, deserved victory. If the matador has fought well and has truly risked his life, then the defense thrown up by the ego is convincing, the superego is placated, and the corrida is a deeply satisfying experience. On the other hand, if the matador is a coward, the spectator feels himself threatened by guilt feelings and will cruelly boo and insult the bullfighter. However, the validity of this process in which one escapes guilt feelings for the parricide is dependent upon an illusion. Hunt explains, "It is the illusion of a fair and equal struggle that makes it possible to act out the murder of the father in as full and direct a form as is done in the bullfight." Since it is generally taken for granted that the bull is stronger than the matador, I wonder why the author sees the essence of the bullfight as a struggle that is "fair and equal."[7]

The author presents another interesting thesis: the public, in addition to identifying with the matador, also identifies—but less so—with the bull. Since the animal suffers pain and death, this identification also implies masochism and the desire to die. The Spaniard would like to die not as 99 percent of the people, ingloriously, but as the toro bravo dies—with dignity and nobility, and with "style." The death of the bull in this way is an admirable one, a way in which a man would be proud to die. In Hunt's words, "It is a great satisfaction to identify with the bull who looks to us as if he is granted the pleasure of death without having to feel ashamed of the manner of dying."[8]

The article ends with an extremely provocative question: "Why is it that the bullfight exists only in Spain and in countries greatly influenced by Spanish culture?" The origin of the toro bravo in the Iberian peninsula (although even this is somewhat clouded in controversy) may explain the birth of bullfighting on foot in Spain, but not its failure to be taken up by other cultures. Leaving the question unresolved, the author merely suggests that the answer may lie in a complex of factors involving the degree of industrialization, the nature of the Spanish family, and that vague and imprecise matter of "national character."[9]

Despite its title, "On Bullfighting and the Future of Tragedy" by Martin Grotjahn examines the religious symbolism of the bullfight. He begins with the observation that the Fiesta Nacional represents the psychoanalytical concept known as "seduction of the aggressor" and explains that "in its deepest, unconscious meaning, the bullfight is a Christian festival, almost a modern Passion Play."[10] Developing this idea, Grotjahn writes: "The Christian drama, in contrast to the classical tragedy, is essentially a reenactment of the incarnation and the victory of Jesus Christ, his death and final resurrection. In a sense it is the last of all tragedies because, through Christ's atonement for original sin, no further tragic struggle is necessary. To believe in him and hope for his grace replaces the tragic struggle between human frailty and divine perfection. The bullfighter with his death dance represents such a distorted Passion Play."[11] Interestingly, Federico García Lorca, in his 1930 lecture "Teoría y juego del duende," spoke of the bullfight as an "authentic religious drama."

In his article "On the Bullfight," Ujamlal Kothari refers to and, in part, agrees with Winslow Hunt's theories. Both writers view the bullfight as a projection of the basic inner human conflict between the id (the part of the psyche that is the source of instinctive energy; it is wholly unconscious, receiving repressed material from the conscious and is dominated by the pleasure principle) on one side (the bull), and the ego and superego (the matador) on the other, with the victory going to the latter, the forces of repression and sublimation. Kothari, however, rejects Hunt's interpretation of the corrida as an oedipal drama, principally because the mother figure is lacking. He does not accept the symbolism of the crowd representing the mother: "In the Oedipus complex, it is the son's wish to kill his father and possess the mother rather than the wish of the mother to adore the son who killed her own husband. The audience here, I believe, identifies with either the 'matador' or the 'bull,' depending on each individual's own emotional needs. The audience, while cheering and giving gifts and showing love, through its identification with the 'matador,' celebrates its own victory over the instincts."[12]

Briefly addressing Hunt's unresolved question concerning the absence of bullfighting in non-Hispanic countries, Kothari suggests that these cultures may have developed psychologically equivalent substitutes for the Fiesta. In the circus, for example, which is popular in many countries, "we see a mass dramatization of this wish fulfillment of the human race to kill and control its instincts in the animal show, where the trainer (ego) with the help of a whip (superego) controls and makes the animals (id) execute the tricks he wants performed." For the author, the rodeo serves the same purpose in the United States, with the cowboy (instead of the matador) representing the ego and the wild animals (replacing the bull) representing the id. Hunting and killing animals would also be, in psychoanalytical terms, an equivalent activity. Kothari ends his article with this plea: "The bullfight, because of its symbolic meaning and the emotions it arouses, deserves much more attention by psychologists and psychoanalysts than it has been given so far."[13]

John Ingham, in an article which appeared in 1964, "The Bullfighter: A Study in Sexual Dialectic," emphasizes the sexual symbolism in the corrida de toros. Thinking more of Mexico than Spain, he speaks of the strong cult of machismo (somewhat comparable to the Spanish *donjuanismo*), pointing out that one of its salient characteristics is a type of "verbal duel" in which the Mexican male participates daily. This duel suggests, according to the author, two men "stabbing" each other with their penises; the verbal content of the "duel" always involves one man accusing the other of being effeminate and homosexual. "In other words," according to Ingham, "the *machos*, in verbal dueling, are engaged in a sublimated homosexual encounter while in the very process of attempting to defend themselves against an accusation of homosexuality. Bullfighting is subject to this same interpretation. If this interpretation is correct, then bullfighting is merely a ceremonial elaboration of everyday discourse in Latin American countries." Ingham specifically uses Mexico as the model for this theory; it seems problematical to apply it to Spain and the Spanish corrida.[14]

Ingham's ideas on the sexual ambivalence of both matador and bull postulate that the torero is "masculine" and the toro "feminine" at the moment the sword penetrates. The matador, however, is also "feminine" in pink stockings and an ornate suit of lights and becomes "homosexual" as well during penetration of a male animal with his sword (phallus). And the toro bravo, symbol of extraordinary male sexual powers, becomes "feminine" at the moment of death—dramatically so if, symbolically castrated, his ears or ears and tail are cut. This blurring of sexual identity is a gradual process. When the bull first enters the ring, the matador leans toward "feminine" passivity but becomes progressively more aggressive and "masculine" while his antagonist goes through the reverse (active to passive) process. In size and shape, the fighting cape used by the matador during the first part of the bullfight resembles the female genitalia; later, along with the muleta, he carries the sword, symbol of the phallus.[15]

The above symbolism, according to the author, explains why Hispanic people find such deep meaning in the corrida. Its dramatic conflict is based on the tension generated by the problem of whether masculinity will prevail over femininity, whether the matador will secure his masculinity by moving progressively from a passive attitude to an active one. Yet, whether the bull or bullfighter dies, it is masculinity that triumphs, for it is the phallus—horn or sword—that kills. In this sense, the audience has nothing to lose; but, of course, the symbolism and probable outcome weigh heavily in favor of the bullfighter. Yet homosexuality persists as the fundamental pattern, since two males are engaged in the conflict.[16]

At the conclusion of his article, Ingham also comments briefly on Winslow Hunt's question concerning the absence of bullfighting in non-Hispanic cultures. He suggests that this enigma "will be closer to a functional solution when it can be explained why Catholicism goes with family structures that tend to produce males with problems in sex-role identification."[17]

A number of interesting ideas are discussed by Enrique Guarner in his article "Some Thoughts on the Symbolism of Bullfights." After summarizing the principal theories of Desmonde, Hunt, Grotjahn, and Ingham, the author begins by randomly listing a series of symbolic interpretations that complement those of his predecessors: the bullfight resembles a pagan rite, with three priests officiating and even minor details compulsively regulated; the symbolic castration ceremony of the removal of the *coleta* (false pigtail) at the end of a matador's career recalls the Sampson myth; the matador expresses qualities of narcissism and exhibitionism in a variety of stylized poses; anal aspects are evidenced by back passes, "which imply a contact with the matador's buttocks"; "genitality" is present when the matador strives to pass the bull as close as possible to the front of his body;

aggression is most apparent when the matador goes in for the kill; the bull, with banderillas in place, resembles Christ crowned with thorns.[18]

Guarner believes that the matador (and, by extension, the spectators) has a strong drive to attain omnipotence. "The bullfighter is but a man who can fall, wounded, in the arena. He must fight on the ground of an enemy six times larger yet agile. It is only when he manages to dominate the animal and strike him with the sword that he becomes transfigured into an omnipotent being, a king of superman, who shows his strength in the face of power." Thus, for Guarner, the esthetic beauty created by the matador during the corrida is simply his way of relieving the intolerable tensions produced by the fear of death; by triumphing over the object of that fear (the bull), the bullfighter achieves the sense of omnipotence he was subconsciously striving for. To support this idea, Guarner discusses the concept of death in Western society and explains that open recognition of the possibility of one's non-existence is necessary for the full integration of the personality: "The id—the repository of wishes—is narcissistically oriented, and contains no conception of death, but only of physical . . . mutilation. Acceptance of one's own extinction is a step necessary for emotional maturity and the integration of the ego." While it is easy enough to accept Guarner's contention that American society is, in general, characterized by a denial or avoidance of death, it is quite difficult to accept his assertion that "the Spaniard has an almost pathological fear of death." If anything, the opposite seems closer to the truth. Many examples of Spanish life and art reveal a people who do not shy away from strong feeling or from human tragedy, a people who accept death as natural.[19]

The final article is by Raphael Pollock, entitled "Some Psychoanalytic Considerations of Bull Fighting and Bull Worship." For the audience, according to the author, the bullfight is an aesthetic spectacle, providing pleasure and "voyeuristic satisfaction in a socially sanctioned context." The spectators, identifying with the matador and/or the bull, can experience vicarious release from subconscious tensions. The fighting bull symbolically represents several levels of "object encounter": "Sibling competition, Oedipal rivalry, and sexuality are all embodied in the drama between man and animal." The matador manifests both male and female components. "Dressed in ruffled shirt, shoes similar to ballet slippers, high stockings, and tight-fitting, light-colored pants and tunic, the matador has a definitely feminine appearance. The various sweeping passes that the matador completes have decidedly feminine overtones. But the matador is a man who, in the most intimate moment of the contest, actually penetrates the bull with his symbolic phallus—the sword." Although his description of the matador is similar to Ingham's, Pollock makes no specific reference to any homosexual element.[20]

The author's interpretation of the contest itself is the most provocative part of his essay. The three divisions of the bullfight are seen as a symbolic seduction scene. The following is Pollock's description and interpretation:

> The first segments of the fight may be likened to foreplay with its tension, increasing flirtation and contact. And then in the *último tercio* the matador, facing the bull by himself, may be thought of as engaging in a symbolic sexual intercourse with the animal . . .
>
> As the contest progresses to the moment of truth, the sexual element intensifies. Facing the animal head-on, the matador must insert his sword into a specific anatomical locus-orifice. . . . With the successful impalement, the bull twitches in an orgiastic-like frenzy and then slumps into death, which has been equated traditionally with the post-orgasmic quiescence. In this encounter the matador risks laceration, especially in the groin area. This might be likened to castration. . . .
>
> In this context the audience may then be considered as the witness to the primal scene, and their excitement can be viewed as corresponding to the excitement children have when witnessing parental sexual intercourse.[21]

Concluding his essay, Pollock briefly suggests a different, more philosophical interpretation of the corrida. Since every bullfight is succeeded by others, there is no finality—death is not the end. "As such, the bullfight, in microcosmic fashion, is a reenactment of the life-death drama which touches on the basic existential conflict that man has been involved with from earliest times to the present."[22]

Spanish-Language Commentary

If we put aside this handful of interesting, albeit highly subjective and debatable, interpretations of the bullfight, the overwhelming majority of serious analyses have come from Spanish-speaking writers. (This is not to detract from the value of certain writings of Ernest Hemingway, especially his 1932 work, *Death in the Afternoon*, which hits the mark on many essential aspects of what constitutes bullfighting—and this at a time when most Americans knew absolutely nothing about the spectacle.) Although the bullfight has made its appearance over the centuries in Spain in all literary genres, it is above all in the essay, and specifically that of the twentieth century, where some of the country's most renowned writers have best expounded their own personal analyses and unique interpretations of the corrida.

These essayists can be classified into one of three general groups according to the author's attitude toward bullfighting—opposed, in favor, or objectively neutral. The "against" group seems generally to correspond to the first important Spanish literary movement of the twentieth century, the so-called "Generation of 1898," the "for" group to their successors, sometimes referred to as "novecentistas," and the noncommittal faction to those outstanding thinkers of the last thirty years. To give the reader a taste of these three tendencies I shall give a brief overview of two authors from each of the first two trends and one from the last.

Vehemently opposed to bullfighting and deeply concerned about the fate of his country and its people, Miguel de Unamuno (1864–1936) is the quintessential "rebel with many causes" (one of his books of essays is entitled *Against This and That*), a perfect representative of the Generation of '98. In fourteen newspaper articles, five letters, and two short essays, Unamuno objects to the bullfight on many different grounds. Perhaps his principal one is that it causes Spaniards to waste so much time discussing particular corridas as well as the whole bullfight world, when they could—and should—be talking about more elevated and transcendental topics. "Let them attend the spectacle if that's where they can go to forget their worries and have a good time, good for them; but, my God, they shouldn't spend the hours, days, months and years talking about it!"[23] Another important objection that Unamuno has to the celebration of bullfights is of a more practical sort: the economic waste of devoting much grazing area, feed, water, and so on to raising a fighting bull to maturity as opposed to raising cattle for dairy products or slaughter.[24] For Unamuno, this misuse of resources is the true "barbarity" of bullfighting, contributing to the economic ruin of the country. It is interesting that Unamuno specifically excludes cruelty or barbarity as grounds for his criticisms: "I do not find the [taurine] spectacle barbaric, nor is it because of its cruelty that it undermines and corrupts Spain. . . . I don't believe that the bullfight spectacle is any more barbaric than many others."[25]

Considering Unamuno's preoccupation with Spain and its future ("Spain as a problem") and what he saw as the urgent need to find solutions to its problems, it is understandable that he criticizes bullfighting for maintaining the status quo, for being a reactionary activity that does not give the people anything to think about.[26] In his poetry, novels, short stories, and drama, as well as his essays, Unamuno sees the philosophical center around which everything revolves as the question of human immortality and, by extension, the existence of God. For Unamuno, this is the *only* important question, the true human tragedy. If an aficionado were to argue that the Spaniard likes tragedy, and that the bullfight is the only truly tragic fiesta, Unamuno would quickly reply: "And the other one, my dear sir, the other one?; the tragedy of our lives, I mean."[27]

The connection that Unamuno makes between tauromachy and religion bears examination. His interpretation of the corrida is that it is like "the persistence of a terrible pagan, almost prehistoric, religious cult . . . a propitiatory sacrifice to who knows which divinity that thirsts for blood . . . and that, in a way, once again renews the ancient tradition of popular barbarism, or rather, savagery."[28] The author maintains that the underlying, hidden religious aspects come to the surface especially during the informal bullfights (capeas) held in small towns. It is here that the common people savagely punish the young bull, stabbing it all over, in order to see its blood run and thus satisfy a type of religious instinct emanating from some shadowy religion of the ancient past. Unamuno states that, deep down, the bullfight is essentially tragedy and fanaticism, a sort of religious fanaticism, not of Christianity or any theological religion, but rather a prehistoric religion of blood sacrifices.[29]

Unamuno's ideas strongly influenced another taurine critic, Eugenio Noel (1885–1936). Although belonging to the next generation, Noel epitomizes the themes of analysis, criticism, and desire for reform in Spain that characterize the Generation of '98. Of the five Spanish intellectuals we are treating in this section, Noel undoubtedly is the least well known and takes a back seat as far as literary quality. It is he, however, who dedicated the greatest part of his literary production to our topic. Indeed, it can be said that he dedicated his whole adult life to writing and lecturing on bullfighting. A fascinating study in contrasts and inadaptation, Noel bitterly excoriated bullfighting every chance he got.

Although the author of more than thirty short stories and one full-length novel, Noel is best known for his anti-bullfighting books of essays and newspaper articles. His literary style matches his personal style—emphatic, vehement, passionate, and exaggerated; he is boastful and exclamatory, and often low-class and uncouth. In sum, he was a singular person as well as having a literary style that is picturesque and evidences great expressive power.

Like the writers of the Generation of '98, Noel characterizes the teens and twenties in Spain as a period of decadence and crisis, lacking ideals, ideas, science, creative energy in all fields, and an interest in becoming part of modern Europe. Noel comments sadly that all of Spain's energy is focused on one place—the bullring. In his mind, the bullfight is not merely a symptom of what is gravely wrong with Spain, but is the actual root cause of the nation's problems. An example of this, as well as an illustration of the element of exaggeration in his style, can be found in a newspaper article of 1914:

> From the bullrings we get the following characteristics of our race: the majority of crimes committed with a knife; the *chulo* [lower class native of Madrid]; the man who puts the personal impression he creates above any other moral consideration; swearing; bad manners; pasodoble music [the bullfight quickstep march] and its derivatives; deep song [*cante hondo*] and other knavery of flamenco dancing, with the guitar as its accomplice; disrespect for the law; banditry; that strange concept of bravery that is represented by the word "kidneys" and that has been and will be the cause of all of our misfortunes; that delirious laughter, having a good time, taking vacations, that characterizes our people; the worship of physical valor and disdain for anything involving struggle, dignity, pride, irreverence; the liberty of being able to do whatever one pleases; the spewing out of one's mouth all manner of low-class and slang words; . . . pornography without voluptuousness, art, nor conscience; political corruption; all, absolutely all aspects of bossism and godfatherism; the complete lack of respect for a pure idea; . . . the cruelty of our feelings; the desire to make war; our ridiculous Don Juanism; . . . and, in sum, whatever has to do with enthusiasm, grace, arrogance, sumptuousness, everything, everything is made negative, corrupted, bastardized, deteriorated, because of those emanations that come from the bullrings to the city and from here to the countryside.[30]

In various essays, Noel brings up an objection to the bullfight spectacle that we have already seen mentioned by Unamuno: the raising of fighting bulls and celebrating of bullfights causes irreparable harm to the nation's economy. What angered Noel most was the tragic paradox of the nation suffering so many problems while at the same time spending millions of pesetas on bullfights. As early as 1912, he was already armed with an impressive arsenal of facts and figures to support his position. Of approximately nineteen million inhabitants, he says, more than eleven million are illiterate; towns are abandoned and desolate; there are no forests, rivers overflow, and there are no decent roads; the country is severely lacking in schoolteachers and public libraries. What the country does have, however, are 396 bullrings in which 872 bullfights are held annually, attended by about seven million Spaniards who spend a total of 150,000 pesetas to see 4,394 bulls and 5,618 horses killed.[31]

Noel's censure is not directed primarily at the bullfighters (they are the ones least culpable) but rather at the general public, those who attend corridas. The Spanish public seems to Noel to exist in a state of walking unconsciousness, not really grasping what is happening to their country as they merrily go off to the bullfight to have a good time and make idols of their bullfighters. This contrast was never more apparent than in 1898, while Spain was losing its last colonies in the New World, in what we know as the Spanish-American War. News of Spain's defeat at Manila arrived in Madrid the very day an important bullfight was held in the Carabanchel bullring. The people weren't worried at all about what was occurring in Manila Bay; they were preoccupied with the bullfight of the day. Sarcastically, Noel comments on this inversion of values and priorities: "Spain doesn't need anything more. It has bullfighters to acclaim, and what does anything else matter? . . . No more universities! What are they good for?"[32]

Given the missionary zeal with which Eugenio Noel went about trying to convince the Spanish-speaking public of the negative effects of the bullfight spectacle (and this during the "Golden Age" years of Joselito and Belmonte), it is logical to ask how successful he was. In general, he maintained an optimistic attitude, pointing to the immense popularity of his public lectures, the progressive physiological deterioration of those who become bullfighters, and the great success of comic bullfights. He was intimately involved enough with the bullfight world to know, however, that during the years 1913, 1914, and 1915 the total number of corridas celebrated increased each year, a fact that greatly depressed him. Nevertheless, he did not lose hope, for in 1924, after the death in the ring of Joselito (1920), he wrote that bullfighting was languishing in a complete state of degeneration. The main reason he gave was that the spectacle, for business reasons, had become merely a simulation, a parody of former barbaric times.[33]

In truth, most Spaniards of the time probably saw Noel more as a colorful fanatic, a laughable eccentric, than a successful anti-bullfight campaigner. His vigorous, sustained, and, yes, brave activities against bullfighting and "flamencoism" had no permanent effect on the taurine spectacle. Paradoxically, several respected authors of the time (Azorín, Ramón Gómez de la Serna, Gonzalo Torrente Ballester) pointed out that Noel in his writings and lectures was like a bullfighter, fighting the "bull" of a hostile public and employing myriad details of the taurine and flamenco worlds that he knew so well and was criticizing. Azorín described this basic Noelian paradox as early as 1913:

> Nobody doubts that Eugenio Noel is a dyed-in-the wool adversary of bullfight-ing and of flamencoism. But the reading of his works quite often produces in us the effect of an exaltation of that which he is trying to berate and condemn. We don't know how to explain this, but it's the truth. If we were lovers of bullfight-ing, perhaps we would experience more pleasure in reading Noel's books than if we were adversaries. Noel knows everything related to bullfighting, in detail. . . . There isn't anything that escapes him. Nobody informs us so well about the characteristics and goings-on of flamencoism as he does. . . . What mystery is this?[34]

The decidedly "anti" attitude of Noel and Unamuno is counterbalanced by the views of the first Spanish thinker who began (the task was left unfin-ished) a true intellectual confrontation with the topic of bullfighting, in the sense of its historical and problematic nature—José Ortega y Gasset (1883–1955). As Spain's most important philosopher of the twentieth cen-tury, Ortega approached the phenomenon of bullfighting as one would expect of a strong Spaniard who had received his philosophical training in Germany—that is, with controlled passion, a favorable attitude, and the open-mindedness and serene objectivity of one who did not consider any human topic as unworthy of serious thought. For many years, beginning at least as early as 1914, Ortega on various occasions promised readers the publication of an in-depth, definitive work on the phenomenon of bull-fighting in Spain, to be entitled *Paquiro, o de las corridas de toros*. For un-known reasons, the work was never written although various short pieces on the subject, some unfinished or in rough draft, were published posthu-mously as part of the volume *La caza y los toros*.

Ortega considered bullfighting to be "a reality of the first magnitude in Spanish history since 1740" that must be carefully analyzed and clearly un-derstood if one was fully to comprehend the history and social reality of Spain since 1650.[35] Surely Oretga was a keen observer of the bullfight world, but even though published photographs show him caping a young bull at the ranch of the excellent bullfighter of the 1930s Domingo Ortega, a good friend, he himself admitted that he could not be characterized as an aficio-nado. If one understands by this word one who regularly attends corridas, then he certainly did not belong to that group, for he attended only a se-lect, small number of them, "only those that were strictly necessary to get an idea of 'how things were going.' "[36]

Perhaps due to his decidedly aristocratic and elitist air, Ortega not only dismissed the importance of previous taurine writers (because they were all writing from the point of view of the aficionado and not of the "analyzer of the humanities") but even went so far as to declare that "knowing, what we can call really knowing what a bullfighter is, no one in Spain—and therefore in the world—knows this except I."[37] In his book entitled *Veláz-quez*, composed of various writings from 1934, 1947, and 1954, Ortega makes the same boast concerning his knowledge of the history of bullfight-ing.[38] It is after reading these claims that one more acutely feels the frustra-tion of Ortega's never having written his *Paquiro* and his leaving us with so few pages on the subject.

Probably Ortega's greatest contribution to the topic of bullfighting is his insistence on the importance of the bullfight spectacle because of its popular, economic, historical, literary, musical, artistic, and social impact on Spain over the centuries. Ortega ignores the personal question of being either "for" or "against" bullfighting. Instead, he maintains that applying "historical reason" to the bullfighter and to the history of bullfighting in Spain reveals certain fundamental secrets concerning the nation's modern history. In effect, the evolution of the spectacle has caused a complete in-version of the social structure of Spain, lasting more than two centuries, which "has given to Spanish society characteristics that are opposite those that other European nations have had."[39] He concludes that "the history of bullfighting turns out to be . . . an ideal scientific paradigm, because of its simplicity and transparency, applicable to the evolutions of every other art form—architecture, painting or poetry."[40] Unfortunately, Ortega does not support or develop this idea further. Questions such as: *Every* other art form? Only in Spain? What are the scientific proofs for this affirmation? are left unanswered.

The question of the morality or ethics of bullfighting is also commented on by Ortega, quite often when speaking directly about hunting and only indirectly about bullfighting (as in "Sobre la caza," in *La caza y los toros*). The ethics of death, he comments, is probably the most difficult aspect of ethics to deal with, because "death is the least intelligible fact that man comes across."[41] Ortega comes to no final resolution of this question of ethical treatment of animals by human beings for the former represent a special situation: they are (living) "things" but at the same time are some-what like humans, without being human. He speaks specifically about bull-fighting in his criticism of the Animal Protection Society:

Is it more ethical that the fighting bull . . . should disappear as a species and that they should die individually in the field without demonstrating their glorious bravery? It is an error to believe that the capacity to feel in ourselves the echo of the pain suffered by an animal should serve as a measure for our moral treatment of the animal. Apply the same principle to the treatment of human beings and its falseness will be seen. The avoidance of suffering is an ethical norm; but it is only one [norm], and it can only achieve the dignity of a guideline when it is articulated along with the others.[42]

The question of the morality of bullfighting, in Ortega's opinion, cannot be judged through a system of fixed, limited criteria, but must be considered from the perspective of Spanish historical reason. This, unfortunately, along with the question of death, was to be included in his oft-promised book.

Unlike Unamuno, who complains about the great "wasting of time" by fans who attend and interminably discuss corridas, Ortega insists that the primary role and even "mission" of aficionados is precisely to discuss the spectacle, "not seriously, but passionately." He then adds:

If they didn't they wouldn't be fulfilling their obligation, and a whole hemisphere of bullfighting would be amputated. This hemisphere consists of the unending resonance of what happens within the bullrings, in the tenacious and incessant discussions around the tables of taverns and cafes, in social clubs, discussion groups and in newspapers. One of the greatest attractions of bullfights is that, even though bullfighting is a silent occupation, which is practiced taciturnly, nevertheless it provokes an enormous amount of talk.[43]

What Ortega y Gasset left us was a tantalyzingly frustrating series of suggestions, of indications without further development. In his excellent article "Ortega y los toros," José Carlos Arévalo examines the philosopher's analyses of the bullfight in greater depth than I have been able to here. He correctly points out that the implied Ortegan challenge, to continue and fully develop what he was only able barely to initiate, has not been accepted by anyone. (The closest we get is a superb—but extremely brief—essay by Pedro Laín Entralgo, to be discussed shortly.) Arévalo lists ten unresolved aspects of the topic brought up by Ortega that should be further researched and treated in written form. They are: the Spanish people who look upon their collective existence as essentially ludic, a representation; theatrical and narrative elements in the corrida, especially during the Enlightenment; a type of political and social regeneration, with the common people taking over the bullfight from the nobility; the social character of the group of matador's helpers, his cuadrilla; bullfight fans beginning to catalogue the regional contributions to the art of bullfighting; the role of genetics in the breeding of fighting bulls, and bravery as a cultural invention; the people adopting the bullfighter as their principal imaginary hero; a sacred aura being conferred upon bullfighting with the invention of the suit of lights; parallelisms between the bullfight fiesta and Spanish society; and the transition of the bullfight from a land-and-cattle rural festival to an urban spectacle.[44] Despite these and other unresolved questions, let us reiterate Ortega y Gasset's principal contribution to the theoretical aspects of bullfighting—the open-minded attitude evidenced by these words of his: "It is not a question of being a fan or disliking it, or of whether this unusual spectacle seems right or wrong. Whatever one thinks of it . . . , there is no choice but to elucidate it."[45]

Born two years before Ortega, Ramón Pérez de Ayala (1881–1962) was a superb novelist and essayist who wrote a work entitled *Politics and Bullfighting (Política y toros)* in 1918. Although not a philosopher, he shared Ortega's open-mindedness and strong desire to learn and to understand the most varied things. Salvador de Madariaga once described him as a "modern humanist, who possesses a synthetic sense of history and a serene understanding of the world and of life. His favorite stance is that of the spectator . . . whose spirit is open to the four winds."[46] Unlike Ortega, Pérez de Ayala did consider himself an aficionado, becoming a special friend and admirer of Juan Belmonte. Despite this, however, in his writings on the subject he evidences a fundamental ambivalence in his attitude toward bullfighting.

Ayala's posture is not due to indecision, nor to a change in position as a result of the evolution of his thinking over the years. Rather, it is a basic, radical duality that he clearly declares almost at the beginning of the bullfighting section of *Politics and Bullfighting* with these words:

> Since I am an aficionado, one should not assume that I cannot deal with this subject dispassionately. If I were dictator of Spain, I would do away with bullfights with the stroke of a pen. But as long as they exist I continue attending. I would do away with them because it is my opinion that, socially, they are a harmful spectacle. I continue to attend because, aesthetically, they constitute an admirable spectacle and because personally, for me, they are not harmful; rather, they are extremely useful, as a text in which to study the psychology of the Spanish people.[47]

Thus, Pérez de Ayala's essays on bullfighting deal primarily with its sociological and psychological aspects, concentrating on the bullfight public.

In what ways, then, does Ayala feel that bullfights are harmful to the Spanish people? After first affirming that the bullfight, as a "popular diversion," is a perfect place to study the average Spaniard, who is spontaneously being his true self, he summarizes the harmful aspects under the following three categories: people accustom themselves to being disrespectful of authority that is just, while being weak in the face of abusive and arbitrary authority; at a bullfight, people practice impulsive—not reflexive—justice; bullfights foment the typically Spanish vice of endlessly discussing things that are incapable of being discussed.[48] (We hear an echo of one of Unamuno's principal objections to the corrida.) These negative characteristics that bullfight spectators learn would not be so bad if they were limited to the bullrings, but they are not. In effect, for Ayala, this type of taurine psychology spreads itself to all areas of Spanish life; the Spanish public *is* the bullfight public. Its sociopsychological traits include an ignorance of its own ignorance with respect to what it is viewing and an exaggerated sense of individualism and of being the ultimate authority, each one feeling that "*I* am the public."[49] It is interesting to note that Ayala, unlike Eugenio Noel, does not believe that bullfights constitute the root cause of the nation's problems nor of the Spanish public's being the way it is: "Is bullfighting the cause of our barbarity and insensitivity, . . . of our decadence, as some of its detractors would have it? . . . Our historical decadence and bullfights are, in my opinion, separate phenomena."[50]

Although he evidences an underlying ambivalence in his attitude toward the spectacle, Pérez de Ayala is unequivocal on one point: he considers bullfighting an art, just as painting, sculpture, dance, and music are arts. What makes this particular human diversion especially rich and enjoyable is its complexity of elements. These fall into two general categories: the sensual and aesthetic elements (the light, color, movement, body poses, beauty of the passes, musicality of the whole) and others of an elementary human order (the enthusiasm, anguish, terror, and death—a true tragedy). Even though the latter, when the risk is real and not faked, can be easily perceived and felt by any spectator (as in the bullfighting of El Cordobés, to choose a recent example), Ayala stresses that the complex of aesthetic emotions (of "style") is clearly of higher value and survives any ethical considerations unscathed. Once again we see the basic bipolarity of his attitude when he states that the aesthetic emotion consists of "a flavor, grace, who knows what; a certain divine something that causes bullfights, in addition to being repugnant, barbaric, and stupid, to also be beautiful."[51] Ayala defines bullfighting as the temporal art *par excellence*, the only one that is strictly temporal and improvised, in which "the work of art is the artist himself."[52] Summing up his definition of this unique, wholly Spanish art form, the author characterizes bullfighting (when it is good) as "dynamic sculpture in movement."[53]

Finally, we observe that Pérez de Ayala touches upon the deeper symbolism of the bullfight. It is the destiny of all human beings to die, to see Nature finally triumph over us; this is the tragedy of our lives. For Ayala, the corrida presents us, "live" and before our very eyes, this natural tragedy that is our fate. Even though the matador almost always triumphs, it is the bull (representing Nature) that will in the end be victorious. The art of bullfighting, then, is in a sense superior to other human art forms, for it is a metaphysical as well as an aesthetic condensation of the ultimate meaning of each human life; the bullfight is no less than an "esthetic paradigm of human life itself."[54]

As representative examples of the varying attitudes toward and theoretical explanations of bullfighting on the part of Spanish writers of this century, we have examined two who clearly look upon the spectacle as something negative and harmful (Unamuno and Noel), and two who are rather positively disposed toward it, though not without a certain amount of ambivalence (Ortega y Gasset and Pérez de Ayala). It remains for us to examine a third, though minor, tendency: those who are neutral on the subject, being neither clearly "for" nor "against," but rather "uninterested." Because of the very nature of this category, these authors have written practically nothing on the subject. The author I have chosen as representative of this group, the one who has written the most on our topic (although a mere five pages), is Pedro Laín Entralgo (born 1908).

Laín Entralgo belongs chronologically to a group of thinkers who made their mark on the Spanish intellectual landscape beginning shortly after the Civil War of 1936–1939 and were originally classified as the "followers (or disciples) of Ortega y Gasset," having studied under him at the University of Madrid. Interestingly, the others—José Luis Aranguren, José Ferrater Mora, and Julián Marías—can also be included, along with Laín, as amongst those writers relatively unconcerned or indifferent to the topic of bullfighting. Laín's brief excursion into the topic is a magnificent one, however. His article, "The Essence of Bullfighting" ("Esencia del toreo"), published in 1969 in volume 3 of the superb anthology *Los toros en España*, is perhaps the best-organized and most intellectually penetrating writing on our topic since Ortega.

The author begins by defining the essential terms of his title: "essence" (that which is permanent and invariable) and "bullfighting" (not merely the matador provoking the bull to charge and executing artistic passes). Laín sets out to determine if, in effect, throughout the varied styles and modes (on horseback, on foot) that constitute the history of bullfighting, there exists a basic essence that remains unalterable. In order to understand the bullfighter and what he does, one must understand the complex world that surrounds the man and the bull, their—to use the quintessential Ortegan term—"circumstances":

> No, I cannot truly understand what the bullfighter is doing in the center of the ring without keeping clearly in mind how the world in which he now exists— the expectant, chattering crowd, the silent and well-organized operating room . . . , the complex network of economic interests surrounding the bullring—belongs to the reality of the cape pass, and in a sense determines it.

While recognizing the importance of the surrounding "circumstance," Laín restricts himself to "peeling away the outer layers, . . . the series of surrounding realities of that complex that is bullfighting, and then fixing an attentive gaze on the essential nucleus that remains."[55] For Laín Entralgo, what is *not* part of the essential nucleus, what is merely the outside shell, includes the business aspects of bullfighting, the spectacle aspects (the artistic "showing off" of the protagonist), and the ritual aspects (it being a festive custom with deep roots in ritual tradition). The basic elements that *do* constitute the essence of *toreo* can be reduced to four: play, challenge, power, and drama. The play element is shown principally in the first part of the bullfight, the cape passes (specifically, the *verónica*). "To play is, amongst other things, to demonstrate a superiority over one's surroundings that are not vital necessities." Challenge, on the other hand, is "deliberately confronting a dangerous reality, one being more or less vulnerable to the danger it entails but with the clear intention of emerging unscathed from the encounter." The section of the bullfight that best exemplifies this is the placing of the banderillas, since the bullfighter (usually one of the matador's helpers, a *banderillero*) goes out unarmed and with no cloth to control the bull's charge. The element of power or control is best exemplified, explains Laín, by a well-executed *natural* pass done with the muleta in the left hand. This is the most classical and dangerous of the passes done with the small, red cloth and requires a maximum amount of intelligence and courage on the part of the man to be able to control the animal's brute force. Drama, the last of Laín's four elements constituting the essence of *toreo*, consists of the tension created by the combination of real danger and potential tragedy—the possibility of a goring. The matador is most at risk during the final act, the "moment of truth," the sword thrust.[56]

In line with the general category in which we have placed him, it is interesting to note that Laín, after bringing up the question of the extent to which bullfighting today contains these four essential elements, exempts himself from answering, confessing, "I am unable to respond, because it's been years since I've seen a bullfight."[57] Once again, we see that general indifference toward the topic of bullfighting characteristic of the other Spanish thinkers of his generation. A further proof of his attitude—if one were needed—is that in 1970–1971 I communicated on two occasions with Laín, presenting him with a series of follow-up questions to his article. In both cases, the response was the *summum* of indifference—silence.

Among the mature Spanish thinkers of the last few years, Pedro Laín Entralgo is probably the author best capable of undertaking the formidable task of writing the *Paquiro* that Ortega y Gasset never got around to. Undoubtedly he has the intellectual capacity to do so. The other consideration, whether he possesses the technical and historical knowledge as well as the inclination to do it, is something we cannot judge.

Recent Discussions

Having said that the group of important Spanish philosophical thinkers whose representative figure is Laín Entralgo are relatively uninterested in the topic of bullfighting, I seem to be implying that the current Spanish intellectual attitude toward *toreo* is one of indifference. In reality, nothing could be further from the truth, especially if we examine the quantity (if not always the quality) of articles in professional journals and books on the subject published in the last ten years or so. A major editorial spurt has occurred in Spain in only the last five years, propelled by the Madrid publishing house of Espasa-Calpe, publisher of the successful multi-volume encyclopedic work that began in 1943, the "Cossío," *Los toros: Tratado técnico e histórico*. As a result of the death in the ring, in September 1984, of the popular matador Paquirri, Espasa-Calpe in April 1985 rushed into publication a well-documented biography of Paquirri, *Born to Die (Nacido para morir)*. This successful volume, now in its fourth edition, initiated a series of taurine books by reputable authors that Espasa named the "Colección La Tauromaquia." As of 1990, this series numbers twenty five volumes, in addition to four others that give detailed reviews of the bullfight seasons of 1985 through 1988. A comparable spurt of journal articles began in 1977 with the publication by Ginés Serrán-Pagán of "The Ritual of the Bull in Spain" ("El ritual del toro en España"), and continued in 1984 with an article published in *Revista de Occidente* by the respected anthropologist Julian Pitt-Rivers, another the same year by Carrie B. Douglass in the *American Ethnologist*, an in-depth, wide-ranging piece in a 1986 issue of *Journal of American Folklore* by Timothy Mitchell, and an article by César Graña in 1987 published in *Society*. Let us now briefly review some of the principal ideas of these articles.

The 1977 article by Ginés Serrán-Pagán, "El ritual del toro en España," is subtitled "Algunos errores de análisis y método" ("Some errors of analysis and method"). This is significant, for it seems that authors writing in the fields of sociology, anthropology, folklore studies, and Hispanic culture in general have come to the realization that it is time to take stock and, in some cases, to sound the note of alarm concerning the body of varied and contradictory interpretations of bullfighting. Serrán-Pagán initiates the debunking of many of the long-standing scholarly myths surrounding our topic brought to its supreme level nine years later in Mitchell's 1986 article.

Serrán-Pagán begins by running through the gamut of "contradictory theories concerning the rite of the bull." Since most cultural rites mask a complex symbolism, says Serrán, it is understandable that taurine literature, although extensive, should be vague and unable to reach serious and objective conclusions. In addition, he criticizes many taurine writers for a "lack of scientific seriousness."[58] The "errors of analysis and method" that Serrán perceives can be summarized as follows:

> They have isolated cultural elements by taking them out of context, even at the risk of distorting their meaning, in order to prove a theory. They have not taken into account that societies that are compared can be different in their languages, their systems of ideas and values, in a word, in their cultures and structures. Thus, they have put all their emphasis on pointing out similarities, but not differences, and even less, differences in social organization.[59]

The bulk of Serrán's article consists of a factual, folkloristic description of a number of bull-related festivals in Spain, some of which no longer take place. Special attention is devoted to the popular bull festival held annually in the small mountain town of Grazalema (Cadiz province), the same town that forms the basis of Pitt-Rivers' pioneering study of 1954. Serrán-Pagán's work in this area was later expanded and, along with photos by

A. Muntadas, published in book form in 1980. In conclusion, he opts for a more direct, in-depth study of certain ancient bull-rites that still persist, basically in their original form, in many small towns in Spain. As he says at the end of his article, "We have more than enough studies done in libraries; what we need are studies based on fieldwork. There is an excess of suppositions and a lack of conclusions, theories based on ethnographic data."[60]

Julian Pitt-Rivers, the British social scientist who, in Mitchell's words, is "the most prestigious modern anthropologist to take an interest in bullfighting,"[61] has written on Spanish subjects for the last thirty years. In his 1984 article, "The Sacrifice of the Bull" ("El sacrifico del toro"), he presents us with a somewhat disorganized and highly debatable analysis of the bullfight as a combination of Freudian sexual symbolism (with male-female roles between bull and bullfighter that fluctuate back and forth during the course of the corrida) and the celebration of a religious rite (the killing of the animal being a sacrifice).

In a brief introduction Pitt-Rivers astutely observes that it is human culture, and not Nature, that has created the image that we have of the fighting bull in the ring, a creation that is part Minotaur, part wild beast, part human invention and that "belongs more to the world of political economics."[62] For Pitt-Rivers, as an anthropologist, the bullfight has to do with sacrifice, which leads him to the observation that a sacrifice normally is part of a religious rite. Mitchell, with whom I agree, dissents from Pitt-Rivers' attribution of deep religious significance to the taurine spectacle. Although the music, costumes, and prescribed movements may make the bullfight *seem* like a ritual, says Mitchell,

> the insiders—*cuadrilla*, aficionados, critics—do not attribute any sort of symbolic meaning to their actions. In a true ritual, like the Mass, the officiant and his communicants are engaged in symbolic activity; their every word and action has an agreed-upon spiritual referent. Participants in a Mass take note of, but do not define as central, the skillfulness with which the priest elevates the chalice, or his style in distributing hosts, or the aplomb with which he consecrates the blood of Christ. But in the "ritual" of the bullfight, the entire point is to evaluate the external behavior of the "officiant." Skill, grace and sang-froid are precisely the qualities on display and they do not stand for anything beyond themselves. Thus it would be—and is—ludicrous to place the bullfight on the same spiritual plane as the Mass, to call it a religious rite, a sacrifice.[63]

Pitt-Rivers' justification for his religious interpretation of the bullfight is his assertion (once again, highly debatable) that "a rite must maintain its own coherence throughout its transformations of meaning; otherwise, it would run the risk of being abandoned."[64] Thus, his implication is that the bullfight spectacle has continued to exist and prosper precisely because it has continued to preserve its ultimate essence as a religious rite.

In his sexual analysis of the corrida, Pitt-Rivers harks back to some of the schizophrenic, any-thing-goes psychoanalytic interpretations of the 1950s and 1960s we have already examined. The matador in the first part of the corrida appears as a feminine figure, the bull as masculine. Later, as he dominates the animal and eventually kills it, the man becomes fully masculine, the bull feminine. At the moment of the sword thrust, the man "rapes" the bull and also breaks the traditional taboo against sexual relations when the woman is "indisposed" (menstruating), by penetrating the "vagina-wound" between the animal's shoulder blades with his sword (penis).[65] Mitchell, with whom I concur wholeheartedly, once again disagrees with this analysis, pointing out that "Pitt-Rivers begins with an erotic theory of the sacred and proceeds through a mechanical distortion of the data to 'reveal' the true essence of the bullfight, its hidden reality, its fundamental structure."[66]

Even more unfortunately, Pitt-Rivers extracts certain aspects from the bullfight (which he confesses, he used to frequent . . . thirty years ago),[67] as a result of his sexual/religious interpretation and applies them to Andalusian men and the relations between the sexes in that southern region of Spain. He even goes so far as to declare that "the whole tragedy of the masculine condition in Andalusia is expressed through the bull's situation."[68] According to Pitt-Rivers, the bullfight presents a representation of a sexual interchange between torero and toro and the (real) final sacrifice of the latter, resulting in a transmission of the bull's procreative power to the man. The animal's sexual capacity is the "emblem of bestial masculinity, which is the source of the virtue of the male animal amongst Andalusians."[69] The matador's symbolic violation of the menstrual taboo is what restores to both sexes their natural rights: "Men go back to being true men, since they are no longer afraid of women, and women transform themselves into true female animals, finally capable of signing a peace pact in the war between the sexes."[70] As Mitchell points out, Pitt-Rivers (and he is not alone in this) commits "the logical error of taking the metaphor for the essence," and then compounds this by incurring in "the methodological error of inventing the informant."[71]

In her article of the same year (1984) entitled "*Toro muerto, vaca es*: An Interpretation of the Spanish Bullfight," Carrie B. Douglass opens herself up to some of the same types of criticisms as those we have seen applied to Pitt-Rivers. In effect, she again "takes the metaphor for the essence," thus arriving at the fascinating and, in my opinion, unjustified conclusion that "the theme of the bullfight itself is 'honor' " and that "the bullfighter is to the bull as man is to woman."[72]

After pointing out that there is no consensus among writers as to the meaning of the bullfight, Douglass briefly reviews statements on and analyses of the bullfight by a series of Spanish and foreign writers: Antonio Machado, Federico García Lorca, Winslow Hunt, Jack Randolph Conrad, John Ingham, and Julian Pitt-Rivers. She then arrives at a statement of the essence of her theory:

> I argue that ideologically, at least, the bull is female, an animal structurally equivalent to a woman. The role of the male is to control, contain and finally kill the bull. I show that the popular image of females in (southern) Spain is that if not controlled by men, they are extremely dangerous and upsetting to the social order due to their sexual nature. It is through the treatment of the bull and the transference of language usually reserved for the *toro bravo* and the bullfight to women and the erotic relations between the sexes that the parallels between the bull and the female can be seen.[73]

Like Pitt-Rivers, Douglass limits her observations to Andalusia, thus eliminating those other Spanish regions where corridas are held and also invalidating her implication that these conclusions can be applied to Spanish men and women as a whole.

The metaphorical and linguistic "evidence" the author uses to buttress her arguments has serious flaws. Her "proofs" are drawn primarily from the brief essay "Los toros, acontecimiento nacional" (1951) by the Spanish socialist, sociologist, and former mayor of Madrid Enrique Tierno Galván, who discusses the use of taurine vocabulary in a sexual context. She also employs, in her title and argumentation, the proverb *"toro muerto, vaca es"* (which she translates as "the dead bull is a cow.") Our peripatetic critical debunker of taurine scholarly myths, Timothy Mitchell, has strong comments on Douglass's argumentation:

> In actual usage this saying does not refer to the bullfight, nor to the *brave* bull, nor to male-female relations. Best translated as "dead bull is cow," the phrase derives from the fact that the meat of a dead bull is prepared, packaged and sold in exactly the same way as cow meat, and is used in contexts similar to those of the English "six of one and a half-dozen of the other." . . .
>
> Douglass falls into graver error with the one-way metaphorical evidence she

borrows from Tierno. "What does it mean," asks Tierno, "that *the Spaniard* sees the conquest and possession of a woman the same as he sees the conquest and defeat of a brave bull?" [emphasis mine] . . . A cursory examination of Spanish folklore reveals that the metaphor is entirely interchangeable: both men and women can and do picture themselves as the bullfighter and the opposite sex as the bull. . . . Any sphere of culture can give and take words to and from any other; it does not follow that therefore some profound structural connection exists. Douglass refers to Tierno as the one scholar who "has seen the event of the bullfight in its fundamental and principal essence as a confrontation between male and female." (Douglass 1984: 252). Tierno does nothing of the sort; while indicating that taurine vocabulary lends itself to sex relations, he does not turn around and assert that therefore sex relations are the essence of the bullfight. This is Douglass's own hasty non sequitur, compounded by a tortuous analysis of "the Spanish Honor Code."[74]

Douglass's conclusion seems to stretch things in its application to Spanish society and "the proper relationship between the sexes." She states that the bullfight actually can be applied to "all the social meanings (and ambiguities) of honor." This is the way she sums up her theory:

> If the bullfight is a metaphor for social relationships in Spain, its message is that precedence is more powerful than virtue. This is what makes the bullfight so encompassing. In the analogy between the sexes and the bullfight, bull-female-virtue-equality and the torero-male-precedence-hierarchy; the social structure is really based on hierarchy, not equality (it is sacrificed), yet honor contains both. . . . This double meaning of honor is the key to the bullfight. The male/female relationship, though basic, is a projection of the relationship of the individual to society, in which honor is the encompassing idiom.[75]

In our discussion of the previous two articles, we have quoted from and referred to the opinions and observations contained in the superb essay of 1986 by Timothy Mitchell, "Bullfighting: The Ritual Origin of Scholarly Myths." Let us turn now to some of Mitchell's thoughts on bullfighting in general and the confused interpretations that the spectacle elicits, as well as how he defines tauromachy, once stripped of its mystifications.

After summarizing the sorry state of affairs with an abundance of others' confused and improbable interpretations of the bullfight, Mitchell states that, despite all this obfuscation, there does exist an "unequivocal essence of tauromachy." He continues: "Bullfighting is not the hypermasculine metaphor it has been made out to be."[76] We must look to the areas of folk art and folk craft, he says, rather than to religious rites or sexuality, to better understand what modern bullfighting is. As a folk craft, bullfighting "constitutes a traditional body of knowledge and practices transmitted orally. . . . It requires a highly sophisticated understanding of animal behavior, adherence to very specific norms and procedures, and a fair degree of nerve in carrying them out."[77]

Bullfighting is an extremely complicated event, "a cultural phenomenon that is multilateral, dense and contradictory," in Mitchell's words. The existing "interpretations" of the spectacle, some of which we have examined, have as their principal defect, in Mitchell's opinion, their exclusivity and one-sidedness.[78] How then does Mitchell define bullfighting, define "the entirely unambiguous essence of tauromachy"?[79] The answer may be somewhat surprising, simply because it is a much more prosaic definition than most other analyists have come up with, but infinitely more accurate and "real":

> Tauromachy, as defined by numerous matadors and aficionados, is nothing more nor less than a standardized set of norms and procedures which, if executed properly and with a certain degree of nerve, will lead to the swift demise of the bovid with something approaching mathematical certainty. Note that I say nerve, not valor or courage or bravery. . . . Nerve can be defined, at least in the case of bullfighting, as the quality required for carrying out a series of prearranged acts which have been developed to reduce personal risk to a minimum![80]

Certainly an interesting and untraditional definition, to say the least. After twenty-eight years of contact with bullfighting and the bullfight world, without claiming to be the "ultimate expert," I would venture to say that matadors themselves would not talk about the *nervio* (nerve) it takes to fight and kill a bull, but rather they recognize that an essential prerequisite for fighting a bull is *valor* (bravery). Of course, if we stick to Mitchell's definition of "nerve," then this certainly is the quality needed to face a fighting bull. The above is merely a semantic quibble. But I am troubled by a serious omission in this definition: the lack of any mention of the bullfighter's artistic goal. Even today's most uneducated matador (or aspirant) is very conscious of his principal reason for fighting bulls (along with the economic motivation): to create art, to invent an aesthetically pleasing performance with a somewhat unpredictable animal that is trying to kill him.

Mitchell, in his conclusion, once again reminds us of the multifaceted nature of the bullfight-event, and stresses that further research is needed. Investigation cannot advance in a serious way, he cautions, unless and until the true essence of bullfighting (as just defined) is kept in mind and clearly kept separate from "the highly ambiguous psychological and cultural resonances of the bullfight-event." Areas where further research is needed include: the various runnings of the bulls in small towns and their link with civil and religious institutions; the "intricate web of rituals and superstitions that many bullfighters rely on"; connections between *toreo cómico* and the regular kind; connections between folk aspects of flamenco and bullfighting; "the matador as a hero of modern mass culture" in Hispanic countries; women as spectators and participants in bullfighting.[81]

Let us conclude this section by briefly examining the article that is chronologically the latest, César Graña's 1987 essay, "The Bullfight and Spanish National Decadence." Graña certainly more than justifies our inclusion of this topic as a major chapter in this book; he introduces bullfighting as no less than "the reigning institution of Spanish popular culture." The author touches upon Ortega y Gasset, Pérez de Ayala, Cossío, and Unamuno, stressing that for centuries in Spain the bullfight has received "theological, moral, socioeconomic, cultural, . . . [and] artistic" attention, not always favorable. He also touches upon linguistic and sociological aspects of the spectacle, pointing out, as we have shown earlier, that "the bullfight represents a peculiar fusion of popular and artistocratic forms."[82]

Although Graña's article is flawed by being too superficial on many different points to be of much value— not containing notes or a bibliography and by devoting only the final two of its five pages to the stated topic of the bullfight—it does contain a provocative idea (undeveloped) that bears quoting. In the author's almost-too-late attempt to address the subject of his title directly, he says about the Spain of about 1860–1920:

> Spain as a "problem" is a wounded and traumatized nation speaking through cries and alarms, thirsting for redeeming visions. The Spain of the bullfight is a Spain curiously euphoric and defiant—ebullient, brilliant, cocky, and self-assured in the native "glory" of the fiesta. The critical "higher spirits" faced with a society in disintegration, the victim of a great historic shipwreck, seek the rediscovery or resurrection of the Spanish nationality, looking to their roots or to the stars for the broad guidelines to the foundations of the Spanish character, identity or destiny.[83]

Ironically—and unfortunately—the author ends his article with a question, a question that should have begun the essay and then been carefully answered in the course of it: "What does the bullfight . . . tell us about the culture of Spain?"[84]

Research Facilities Available

Bullfighting continues to be a polemical topic, both in Spain and, now that the country has become a more equal partner in the European community of nations, among the other countries of Europe. On the one hand, we note an article published in a Madrid newspaper in November 1988, entitled "The European Parliament, Against Bullfights" ("El Parlamento Europeo, contra las corridas"); a month later, the *Philadelphia Inquirer* published an article with the title "Bullfighting Tradition Under Siege by Group Pushing Animal Rights." On the other hand, bullfighting (economically and artistically) is flourishing in Spain, if the number of corridas held and the amount of money involved are any indication. For one intent on pursuing this fascinating subject further (whether with a positive, negative, or neutral inclination), there are many sources available.

One can usually locate a number of the basic, "encyclopedic" sources (in English) at many local public libraries, especially at the main branch. University libraries, particularly in larger cities, and in Texas and California, are another good source. The main branch of the Los Angeles Public Library now possesses probably the most extensive collection in the United States of books on tauromachy published in this century, as the result of a bequest from George B. Smith, who died in February 1986, leaving the library his collection of some five-thousand volumes. The dean of American taurine bibliophiles, Smith was a charter member of the Taurine Bibliophiles of America, one of its past presidents, and an Honorary Member.

Two libraries that I have found to be indispensable are the main branch of the New York Public Library (Fifth Avenue and 42nd Street, New York, N.Y. 10036) and that of the Hispanic Society of America (Broadway and 155th Street, New York, NY 10032). The latter is an unexpected gold mine, for it houses, perhaps still partially uncatalogued (as I found it), the collection of Luis Carmena y Millán (died 1904), an erudite collector who was the father of modern taurine bibliographic activities in Spain.

In the early 1950s, an organization called the Unión de Bibliófilos Taurinos was formed in Madrid. Charter members included José María de Cossío, creator and editor of the first four volumes of *Los toros: Tratado técnico e histórico*. Some ten years later, in 1964, Robert Archibald founded the

Taurine Bibliophiles of America. As of 1990 it was in its twenty-sixth year and flourishing, with some 140 members. The organization, devoted primarily to taurine books in English, publishes a very informative, bimonthly newsletter called *La Busca* (*The Search*), as well as a special year-end issue, edited by the president (Donald K. Conover, President, 2171 Twining Road, Newtown, PA 18940). The year-end special issue usually contains an annual bibliographic update, both of bullfight books in English as well as articles of a taurine nature in magazines. Annual dues are fifteen dollars (Dave Tuggle, Treasurer, 3731 W. Flying Diamond Drive, Tucson, Ariz. 85741). There seems to be a special closeness, despite the miles that separate many of the members, among the American aficionados and taurine bibliophiles of this organization. This organization is highly recommended for anyone interested in maintaining contact with the intellectual side of bullfighting in the United States.

To those who are relatively new to the subject of tauromachy, especially American readers, I would like to point out that the bullfight is not native to the culture of the United States; as a matter of fact, it seems to be in direct opposition to some of our basic cultural values and perceived sensitivities. An intellectual open-mindedness and willingness to learn are, therefore, two essential preconditions to approaching the topic. Ernest Hemingway, as an American, was well aware of the innate difficulties his compatriots would have in coming to terms with the subject. I leave my final words to him, taken from the opening paragraph of the book that began so many of us on the road to tauromachy, *Death in the Afternoon*:

> I suppose, from a modern moral point of view, that is, a Christian point of view, the whole bullfight is indefensible; there is certainly much cruelty, there is always danger, either sought or unlooked for, and there is always death, and I should not try to defend it now, only to tell honestly the things I have found true about it. To do this I must be altogether frank, or try to be, and if those who read this decide with disgust that it is written by some one who lacks their, 'the readers', fineness of feeling I can only plead that this may be true. But whoever reads this can only truly make such a judgement when he, or she, has seen the things that are spoken of and knows truly what their reactions to them would be.[85]

Notes

1. William H. Desmonde, "The Bull-fight as a Religious Ritual," *American Imago* 9 (1952): 194.

2. Ibid., pp. 179–187.

3. Ibid., pp. 174–176.

4. Ibid., p. 176.

5. Winslow Hunt, "On Bullfighting," *American Imago* 12 (1955): 343.

6. Ibid., p. 346.

7. Ibid., pp. 349–350.

8. Ibid., pp. 351–352.

9. Ibid., p. 352.

10. Martin Grotjahn, "On Bullfighting and the Future of Tragedy," *International Journal of Psycho-Analysis* 40 (1959): 238.

11. Ibid., p. 239.

12. Ujamlal C. Kothari, "On the Bullfight," *Psychoanalysis and the Psychoanalytic Review* 49 (1962): 126.

13. Ibid., p. 127.

14. John Ingham, "The Bullfighter," *American Imago* 21 (1964): 97.

15. Ibid., pp. 97–98.

16. Ibid., p. 99.

17. Ibid., p. 101.

18. Enrique Guarner, "Some Thoughts on the Symbolism of Bullfights," *Psychoanalytic Review* 57 (1970): 19–20.

19. Ibid., pp. 20, 26.

20. Raphael E. Pollock, "Some Psychoanalytic Considerations of Bull Fighting and Bull Worship," *Israel Annals of Psychiatry and Related Disciplines* 12 (1974): 65.

21. Ibid., pp. 65–66.

22. Ibid., p. 66.

23. Miguel de Unamuno, "La obra de Eugenio Noel" (orig. pub. 1912), *Obras completas*, vol. 3 (Madrid: Escelicer, 1967), pp. 1135–1136 (my translation).

24. Unamuno, "La obra de Noel," p. 1137.

25. Unamuno, "Si yo fuera autócrata . . ." (orig. pub. 1911), *Obras completas*, vol. 7 (Madrid: Escelicer, 1967), pp. 961–962 (my translation).

26. Ibid., p. 962.

27. Unamuno, "El deporte tauromáquico" (orig. pub. 1914), *Obras completas*, vol. 7, p. 974 (my translation).

28. Unamuno, "Huichilobos y el bisonte de Altamira" (orig. pub. 1936), *Obras completas*, vol. 7, p. 981 (my translation).

29. Ibid., pp. 981–983.

30. Eugenio Noel, *Escritos antitaurinos* (orig. pub. 1914; Madrid: Taurus, 1967), pp. 161–162 (my translation).

31. Eugenio Noel, *El flamenquismo y las corridas de toros* (Bilbao: 1912), pp. 3–4.

32. Eugenio Noel, "¡Oh, el arte de los toros!" *Escritos antitaurinos*, p. 106 (my translation).

33. Eugenio Noel, *Raza y alma* (Guatemala, 1924), pp. 54–55.

34. Azorín (José Martínez Ruiz), "Toritos, barbarie," *Los valores literarios* (orig. pub. 1913; 2d ed.; Buenos Aires: Losada, 1957), p. 171 (my translation).

35. José Ortega y Gasset, *Una interpretación de la historia universal: En torno a*

Toynbee (orig. pub. 1948; 2d ed.; Madrid: Revista de Occidente, 1966), pp. 177–178 (my translation).

36. José Ortega y Gasset, "Enviando a Domingo Ortega el retrato del primer toro," afterword to Domingo Ortega, *El arte del toreo* (Madrid: Revista de Occidente, 1950), p. 55 (my translation).

37. Ortega y Gasset, *Una interpretación de la historia universal*, p. 174 (my translation).

38. José Ortega y Gasset, *Velázquez* (orig. pub. 1950; Madrid: Revista de Occidente, 1959), p. 156.

39. Ortega y Gasset, *Una interpretación de la historia universal*, pp. 177–178 (my translation).

40. Ibid., p. 178 (my translation).

41. José Ortega y Gasset, "Sobre la caza" (orig. pub. 1943), *La caza y los toros* (Madrid: Revista de Occidente, 1960), pp. 74–75 (my translation).

42. José Ortega y Gasset, "Sobre el vuelo de las aves anilladas" (orig. pub. 1929), *La caza y los toros* (Madrid: Revista de Occidente, 1960), p. 181 (my translation).

43. José Ortega y Gasset, "[Notas para un brindis]," *La caza y los toros*, p. 162 (my translation).

44. José Carlos Arévalo, "Ortega y los toros," *Revista de Occidente* 36 (1984): 56–59.

45. Ortega y Gasset, "Enviando a Domingo Ortega el retrato del primer toro," p. 56 (my translation).

46. Salvador de Madariaga, *De Galdós a Lorca* (Buenos Aires: Sudamericana, 1960), p. 117 (my translation).

47. Ramón Pérez de Ayala, *Política y toros* (*Obras completas*, vol. 3; Madrid: Aguilar, 1963), p. 805 (my translation).

48. Ibid., p. 811.

49. Ibid., pp. 811–830.

50. Ibid., p. 811 (my translation).

51. Ibid., pp. 800–809 (my translation).

52. Ibid., p. 1276 (my translation).

53. Ibid., p. 1278 (my translation).

54. Ibid., pp. 1273–1277 (my translation).

55. Pedro Laín Entralgo, "Esencia del toreo," in *Los toros en España*, vol. 3, ed. Carlos Orellana (Madrid: Orel, 1969), pp. 71–72 (my translation).

56. Ibid., 73–75 (my translation).

57. Ibid., p. 75 (my translation).

58., Ginés Serrán-Pagán, "El ritual del toro en España: Algunos errores de análisis y método," *Revista de Estudios Sociales* 20 (1977): 92 (my translation).

59. Ibid., p. 90 (my translation).

60. Ibid., p. 99 (my translation).

61. Timothy Mitchell, "Bullfighting: The Ritual Origin of Scholarly Myths," *Journal of American Folklore* 99 (1986): 401.

62. Julián Pitt-Rivers, "El sacrificio del toro," *Revista de Occidente* 36 (1984): 29 (my translation).

63. Mitchell, "Bullfighting," pp. 401–402.

64. Pitt-Rivers, "El sacrificio del toro," p. 32 (my translation).

65. Ibid., pp. 38–40.

66. Mitchell, "Bullfighting," p. 402.

67. Pitt-Rivers, "El sacrificio del toro," p. 32.

68. Ibid., p. 37 (my translation).

69. Ibid., p. 39 (my translation).

70. Ibid., p. 40 (my translation).

71. Mitchell, "Bullfighting," p. 402.

72. Carrie B. Douglass, "*Toro muerto, vaca es*: An Interpretation of the Spanish Bullfight," *American Ethnologist* 11 (1984): 243.

73. Ibid., p. 243.

74. Mitchell, "Bullfighting," pp. 399–400.

75. Douglass, "*Toro muerto, vaca es*," 254–255.

76. Mitchell, "Bullfighting," p. 394.

77. Ibid., p. 396.

78. Ibid., p. 411.

79. Ibid.

80. Ibid., p. 406.

81. Ibid., p. 411.

82. César Graña, "The Bullfight and Spanish National Decadence," *Society* 24 (1987): 36–37.

83. Ibid., p. 37.

84. Ibid.

85. Ernest Hemingway, *Death in the Afternoon* (New York: Charles Scribner's Sons, 1932), p. 1. Reprinted with permission of Charles Scribner's Sons, an imprint of Macmillan Publishing Company, from *Death in the Afternoon* by Ernest Hemingway. Copyright 1932 by Charles Scribner's Sons, renewed 1960 by Ernest Hemingway.

Bibliography on Bullfighting

Compiled by Rosario Cambria

Abad Ojuel, Antonio. *Estirpe y tauromaquia de Antonio Ordóñez*. Madrid: Espasa-Calpe, 1987.

Abad Ojuel, Antonio, and Emilio L. Oliva. *Los toros*. Barcelona: Argos, 1966.

Abarquero Durango, R. *Para-taurinismo, papanatismo y para-manoletismo*. Madrid: Talleres Gráficos Juan Torroba, 1961.

————. *El toro no es una fiera, ni la fiesta nacional una barbarie: Ideas biológicas taurinas de los ganaderos*. Madrid: Talleres Gráficos Juan Torroba, 1963.

Abenámar (Santos López Pelegrín). *Filosofía de los toros*. Madrid: Boix, 1842.

Acquaroni, José Luis. *La corrida de toros*. 3rd ed. Barcelona: Noguer, 1960.

Alameda, José. *Al hilo del toreo*. Madrid: Espasa-Calpe, 1989.

————. *Crónica de sangre: 400 cornadas mortales y algunas más*. México, D.F.: Grijalbo, 1981.

————. *Los heterodoxos del toreo*. México, D.F.: Grijalbo, 1979.

Alberti, Rafael. *Suma taurina*. Barcelona: RM, 1963.

Alcázar, Federico M. *Tauromaquia moderna: Primer tomo (del toreo)*. Madrid: Sucesores de Rivadeneyra, 1936.

Alvarez de Miranda, Angel. *Ritos y juegos del toro*. Madrid: Taurus, 1962.

Alvarez Vara, Ignacio (Barquerito). *Larga cambiada: Temporada taurina 1988*. Madrid: Espasa-Calpe, 1989.

Amicis, Edmondo de. *Spain and the Spaniards*. New York: Putnam's, 1881.

Amorós, Andrés. *Toros y cultura*. Madrid: Espasa-Calpe, 1987.

Anasagasti, Victorio de (Dr. Anás). *Los ojos del toro: Nuevas orientaciones; Estudio científico del toreo*. Madrid: Pueyo, n.d.

Apelt, Wilfredo. *Corrida de Toros: Stierkampf in der Kunst Europas*. Düsseldorf: LTU, 1982.

Araúz de Robles, Santiago. *Sociología del toreo*. Madrid: Prensa Española, n.d.

————. *Pepe Luis: Meditaciones sobre una biografía*. Madrid: Espasa-Calpe, 1989.

Arévalo, José Carlos. "Ortega y los toros." *Revista de Occidente* 36 (1984): 49–59.

Arévalo, José Carlos, and José Antonio del Moral. *La guerra secreta: Temporada taurina 1986*. Madrid: Akal, 1986.

————. *Nacido para morir*. 2d ed. Madrid: Espasa-Calpe, 1985.

————. *Repóquer: Temporada taurina 1985*. Madrid: Espasa-Calpe, 1986.

Arruza, Carlos (with Barnaby Conrad). *My Life as a Matador*. Boston: Houghton Mifflin, 1956.

Arte y tauromaquia. Universidad Internacional Menéndez Pelayo, ed. (Madrid: Turner, 1983).

Ascasubi, Luis. *Of Bulls and Men*. New York: Thomas Nelson & Sons, 1962.

Aubier, Dominique (text), and Inge Morath (photos). *Fiesta in Pamplona*. Paris: Delpire, 1956.

Azorín (José Martínez Ruiz). "Toritos, barbarie." *Los valores literarios*. Orig. pub. 1913. 2d ed. Buenos Aires: Losada, 1957.

Bagüés, Ventura (Don Ventura). *Historia de los matadores de toros*. 2d ed. Barcelona: De Gassó, 1973.

Barbadillo, Manuel. *La gracia de los toreros y de sus compañeros*. Jerez: Sexta, 1980.

Barga Bensusán, Ramón. *El Afeitado: Un fraude a la fiesta brava*. Madrid: Nacional, 1972.

———. *Taurología: La ciencia del toro de lidia*. Madrid: Espasa-Calpe, 1989.

Bates, Katharine Lee. *Spanish Highways and Byways*. Chautauqua, N.Y.: Chautauqua Press, 1920.

Beamish, Huldine. *Cavaliers of Portugal*. New York: Taplinger, 1969.

Bergamín, José. *El arte de birlibirloque, La estatua de Don Tancredo, El mundo por montera*. Orig. pub. 1930, Mexico, D.F.: Stylo, 1944.

———. *El arte de birlibirloque, La estatua de Don Tancredo, El mundo por montera*. Santiago de Chile: Cruz del Sur, 1961.

———. *La claridad del toreo*. Madrid: Turner, 1985.

———. *Ilustración y defensa del toreo: El arte de birlibirloque, la estatua de Don Tancredo, El mundo por montera*. Málaga: Litoral, 1974.

———. *La música callada del toreo*. Madrid: Turner, 1981.

Blasco Ibáñez, Vicente. *The Blood of the Arena*. Chicago: McClurg, 1911.

———. *Sangre y arena*. 5th ed. Madrid: Espasa-Calpe, 1964.

Bollaín, Adolfo. *Los detractores*. Madrid: Los de José y Juan, 1955.

Botán, Fernando. *Crónica Taurina Gráfica, 1967*. Madrid, 1968.

———. *Crónica Taurina Gráfica, 1972*. Madrid, 1972.

———. *Crónica Taurina Gráfica, 1974*. Madrid, 1974.

———. *4 toreros, 4 estilos*. Madrid: Artes Gráficas Ibarra, 1966.

Botsford, Keith. *Dominguín*. Chicago: Quadrangle, 1972.

Broer, Lawrence R. *Hemingway's Spanish Tragedy*. University: University of Alabama Press, 1973.

Buckley, Peter. *Bullfight*. New York: Bonanza, 1958.

Camaño, Angel (El Barquero). *Toros, toreros y aficionados: Relatos históricos*. Vol. 16, no. 788 of *Los Contemporáneos* 28 Feb. 1924.

Camacho Padilla, José Manuel. *El toro, el torero, el público y Manolete*. Córdoba: La Ibérica, 1952.

Cambria, Rosario. "Federico García Lorca, aficionado taurino y poeta del toro." *García Lorca Review* 2 (1974): 54–56.

———. "El torero Ignacio Sánchez Mejías como dramaturgo: *Sinrazón*." *Hispanófila* 78 (May 1983): 43–52.

———. *Los toros: tema polémico en el ensayo español del siglo XX*. Madrid: Gredos, 1974.

Campo, Luis del. *El encierro de los toros*. Pamplona, n.d.

———. *Psicología del corredor en el encierro de los toros en Pamplona*. Barcelona, n.d.

————. *El traje del torero de a pie: Evolución, psicología*. Pamplona: "La Acción Social, 1965.

Campo Jesús, Luis del. *El encierro de los toros*. Pamplona: Diputación Foral de Navarra, 1968.

Campos Carranza, Félix. *Un día de toros*. 2d ed. Madrid: Publicaciones Españolas, 1958.

————. *Un día de toros*. 3d ed. Madrid: Publicaciones Españolas, 1963.

Campos de España, Rafael. *Calendario de ferias taurinas España 1970*. Pamphlet in Spanish, German, French, English. Madrid: Ministerio de Información y Turismo, 1970.

Carmena y Millán, Luis. *Estocadas y pinchazos*. Madrid, 1900.

Caro Baroja, Julio. "Toros y hombres." *Revista de Occidente* 36 (1984): 7–26.

Casero, Antonio. *La tauromaquia de Antonio Casero*. Madrid: Ayuntamiento de Madrid, 1982.

Casteel, Homer. *The Running of the Bulls*. New York: Dodd, Mead, 1953.

Cau, Jean. *Por sevillanas*. Madrid: Espasa-Calpe, 1988.

Cela, Camilo José. *Toreo de salón: Farsa con acompañamiento de clamor y murga*. Barcelona: Lumen, 1963.

Chatfield-Taylor, H. C. *The Land of the Castanet*. Chicago: Herbert S. Stone, 1896.

————. *Tawny Spain*. Boston: Houghton Mifflin, 1927.

Chaves Nogales, Manuel, and Juan Belmonte. *Juan Belmonte, Killer of Bulls*. Trans. Leslie Charteris. New York: Doubleday, Doran, 1937.

————. *Juan Belmonte, matador de toros*. Orig. pub. 1935. Madrid: Alianza, 1969.

Cintrón, Conchita. *Memoirs of a Bullfighter*. New York: Holt, Rinehart & Winston, 1968.

————. *¿Por qué vuelven los toreros?* México, D.F.: Diana, 1977.

Claramunt, Fernando. *Historia ilustrada de la tauromaquia*. Vol. 1: *De la prehistoria a los toreros del 98*. Madrid: Espasa-Calpe, 1989.

————. *Historia ilustrada de la tauromaquia*. Vol. 2: *De la Edad de Oro a nuestros días*. Madrid: Espasa-Calpe, 1989.

Claramunt López, Fernando. *Azorín, Miró y Hernández ante el toro*. Alicante: Instituto de Estudios Alicantinos, 1981.

Clarín Taurino. Bilbao, 1969, 1972, 1973, 1974, 1975, 1976, 1977, 1978, 1979, 1980, 1981, 1982.

Clergue, Lucien. *Toros muertos*. New York: Brussel & Brussel, 1966.

Collins, Larry, and Dominique Lapierre. *Or I'll Dress You in Mourning*. New York: Simon & Schuster, 1968.

————. *Or I'll Dress You in Mourning*. New York: New American Library, 1969.

Conrad, Barnaby, *The Death of Manolete*. Boston: Houghton Mifflin, 1958.

————. *Encyclopedia of Bullfighting*. Boston: Houghton Mifflin, 1961.

————. *La Fiesta Brava: The Art of the Bull Ring*. Boston: Houghton Mifflin, 1950.

————. *Gates of Fear*. New York: Bonanza, 1957.

————. *How to Fight a Bull*. Garden City, N.Y.: Doubleday, 1968.

————. *Matador*. Boston: Houghton Mifflin, 1952.

Conrad, Jack Randolph. *The Horn and the Sword: The History of the Bull as a Symbol of Power and Fertility*. New York: E. P. Dutton, 1957.

Córdoba, José Luis de. *"Manolete" en el recuerdo*. 2d ed. Córdoba: Monte de Piedad y Caja de Ahorros, 1984.

———. *Primeras crónicas sobre Manolete*. Córdoba: Ayuntamiento de Córdoba, 1972.

Corrochano, Gregorio. *Cuando suena el clarín*. 2d ed. Madrid: Alianza, 1966.

———. *¿Qué es torear? Introducción a la tauromaquia de Joselito*. Madrid, 1953.

———. *Teoría de las corridas de toros*. Madrid: Revista de Occidente, 1962.

Cossío y Corral, Francisco de. *Los toros: Tratado técnico e histórico*. Vol. 8 (1986), vol. 9 (1987). Madrid: Espasa-Calpe.

Cossío, José María de. *Los toros: Tratado técnico e histórico*. Vol. 1 (5th ed., 1964), vol. 2 (4th ed., 1965), vol. 3 (6th ed., 1969), vol. 4 (1961), vol. 5 (1980), vol. 6 (1981), vol. 7 (1982). Madrid: Espasa-Calpe.

———. *Los toros en la poesía castellana*. Vol. 1. Madrid: Ibero-Americana, 1931.

———, ed. *Los toros en la poesía*. 3d ed. Madrid: Espasa-Calpe, 1959.

Crónicas taurinas. Comp. and ed. José Altabella. Madrid: Taurus, 1965.

Cuadernos taurinos. Vol. 1: *La tauromaquia en el siglo XVIII* by Bruno del Amo. Madrid: Mon, 1951.

———. Vol. 2: *La tauromaquia en el siglo XIX* by Don Ventura. Madrid: Mon, 1951.

———. Vol. 3: *La tauromaquia en el siglo XX: Los treinta primeros años* by Don Indalecio. Madrid: Mon, 1952.

———. Vol. 4: *La tauromaquia en el siglo XX: Desde 1931 hasta nuestros días* by Don Indalecio. Madrid: Mon, 1952.

Daly, Robert. *The Swords of Spain*. New York: Dial, 1966.

Delgado Guerra, José (Pepe-Illo). *La tauromaquia o arte de torear*. Madrid, 1946.

Delgado Ruiz, Manuel. *De la muerte de un dios: La fiesta de los toros en el universo simbólico de la cultura popular*. Barcelona: Nexos, 1986.

Desmonde, William H. "The Bull-Fight as a Religious Ritual." *American Imago* 9 (1952): 173–195.

Desperdicios (Aureliano López Becerra). *Los italianos y los toros*. Bilbao: Viscaina, 1935.

Díaz-Cañabate, Antonio. *La fábula de Domingo Ortega*. 2d ed. Madrid: Valero, n.d.

———. *The Magic World of the Bullfighter*. London: Burke, 1956.

———. *El mundo de los toros*. 3d ed. León: Everest, 1979.

———. *Paseíllo por el planeta de los toros*. Madrid: Salvat, 1970.

———. *Tipos y sainetillos del planeta de los toros*, 2d ed. Madrid: Prensa Española, 1976.

Díaz-Flores, Florentino. *Mis memorias*. Salamanca, 1983.

Diego, Gerardo. *"El Cordobés" dilucidado y Vuelta del peregrino*. Madrid: Revista de Occidente, 1966.

———. *La suerte o la muerte*. Madrid: Taurus, 1963.

Domecq y Díez, Alvaro. *El toro bravo*. Madrid: Espasa-Calpe, 1986.

Douglass, Carrie B. "*Toro muerto, vaca es*: An Interpretation of the Spanish Bull-fight." *American Ethnologist* 11 (1984): 242–258.

Ellis, Havelock. *The Soul of Spain*. Boston: Houghton Mifflin, n.d.

Epton, Nina. *Love and the Spanish*. Cleveland: World, 1961.

Estefanía, Julio. *Toros en el Puerto*. Puerto de Santa María, Spain: Osborne, 1955.

Esteras Gil, Santiago. *La fiesta de los toros y sus tristes verdades*. 2d ed. Barcelona: T. C. Casals, 1969.

Extraordinario dedicado a los toros. Madrid: Indice, 1958.

Feria del toro Agosto/1969: Bilbao. Pamphlet. Bilbao, 1969.

Fernández, Tomás Ramón. *Reglamentación de las corridas de toros*. Madrid: Espasa-Calpe, 1987.

Fernández de Moratín, Nicolás, and Leandro Fernández de Moratín. *Obras*. New ed. Madrid: Atlas, 1944.

Fernández de Soto, José Manuel (Pepe Castoreño). *Historia de los toros en Cali: Segunda Epoca, 1940–1964*. Cali: Fervia, 1965.

Fernández Salcedo, Luis. *Cuatro conferencias taurinas con aperitivo*. Madrid: Porrúa Turanzas, 1981.

———. *Tres ensayos sobre relatividad taurina*. Madrid, 1948.

Fernández Suárez, Alvaro. *España, árbol vivo*. Madrid: Aguilar, 1961.

———. "Los toros en la sociedad industrial." *Indice* 249 (1969): 22–28.

Ferrater Mora, José. "XXV: Los toros y el microscopio, en Jaén" in *El hombre y su medio y otros ensayos*. Madrid: Siglo Veintiuno de España, 1971.

XXXIX Festival, Club Taurino de Bilbao. Bilbao, 1972.

Fiesta de toros en la Villa de Madrid. Facsimile of 1690 ed. (Madrid). Madrid, 1982.

Frank, Waldo. *Virgin Spain: The Drama of a Great People*. Orig. pub. 1926. New York: Duell, Sloan & Pearce, 1942.

Franklin, Sidney. *Bullfighter from Brooklyn*. New York: Prentice-Hall, 1952.

Fraser, Allan. *The Bull*. New York: Charles Scribner's Sons, 1972.

Fulton, John. *Bullfighting*. New York: Dial, 1971.

Ganivet, Angel. *Idearium español*. 4th ed. Madrid: Espasa-Calpe, 1949.

García Lorca, Federico. *Llanto por Ignacio Sánchez Mejías*. Facsimile of autographed MS. Madrid: Institución Cultural de Cantabria, 1982.

———. "Teoría y juego del duende" in *Obras completas*. 11th ed. Madrid: Aguilar, 1966.

García-Ramos, Antonio, and Francisco Narbona. *Ignacio Sánchez Mejías*. Madrid: Espasa-Calpe, 1988.

García-Ramos Vázquez, Antonio. *20 temas taurinos*. Madrid: Club Fiesta Nacional, 1960.

García Santos, Manuel. *Juan Belmonte: Una vida dramática*. México, D.F.: Prensa, 1962.

García Serrano, Rafael. *Toros de Iberia*. Pamplona: Morea, 1964.

Garland, Antonio. *Lima y el toreo*. Lima: Librería Internacional del Perú, 1948.

Garrido Domínguez, Francisco. *La Plaza de Toros de la Real Maestranza de Ronda*. Ronda, Spain, 1985.

Gil Calvo, Enrique. *Función de toros: Una interpretación funcionalista de las corridas*. Madrid: Espasa-Calpe, 1989.

Gilpérez García, Luis, and Mercedes Fraile Sanz. *El toro bravo: Origen y evolución del toro y del toreo*. Sevilla, 1962.

Giménez Caballero, Ernesto. *Los toros, las castañuelas y la Virgen*. Madrid: Caro Raggio, 1927.

Giraldillo (Manuel Sánchez del Arco). *Filosofía del toreo: España, Portugal, Francia, América*. Madrid: Prensa Española, 1951.

Gómez de la Serna, Ramón. *El torero Caracho*. Orig. pub. 1926. Mexico, D.F., 1945.

Gómez Mesa, Antonio. *Doctrinal tauromáquico: Hacia la depuración de la fiesta de los toros*. Madrid, 1933.

Gómez-Santos, Marino. *El Cordobés y su gente*. 4th ed. Madrid: Escelicer, 1965.

———. *Diálogos españoles*. Madrid: Cid, 1958.

———. *El Viti y su carácter*. Madrid: Escelicer, 1965.

González Climent, Anselmo. *Flamencología: Toros, cante y baile*. Madrid, 1955.

González García, Venancio. *La estética anatómica en la historia del toreo*. Cádiz, 1958.

González Troyano, Alberto. *El torero, héroe literario*. Madrid: Espasa-Calpe, 1988.

Grajal, María Angeles. *Yo me asomé al escote del "Viti."* Salamanca, 1980.

Graña, César. "The Bullfight and Spanish National Decadence." *Society* 24 (1987): 33–37.

Greenfield, Arthur. *Anatomy of a Bullfight*. Reissue. New York: McKay, 1976.

Grotjahn, Martin. "On Bullfighting and the Future of Tragedy." *International Journal of Psycho-Analysis* 40 (1959): 238–239.

Guarner, Enrique. "Some Thoughts on the Symbolism of Bullfights." *Psychoanalytic Review* 57 (1970): 18–28.

Guía del aficionado a los toros: Con ocasión de las ferias taurinas de Medellín-Bogotá-Cali-Manizales 1970. Pamphlet. Medellín: Colina, 1970.

Gutiérrez Alarcón, Demetrio. *Los toros de la guerra y del franquismo*. Barcelona: Luis de Caralt, 1978.

Guzmán, Eduardo de. "Los toros como 'problema' nacional." *Indice* 312 (1972): i–viii.

Hail, Marshall. *Knight in the Sun*. Boston: Little, Brown, 1962.

Haining, Peter, ed. *A Thousand Afternoons*. New York: Cowles, 1970.

Hale, Susan. *A Family Flight Through Spain*. Boston: Lothrop, 1883.

Harris, Miriam Coles. *A Corner of Spain*. Boston: Houghton Mifflin, 1898.

Hatton, Robert W., and Gordon L. Jackson. *The Bullfight*. Detroit: Advancement Press, 1974.

Hay, John. *Castilian Days*. Boston: Houghton Mifflin, 1899.

Hemingway, Ernest. *The Dangerous Summer*. New York: Charles Scribner's Sons, 1985.

———. "The Dangerous Summer." *Life*, 5 Sept. 1960 (pt. 1), 12 Sept. 1960 (pt. 2), 19 Sept. 1960 (pt. 3).

———. *Death in the Afternoon*. New York: Charles Scribner's Sons, 1932.

———. "Bullfighting" in *The Wild Years*. New York: Dell.

Hernández, Miguel. *El torero más valiente, La tragedia de Calisto, [y] otras prosas*. Madrid: Alianza, 1986.

Herrero Mingorance, Rafael. *De Miedo y Oro*. Madrid: Tres-Catorce-Diecisiete, 1980. 1980.

Hjortsberg, William. *Toro! Toro! Toro!* New York: Ballantine, 1975.

Horcajada García, Ricardo. *"Soñador": La corrida según el punto de vista del toro*. Barcelona: Ariel, 1968.

Hoyos y Vinent, Antonio de. *Oro, seda, sangre y sol*. Madrid: Renacimiento, 1914.

Hunt, Winslow. "On Bullfighting." *American Imago* 12 (1955): 343–353.

Iglesias Hermida, Prudencio. *España: El arte, el vicio y la muerte*. Madrid: Pueyo, 1914.

Ingham, John. "The Bullfighter." *American Imago* 21 (1964): 95–102.

Ingram, Rex. *Mars in the House of Death*. New York: Alfred A. Knopf, 1939.

Insúa, Alberto. *La mujer, el torero y el toro*. Barcelona: Favencia, 1971.

Iribarren, José María. *Hemingway y los sanfermines*. Pamplona: Gómez, 1970.

Jiménez Martos, L. *Tientos de los toros y su gente*. Madrid: Rialp, 1981.

Josephs, Allen. *White Wall of Spain: The Mysteries of Andalusian Culture*. Ames: Iowa State University Press, 1983.

Jovellanos, Gaspar Melchor. *Pan y toros*. Madrid: La Ultima Moda, 1898.

Juárez Ugena, Julián. *Las corridas de toros*. Madrid: Dirección General del Turismo, n.d.

Kazantzakis, Nikos. *Spain*. New York: Simon & Schuster, 1963.

Kehoe, Vincent J. R. *Aficionado!* New York: Bonanza, 1959.

———. *Wine, Women and Toros!* New York: Hastings House, 1961.

Kennedy, Bart. *A Tramp in Spain*. New York: Frederick Warne, 1904.

Kothari, Ujamlal C. "On the Bullfight." *Psychoanalysis and the Psychoanalytic Review* 49 (1962): 123–128.

Lafront, A. (Paco Tolosa). *Toreros d'aujourd'hui*. Paris: Art et Industrie, 1959.

Laín Entralgo, Pedro. "Esencia del toreo." *Los toros en España*. Vol. 3. Ed. Carlos Orellana. Madrid: Orel, 1969.

Lalanda, Marcial, and Andrés Amorós. *La tauromaquia de Marcial Lalanda*. Madrid: Espasa-Calpe, 1987.

Landaeta Rosales, Manuel. *Los toros en Caracas desde 1560 hasta . . .* Caracas, 1971.

Lasker, Linda Gail. *El tema de los toros en la novelística española contemporánea*. New York: Abra, 1976.

Laszlo, Andras. *Mi tío jacinto*. Barcelona: Ediciones G.P., 1967.

Lea, Tom. *The Brave Bulls*. Boston: Little, Brown, 1949.

Leaf, Munro. *El cuento de Ferdinando*. New York: Scholastic, 1962.

Leibold, John. *This Is the Bullfight*. Cranbury, N.J.: A. S. Barnes, 1971.

Leonard, Jacques. *Les taureaux: Fête espagnole / The Bulls: Spanish Fiesta / Los toros: Fiesta española*. Barcelona: Barna, n.d.

Lera, Angel María de. *Los clarines del miedo*. 3d ed. Barcelona: Destino, 1967.

Linares, Agustín. *El Cordobés: Torero de época*. Madrid, 1964.

López Pinillos, José (Parmeno). *Las águilas: De la vida del torero*. Madrid: Renacimiento, 1911.

———. *Las águilas: De la vida del torero*. Madrid: Alianza, 1967.

———. *Lo que confiesan los toreros: Pesetas, palmadas, cogidas y palos*. Madrid: Renacimiento, 1917.

López-Valdemoro y de Quesada, Juan Gualberto (Conde de Las Navas). *El espectáculo más nacional*. Madrid, 1900.

Lozano Sevilla, Manuel. *Lo que sabemos de toros*. Madrid: Gregorio del Toro, 1967.

Luján, Néstor. *Historia del toreo*. 2d ed. Barcelona: Destino, 1967.

Lyon, William. *La pierna del Tato: Historias de toros*. Madrid: El País, 1987.

Macnab, Angus. *Fighting Bulls*. New York: Harcourt, Brace, 1959.

Madariaga, Benito. *El toro de lidia*. Madrid: Alimara, 1966.

Madariaga, Salvador de. *De Galdós a Lorca*. Buenos Aires: Sudamericana, 1960.

Mailer, Norman. *The Bullfight*. New York: CBS/Macmillan, 1967.

Mariana, Juan de. *Tratado contra los juegos públicos: Obras del Padre Juan de Mariana*. Vol. 2. Madrid: Atlas, 1950.

Mariscal, Nicasio. *Epístola antitaurómaca: Mis reflexiones*. Madrid: Leopoldo Martínez, 1902.

Marks, John. *To the Bullfight*. New York: Knopf, 1953.

Marrero, Vicente. *Picasso y el toro*. 2d ed. Madrid: Rialp, 1955.

Martínez de León, Andrés. *Los amigos del toro*. Madrid: Aguilar, 1956.

Martínez-Fornés, Santiago. *El público de toros*. Málaga: Gráficas Urania, 1974.

———. *El simbolismo en el toro y en los toros*. Madrid, 1966.

Martínez-Novillo, Alvaro. *El pintor y la tauromaquia*. Madrid, 1988.

Martínez Rueda, Manuel. *Elogio de las corridas de toros*. Orig. pub. 1831. Madrid: Unión de Bibliófilos Taurinos, 1960.

Menéndez Pidal, Ramón. *Los españoles en la historia*. Madrid: Espasa-Calpe, 1959.

Michener, James. *Iberia*. New York: Random House, 1968.

Mitchell, Timothy. "Beauty from Barbarity: The Intellectual Redemption of Tauromachy in Bergamín, Lorca, and Pérez de Ayala." *Hispanic Journal* 8 (1987): 89–101.

———. "Bullfighting: The Ritual Origin of Scholarly Myths." *Journal of American Folklore* 99 (1986): 394–414.

Monserrate, Marita de. *Vengo a torear . . . dijo Antonio Ordóñez*. Madrid, 1966.

Monteira, Félix. "El Parlamento Europeo contra las corridas." *El País* (international ed.), 28 Nov. 1988.

Montes, Francisco (Paquiro). *El arte de torear*. Madrid: Afrodisio Aguado, 1948.

———. *Tauromaquia completa o sea el arte de torear en plaza*. Madrid: Turner, 1983.

Moore, Thomas Ewing. *In the Heart of Spain*. New York: Universal Knowledge Foundation, 1927.

Morales y Marín, José Luis. *Los toros en el arte*. Madrid: Espasa-Calpe, 1989.

Morris, Wright. *The Field of Vision*. New York: Signet, 1957.

Mujica Gallo, Manuel. *Goya, figura del toreo*. Madrid: Cultura Hispánica, 1971.

———. *La minitauromaquia de Picasso o El ocaso de los toros*. Madrid: Prensa Española, 1971.

Muñoz Cortina, José. *Curro Romero: Genio y figura*. Camas, Spain: Peña Taurina Curro Romero, 1984.

Murphy, Bill. *The Red Sands of Santa Maria*. New York: Popular Library, 1957.

Museo Taurino de Madrid. Madrid: Diputación Provincial de Madrid, 1970.

Narbona, Francisco. *Manolete: 50 años de alternativa*. Madrid: Espasa-Calpe, 1989.

Navalón, Alfonso. *Viaje a los toros del sol*. 2d ed. Madrid: Ediciones 99, 1971.

Navarrete, José. "Las fiestas de toros impugnadas," "Sobaquillo" (Mariano de Cavia), and "Las fiestas de toros defendidas." *División de plaza*. Madrid: F. Bueno, 1886.

Nieto Manjón, Luis. *Diccionario ilustrado de términos taurinos*. Madrid: Espasa-Calpe, 1987.

Noel, Eugenio. *Aguafuertes ibéricas*. Barcelona: Maucci, n.d.

———. *América bajo la lupa*. Madrid: EDAF, 1970.

————. *Las capeas*. Madrid: Imprenta Helénica, 1915.

————. *Cornúpetos y bestiarios*. Tortosa: Monclús, 1920.

————. *Diario íntimo: La novela de la vida de un hombre*. 2 vols. Madrid: Taurus, 1962, 1968.

————. *Escenas y andanzas de la campaña antiflamenca*. Valencia: Sempere, 1913.

————. *Escritos antitaurinos*. Orig. pub. 1914. Madrid: Taurus, 1967.

————. *España fibra a fibra*. Madrid: Taurus, 1967.

————. *España nervio a nervio*. Madrid: Calpe, 1924.

————. *El flamenquismo y las corridas de toros*. Bilbao, 1912.

————. *Nervios de la raza*. Madrid: Sáenz Hermanos, 1915.

————. *La novela de un toro*. Santiago de Chile: Nascimento, 1931.

————. *Pan y toros*. Valencia: Sempere, 1912.

————. *El picador Veneno y otras novelas*. Barcelona: Maucci, 1929.

————. *Piel de España*. Madrid: Biblioteca Nueva, 1917.

————. *La providencia al quite*. Madrid: Biblioteca Hispania, n.d.

————. *Raza y alma*. Barcelona: B. Bauzá, 1926.

————. *República y flamenquismo*. Barcelona: A. López, 1913.

————. *Señoritos chulos, fenómenos, gitanos y flamencos*. Madrid: Renacimiento, 1916.

————. *Taurobolios y verdades contrastadas: Hombres e ideas de América y de España*. Santiago de Chile: Nascimento, 1931.

Oag, Shay. *In the Presence of Death: Antonio Ordóñez*. New York: Coward-McCann, 1968.

Olano, Antonio D. *Dinastías*. Madrid, 1988.

————. *Yiyo: Adiós, príncipe, adiós*. Madrid: Delfos, 1985.

Oliver, Federico. *Los semidioses*. In the series *El Teatro Moderno*. Madrid: Prensa Moderna, 1931.

Ordóñez, Valeriano. *San Fermín y sus fiestas*. Pamplona: Diputación Foral de Navarra, n.d.

Orellana, Carlos, ed. *Los toros en España*. Vols. 1–3. Madrid: Orel, 1969.

Ortega, Domingo. *El arte del toreo*. Madrid: Revista de Occidente, 1950.

Ortega Spottorno, José. "Amigo y tocayo." *El País* (international ed.), 6 June 1988, p. 9.

Ortega y Gasset, José. "Enviando a Domingo Ortega el retrato del primer toro." In Domingo Ortega, *El arte del toreo*. Madrid: Revista de Occidente, 1950.

————. *La caza y los toros*. Madrid: Revista de Occidente, 1960.

————. *Goya*. Madrid: Espasa-Calpe, 1963.

————. *Una interpretación de la historia universal: En torno a Toynbee*. Orig. pub. 1948. 2d ed. Madrid: Revista de Occidente, 1966.

————. *Velázquez*. Madrid: Revista de Occidente, 1959.

Pamplona: 100 años de carteles de las fiestas y ferias de San Fermín (1882–1981). 2d ed. (Caja de Ahorros de Navarra, 1982).

Paz Lancha, María. *De Curro al Cordobés*. 2d ed. Sevilla: Católica Española, 1968.

Pereda, Julián. *Los toros ante la iglesia y la moral*. 2d ed. Bilbao: Mensajero del Corazón de Jesús, 1965.

Pérez Calderón, Miguel. *El cuerno y el trapo*. Madrid: Burladero, 1967.

Pérez de Ayala, Ramón. *Política y toros. Obras completas*, vol. 3. Madrid: Aguilar, 1963.

Pérez Delgado, Rafael. "Sobre las corridas de toros: Notas sociológicas." In Antonio Carreira et al., eds., *Homenaje a Julio Caro Baroja*, pp. 843–875. Madrid: Centro de Investigaciones Sociológicas, 1978.

Pérez Lugín, Alejandro. *Currito de la Cruz*. México, D.F.: Buenos Aires, 1946.

Petit Caro, Antonio. *Por la puerta grande*. Barcelona: Marte, 1974.

Picasso, Pablo. *Toros y toreros*. Text by Luis Miguel Dominguín and Georges Boudaille. London: Thames Hudson, 1961.

Pitt-Rivers, Julián. *The People of the Sierra*. Chicago: University of Chicago Press, 1954.

———. "El sacrificio del toro." *Revista de Occidente* 36 (1984): 27–47.

Pollock, Raphael E. "Some Psychoanalytic Considerations of Bull Fighting and Bull Worship." *Israel Annals of Psychiatry and Related Disciplines* 12 (1974): 53–67.

Popelin, Claude. *El toro y su lidia*. Madrid: Calleja, 1956.

———. *Los toros desde la barrera*. 2d ed. Madrid: Rialp, 1966.

Portuguese Bullfight. Lisbon(?): Star Tourism & Travel.

Posada, Juan. *De Paquiro a Paula, en el rincón del sur*. Madrid: Espasa-Calpe, 1987.

Pozo, Raúl del, and Diego Bardón. *Un ataúd de terciopelo . . . para un mito de papel.* *(El ataúd de astracán: El regreso de El Cordobés)*. Barcelona: Zeta, 1980.

Prieto, Gregorio. *El toro*. Madrid: Librería Clan, 1954.

Pritchett, V. S. *The Spanish Temper*. London: Chatto & Windus, 1954.

Puente, J. V. *Arcángel: Novela del torero "Manolete."* Madrid: Rivadeneyra, 1960.

Quiroga, Elena. *La última corrida*. Barcelona: Noguer, 1958.

Ramírez, Guzmán. *El periodismo taurino*. Caracas: Peña Taurina Eleazar Sananes, 1970.

Reglamento de las corridas de toros, novillos y becerros. Madrid: Antonio Ros, 1917.

Reglamento Taurino. Commentary by Edmundo G. Acebal. Madrid: 1967.

Requena, José María. *Gente del toro*. Madrid: Propaganda Popular Católica, 1971.

Rey, Tomas (Pedro de los Palotes). *La tauromanía: Poema bufoépico avinagrado.* Madrid: Diego Pacheco, 1889.

Rey Caballero, José María. *Dos artistas frente a frente*. Madrid: 1950.

Ríos Mozo, Rafael. *El intelectual y el toreo*. 2d ed. Sevilla: Universidad de Sevilla, 1986.

Rof Carballo, Juan. "El juego del toro." *ABC Internacional*, 29 Apr.–5 May 1987, p. 1.

Rojas, Carlos de, and Manuel Vidal. *Cuernos para el diálogo*. Madrid: A.Q., 1976.

Roldán, Mariano. *Poesía Hispánica del toro: Antología siglos XIII al XX*. Madrid: Escelicer, 1970.

Ronda y un torero. nos. 21–22 of *Litoral*. Málaga: Litoral, 1971.

Ruiz Morales, Diego. *Teorías, opiniones y comentarios taurinos de J. Ortega y Gasset*. Madrid: Unión de Bibliófilos Taurinos, n.d.

Sabartés, Jaime. *Picasso Toreros*. Paris: Braziller, 1961.

Saiz Valdivielso, Alfonso Carlos. *La fiesta taurina: Una pasión ibérica*. Bilbao: Proyección, 1972.

Salabert, Miguel de, comp. *Los toros en la literatura contemporánea*. Madrid: Taurus, 1959.

Salinas, Pedro. *Ensayos de literatura hispánica*. Madrid: Aguilar, 1961.

Sánchez, Rafael (El Pipo). *Así fue . . . El Pipo, Manolete, El Cordobés*. Madrid: Sánchez Ortiz, 1981.

Sánchez Dragó, Fernando. *Volapié: Toros y tauromagia*. Madrid: Espasa-Calpe, 1987.

Sánchez Ferlosio, Rafael. *Las semanas del jardín. Semana segunda: Splendet dum frangitur*. Madrid: Nostromo, 1974.

Sánchez Mejía [sic], Ignacio. *Sinrazón*. Madrid: Prensa Moderna, 1928.

———. *Teatro*, ed. Antonio Gallego Morell. Madrid: Ediciones del Centro, 1976.

Sánchez de Neira, J. *Los toreros de antaño y los de hogaño*. 2d ed. Madrid: Pedro Núñez, 1884.

Sancho-Jiménez, Juan. *Defensa de las corridas de toros*. Málaga: Mediodía, 1877.

Santainés, Antonio. *Domingo Ortega: 80 años de vida y toros*, 2d ed. Madrid: Espasa-Calpe, 1987.

Santos Yubero, Martín. *Manolete: El artista y el hombre*. 3d ed. Vitoria: Fournier, 1947.

Sanz Egaña, Cesáreo. *Historia y bravura del toro de lidia*. Madrid: Espasa-Calpe, 1958.

Sastre, Alfonso. *La cornada*. 3d ed. Madrid: Escelicer, 1970.

III Semana Internacional del Toro de Lidia. Salamanca, 1965.

Serrán-Pagán, Ginés. "El ritual del toro en España: Algunos errores de análisis y método." *Revista de Estudios Sociales* 20 (1977): 87–99.

Serrán-Pagán, Ginés, and A. Muntadas. *Pamplona-Grazalema: From the Public Square to the Bullring*. (New York: Enquire, 1980).

Silva Aramburu, José (Pepe Alegrías). *Enciclopedia taurina*. 2d ed. Barcelona: De Gassó, 1962.

Simont, Marc. *Afternoon in Spain*. New York: Morrow, 1965.

Smith, Rex, ed. *Biography of the Bulls*. New York: Rinehart, 1957.

Soberanas, Amadeu J. "*Ensayo o poema sobre el toro en España*: Otro inédito de Federico García Lorca." *El Crotalón* 1 (1984): 717–730.

Spota, Luis. *Más cornadas da el hambre*. México, D.F.: Manuel Porrúa, 1961.

Steen, Marguerite. *The Bulls of Parral*. Garden City, N. Y.: Doubleday, 1954.

———. *Matador*. Boston: Little, Brown, 1934.

Sureda Molina, Guillermo. *De "El Viti" a Santiago Martín*. Palma de Mallorca, 1965.

———. *Ensayos taurinos: Para una fenomenología taurina*. Palma de Mallorca, 1952.

———. *Paco Camino en blanco y negro*. Palma de Mallorca, 1969.

———. *Tauromagia*. Madrid: Espasa-Calpe, 1978.

———. *"El Viti": El hombre y el torero*. Palma de Mallorca, 1963.

Thronbury, Walter. *Life in Spain: Past and Present*. New York: Harper & Bros., 1860.

Tierno Galván, Enrique. "Los toros, acontecimiento nacional." *Desde el espectáculo a la trivialización*. Orig. pub. 1951. Madrid: Taurus, 1961.

Tinsley, Jesse. "Bullfighting Tradition Under Siege by Group Pushing Animal Rights." *Philadelphia Inquirer* 11 Dec. 1988, p. 36-A.

¡Toro! primera tauromaquia en color. Fascículos 1, 3, 6, 7, 8, 11, 12, 13, 17, 20, 21, 24, 25, 26. (Madrid: Codex, 1966).

Los Toros: Bullfighting. [in English] Madrid: Indice, 1974.

Tynan, Kenneth. *Bull Fever.* New York: Harper & Bros., 1955.

————. *Bull Fever.* London: Longmans, Green, 1955.

Unamuno, Miguel de. "El deporte tauromáquico." *Obras completas,* vol. 7. Orig. pub. 1914. Madrid: Escelicer, 1967.

————. "Huichilobos y el bisonte de Altamira." *Obras completas,* vol. 7. Orig. pub. 1936. Madrid: Escelicer, 1967.

————. "La obra de Eugenio Noel." *Obras completas,* vol. 3. Orig. pub. 1912. Madrid: Escelicer, 1967.

————. "Si you fuera autócrata . . ." *Obras completas,* vol. 7. Orig. pub. 1911. Madrid: Escelicer, 1967.

Urrutia, Julio de. *Los toros en la guerra española.* Madrid: Nacional, 1974.

Ustinov, Peter. "A Place in the Shade" in *Add a Dash of Pity.* New York: Signet, 1961.

Valdeón, José Aurelio. *Tragedia y miseria del mundo del toro.* Madrid: Maisal, 1978.

Valle Inclán, Ramón del. *Cartel de Feria.* Barcelona: Ediciones G.P., [1955].

Vargas Ponce, José. *Disertación sobre las corridas de toros.* Madrid: Real Academia de la Historia, 1961.

Vázquez Díaz, Daniel. *El retrato de "Manolete".* Madrid: Afrodisio Aguado, 1961.

Vega, José. *Páginas olvidadas del Madrid taurino.* Madrid: Instituto de Estudios Madrileños, 1953.

Velarde, José. *Toros y chimborazos.* Madrid: Gutenberg, 1886.

Ventas (Las): Cincuenta años de corridas. Madrid: Diputación Provincial de Madrid, 1981.

Verrill Cintrón, Lola. *Goddess of the Bullring.* Indianapolis: Bobbs-Merrill, 1960.

Vidal, Joaquín. *40 años después: Temporada taurina 1987.* Madrid: Espasa-Calpe, 1988.

————. *El toreo es grandeza.* Madrid: Turner, 1987.

Viertel, Peter. *Love Lies Bleeding.* New York: Pocket Books, 1966.

Villa, Antonio de la. *Belmonte: El nuevo arte de torear.* Madrid: Espasa-Calpe, 1928.

————. *Manolete: Otra época del toreo.* México, D.F.: Leyenda, 1946.

Villalón, Fernando. *Taurofilia racial.* Madrid: El Observatorio, 1986.

————. *La toriada: Romances del 800.* Nos. 97–99 of *Litoral.* Torremolinos: 1980.

Wojciechowska, Maia. *Shadow of a Bull.* New York: Atheneum, 1964.

Zabala, Vicente. *La entraña del toreo.* Madrid: Prensa Española, 1967.

————. *Hablan los viejos colosos del toreo.* Madrid: Sedmay, 1976.

————. *Tiempo de esperanza.* Madrid: Espasa-Calpe, 1987.

Zabala, Vicente, Antonio García-Ramos, and José Luis Suárez-Guanes. *75 años de toros a través de ABC.* Madrid: ABC, 197?.

Zimmerman, Jeremiah. *Spain and Her People.* Philadelphia: George W. Jacobs, 1902.

Zumbiehl, François. *El torero y su sombra.* Madrid: Espasa-Calpe, 1987.

Index

This book has been set in Linotron Galliard. Galliard was designed for Mergenthaler in 1978 by Matthew Carter. Galliard retains many of the features of a sixteenth century typeface cut by Robert Granjon but has some modifications which gives it a more contemporary look.

Printed on acid-free paper.